Canadian Evidence Law in a Nutshell

Third Edition

Ronald J. Delisle, Lisa Dufraimont

D1214427

CARSWELL®

Canadian Cataloguing in Publication Date

A cataloguing record for this publication is available from Library and Archives Canada.

ISBN 978-0-7798-2302-4

Printed in Canada by Thomson Reuters

CARSWELL, A DIVISION OF THOMSON REUTERS CANADA LIMITED

One Corporate Plaza
2075 Kennedy Eoad
Toronto, Ontario
M1T 3V4

Customer Relations
Toronto 1-416-609-3800
Elsewhere in Canada/U.S. 1-800-387-5164
Fax 1-416-298-5082
www.carswell.com
E-mail www/carswell.com/email

To Gloria, Donald Albert and Kathy Mae

Preface to the Third Edition

I was delighted to work on the third edition of *Canadian Evidence Law in a Nutshell*. The first two editions by Ron Delisle provided a useful and illuminating overview of this challenging area of law, and the current edition aims to offer a similar blend of brevity and clarity. Consistent with the Canadian courts' approach to evidence, the analysis in this book remains focused on the principles behind the rules.

Of course, much has changed in the seven years since the second edition was published and the book has been thoroughly revised and updated. The new edition updates and expands the analysis on various key topics, including the general approach to the admissibility of evidence, the meaning of prejudice, children's evidence, the confessions rule and the principled approach to hearsay. Numerous significant Supreme Court rulings have been included in the third edition, including *F.H. v. McDougall* (cited as *C.R. v. McDougall*), which clarifies the civil standard of proof, *R. v. J.H.S.*, which offers guidance on reasonable doubt jury instructions, *R. v. Griffin*, which resolves a longstanding uncertainty about the rule in *Hodge's Case* and also sheds light on the state of mind or present intentions exception to the hearsay rule, *R. v. Spence*, which reformulates the law on judicial notice, *R. v. Lyttle* on the scope of cross-examination, *R. v. Stirling* and *R. v. Dinardo* on prior inconsistent statements, *R. v. Khela*, a comprehensive restatement of the law on unsavoury witness warnings, *R. v. Khelawon*, the new leading case on the principled approach to hearsay, *R. v. Trochym* on expert evidence, *Blank v. Canada (Minister of Justice)* on the distinction between solicitor-client privilege and litigation privilege, *Named Person v. Vancouver Sun* on informer privilege, *R. v. Henry*, which rationalizes the law on use immunity under s. 13 of the Charter, *R. v. Singh*, which spells out the relationship between the confessions rule and the right to silence, and *R. v. Grant* and *R. v. Harrison*, which adopt a new approach to the exclusion of evidence obtained in violation of Charter rights.

This edition aims to reflect the law as of October 2009. Thanks are due to Ron for inviting me to be a part of this project, to Don Stuart for his encouragement and to the editors at Carswell for their careful work.

Lisa Dufraimont

Preface to the First Edition

This brief text was initially intended for the use of law students who are beginning their study of the law of evidence and who might benefit from an overall look at this fascinating field. While a good understanding can only be had by a close analysis of the leading cases and the legislation, it is recognized that students can often profit from a look at the forest before and/or after an examination of the trees. Since this was the purpose, the book follows the organization of my coursebook, *Evidence: Principles and Problems*, and hopefully will be considered a useful companion to the same. As the book was being written it was recognized that the book might also be a valuable guide to the experienced practitioner and judge if only as a reminder of some basics that may possibly have been forgotten over time. It is hoped that the book will also be a good, succinct introduction to the subject for the non-lawyer who must frequently wonder what it is that lawyers are about in the courtroom. I have tried to articulate the principles, the common sense, underlying each of the rules so that one might better understand their purpose.

I would like to thank Julia Gulej, Acquisitions Editor at Carswell for encouraging me to write this book, and Kimberly Aiken, Senior Production Editor for her careful editing. I have tried to accurately describe the law as it appeared to be as of May 30, 1996.

R.J. Delisle

Table of Contents

Table of Cases

xvi   *Evidence in a Nutshell*

1

Basic Concepts

1. Introduction

The rules of evidence that we will be examining in this book govern proof of facts in court proceedings, civil and criminal. We will be examining the rules as they are applied when insisted on by the parties to the litigation and when the proceedings are taking place in a courtroom. In other forums, the rules are considerably relaxed. And, indeed, even in the courtroom there is a relaxing of rules at times: at the sentencing stage in criminal matters, for example,[1] or in custody matters when the best interests of the child are being considered.[2] There are, of course, a number of administrative tribunals functioning in Canada and each, by its enacting legislation and by general legislation referable to all administrative tribunals, must follow its own procedures. More often than not these tribunals are more liberal with respect to what evidence might be received. Understanding the basic rules applicable to the courts will, however, assist in appreciating the process before other tribunals.

The rules of evidence are largely judge-made but at times we'll see modifications of the rules by statute. The *Canada Evidence Act*[3] governs federal matters and each province has its own *Evidence Act* governing provincial matters. Roughly speaking, what this means is that evidence in criminal matters is governed by the *Canada Evidence Act* and civil matters are governed by, for example, the Ontario or Alberta *Evidence Act*. Various sections of the *Criminal Code*[4] and the *Canadian Charter of Rights and Freedoms*[5] affect the rules of evidence in criminal trials, and other modifications to criminal and civil evidence rules idiosyncratically appear in other pieces of legislation.

---

1 See *R. v. Gardiner* (1982), 68 C.C.C. (2d) 477 (S.C.C.).
2 See *Children's Aid Society of Metropolitan Toronto v. B. (N.H.)*, [1980] O.J. No. 1982, 1980 CarswellOnt 1771 (Ont. Prov. Ct.).
3 R.S.C. 1985, c. C-5.
4 R.S.C, 1985, c. C-46.
5 Part I of the *Constitution Act, 1982*, being Schedule B to the *Canada Act 1982* (U.K.), 1982, c. 11.

2. The Adversary System

A trial, civil or criminal, provides society with the final forum within which a dispute can be settled. Most disputes, civil or criminal, are settled by negotiation between the parties. It is only when they are unable to reach a settlement by themselves that they turn to the courts or administrative tribunals for help. Oftentimes the dispute centres around different appreciations of the applicable law. The parties are agreed as to what happened but cannot agree on the legal significance of those facts. The court or administrative tribunal, operating with agreed facts, provides a legal answer. More often, however, the dispute is caused by different interpretations as to what in fact occurred between the parties. When the parties cannot agree on the historical facts they turn to one of our institutions and ask a third party to make a determination so that the matter can be settled and the parties can get on with their lives. The method of fact determination that we in the Anglo-Canadian common law tradition have adopted is called the "adversary method".

The adversary method stands in contrast to the fact-finding method employed in civil law countries, which is sometimes called the "inquisitorial method". A key distinction between the two methods is the role of the judge: in the civil law tradition, the judge actively investigates and conducts the inquiry, while the adversary judge remains relatively passive. She does not herself conduct the inquiry and she does not investigate. She presides over a contest between two parties and judges the merits of two positions which are described by witnesses called by the parties. This system has been justified by common law lawyers as promoting the closest approximation to the truth. The diligence of the parties in ferreting out evidence favourable to their side and the vigour with which they attack their opponent's case are seen as better guarantees of approximating the historical truth than giving the problem for resolution to some governmental official whose motivation will rarely be of the same magnitude as the parties'. It is also believed that a judge who stays out of and above the fray is better able to objectively determine what in fact occurred than is a judge who descends into the arena and risks having "his vision clouded by the dust of the conflict."[6]

The adversary system has its critics. It is pointed out that the lawyer representing a party, seeking to win the game, will present only the evidence that is favourable to his client's case and not all the evidence that he might have at his disposal and which might shed additional light on the matter. Also, the ability of the adversary system to gain the truth through a contest presupposes some equality between the parties in their resources and, when this is lacking, the truth may become simply the view of the more powerful.

---

6 See *Yuill v. Yuill*, [1945] 1 All E.R. 183 at 189 (C.A.).

A major impediment to our search for truth is that the facts to be discovered by our courts are almost always past facts. We discover them largely through the oral testimony of witnesses who profess personal knowledge about what happened. Their supposed knowledge, their beliefs as to what happened, may be tainted by possible defects in their memory processes or their powers of perception. The witness may, in addition, have a motive for falsifying. When a witness speaks, his narration, his description, may not truly reflect what happened. The witness may be remembering imperfectly. He remembers the person as having dark hair although at the time he saw it as red. Or, he thought at the time that the car was black but the light wasn't all that good and he only had a fleeting glance and in fact the car was blue. Or, the witness may be insincere and may want to deliberately mislead the trier of fact. Or, the witness may be communicating imperfectly: he says the car was going fast but for him 50 km/hr is fast. The trier of fact may be misled by the language chosen by the witness to describe the incident. All of these possible imperfections are explored on cross-examination in front of the trier of fact. Cross-examination by the adversary is a process that is peculiar to the common law method of fact-finding.

The trier of fact has to guess whether the witness's testimony is an accurate reflection of what occurred. The witness, we've seen, may also be guessing. We cannot be certain as to what actually happened and we accommodate that fact by the device of burdens of proof. We insist that the plaintiff, or the prosecutor, who makes certain allegations and seeks a judgment that will disturb the *status quo*, must persuade the trier to a certain standard of belief. Short of certainty, but a belief nonetheless. The trier of fact has regard to what the witnesses have had to say, how they said it, how they presented under cross-examination, and arrives at a belief as to the correctness of the witnesses's belief. The trier cannot duplicate, as in a laboratory, the historical facts. Facts as found by a trier are then, frequently, guesses upon guesses. This is the best we can do.[7]

While approximating truth may be their pre-eminent goal, our courts also need to settle disputes. The resolution needs to be done in an efficient way. The tribunal does not have the luxury of postponing the decision to a later day when more evidence might be available. The parties and society need a resolution of the matter now. The parties and society also need to believe that the matter was settled in a fair way—fair to the parties, fair to the witnesses and fair in the sense that it protected other important societal interests. The law of evidence seeks to accommodate all of these interests, which are frequently competing in their claims.

Ideally, the trial judge uses the rules of evidence to ensure efficiency, fairness and the closest possible approximation to the truth, and counsel

---

7   See generally Jerome Frank, *Courts on Trial* (1949).

does the same. The rules are there to guide in the endeavour to satisfy the various claims. The wise judge, the wise counsel, recognize that they are but guides and are not to be slavishly and mechanically applied. Compromises must often be made. When the context of a particular case warrants it, the rule must be disregarded. To do this intelligently, the judge and the counsel must not only know the rule, they must understand it. They must appreciate the underlying reason for the rule so that they can decide whether it merits application. Admittedly, the reality of the adversary system is such that, normally, one party will benefit from a rigid application of an evidentiary rule even in circumstances where applying the rule will not advance the policy on which it rests. Counsel is free, and may be ethically bound, to advocate for the application of the rule in the interests of his or her client. Ultimately, the trial judge is responsible for ensuring that the tail does not wag the dog. Judges should always remember that the goals—truth, efficiency and fairness—are pre-eminent. The rules are there to assist in attaining those goals.

Our highest courts have increasingly recognized the centrality of judicial discretion in the application of the rules of evidence.[8] Discretion in the application of the rules of procedure is essential to any model of adjudication. Conscious of the policy on which a rule was based, our courts gauge whether that policy is being advanced by application of the rule in the circumstances of their particular case. Our courts articulate the factors that need to be taken into account if the exercise of discretion is to be sound. Counsel, to be effective, must similarly appreciate the underlying policy of any rule of evidence and the factors to be taken into account in deciding whether or not to apply a rule of evidence if she is to advance intelligent argument in her particular situation and persuade.

3. Exclusion of Evidence

A key question about any piece of evidence is whether or not it is admissible, whether the trier of fact may consider it with the other evidence in reaching a verdict. Much of the law of evidence consists of exclusionary rules. Other kinds of evidence rules also exist, such as the rules governing the qualification and manner of questioning witnesses, the rules stipulating the procedure for admitting physical evidence, and the rules requiring warnings to the jury about certain forms of unreliable evidence. Undoubtedly, however, our law of evidence is preoccupied with questions of admissibility.

---

8 See, *e.g.*, *Morris v. R.* (1983), 36 C.R. (3d) 1; *R. v. Corbett* (1988), 64 C.R. (3d) 1 (S.C.C.); *R. v. Potvin* (1989), 68 C.R. (3d) 193 (S.C.C.); and *R. v. L. (D.O.)*, [1993] 4 S.C.R. 419.

Given this preoccupation, it is useful to lay out a framework for determining the admissibility of evidence. There are, essentially, three steps to resolving any admissibility question. First, only evidence that is relevant to a legal issue in the case is admissible. Put another way, the evidence must be both relevant and material, and if it fails to meet these criteria it should be excluded. Second, there are various exclusionary rules covering specific forms of evidence like hearsay and opinion. Relevant evidence may be excluded because it runs afoul of one of these rules. Finally, even when a piece of evidence is relevant and material and no exclusionary rule applies, it may be excluded in the exercise of the trial judge's discretion.

4. Relevance, Materiality and Discretion to Exclude

Much of the rest of this book is devoted to detailing various exclusionary rules. This section explains the basic concepts underlying the questions of relevance and materiality and the trial judge's discretion to exclude.

(a) Materiality

When parties cannot settle a dispute by themselves and decide to resolve it in the courtroom, they delineate in advance what it is that they allege occurred and why that has meaning according to the substantive law. They select that particular slice of life that they wish to litigate; they do not litigate all of history. In a civil suit, the parties exchange pleadings. The plaintiff alleges that certain things occurred and that by the substantive law, of contract, property or negligence, the defendant is obliged to do something. In response to the plaintiff's allegations, the defendant concedes some and disputes others. In a criminal case, the prosecution alleges that the accused committed a certain crime at a certain time and place. The accused may choose to make formal admissions and, in any event, after disclosure and negotiations, by the time the case comes to trial, the prosecution and accused usually understand what it is that separates them. By this process the parties set out in advance what it is that matters between them. These issues that they have identified are known, appropriately enough, as the "material issues".

Suppose the accused is charged with the provincial offence of possession of undersized lobsters. Defence counsel tenders in evidence a witness who will testify that the accused didn't know that there were undersized lobsters in his catch. What does the prosecutor say? "The evidence is immaterial". Notice that by objecting that the evidence is immaterial the prosecutor is not arguing that the evidence would fail to rationally persuade a trier of fact regarding the accused's state of mind but rather that the accused's state of mind doesn't matter. It's immaterial. Our courts decided, as a matter of substantive law, that there is no *mens rea* requirement for the offence of possession of undersized lobsters; the offence was decided to be one of strict liability.[9] The evidence tendered was relevant to the matter sought to be established but what was sought to be established was beside the point; it was immaterial.

It is not uncommon for our courts to reject immaterial evidence as "irrelevant". This looseness of language is understandable as evidence that does not advance our understanding of a material issue might properly be said to be, in a broad sense, irrelevant. Keeping the concepts separate does, however, yield greater clarity of thought.

(b) Relevance

We regard our present system of fact-finding as a rational system. It's rational at least insofar as we do not engage in the earlier techniques of trial by ordeal or trial by battle. Each of those trials were attempts to call on the Almighty to directly provide us a witness as to who was in the right. Regarding our system as rational, we insist that there be a rational connection between the evidence and the conclusion that the proponent of the evidence hopes to be drawn. We exclude from the trier of fact information that affects only our senses or emotions. We seek to include only those items that have a legitimate influence on reason. The first determination that must be made concerning any information that tendered into evidence is whether the information is relevant. If the judge decides the evidence is not relevant, it is not admissible. If the evidence is found to be relevant, the court will decide whether the law of evidence should operate to exclude this logically probative material.

Relevance exists if there is, logically, probative value within the tendered evidence. The proponent of the evidence must demonstrate that, based on logic and experience, there is a rational connection between the evidence tendered and the proposition sought to be established thereby. Evidence must be relevant only as a matter of logic. There are no degrees of relevance and no special legal tests to be applied. This issue can be confused by the use of the phrase "legal relevance," which sometimes finds its way into the jurisprudence. Sometimes this phrase is just a shorthand for "relevant to a legal issue", a synonym for material. More frequently, "legal relevance" refers to some heightened legal standard of relevance that goes beyond mere

---

9 See *R. v. Pierce Fisheries Ltd.*, [1970] 5 C.C.C. 193 (S.C.C.).

logical relevance, a concept that has been specifically rejected by our highest court.[10] The only relevance insisted on is logical relevance.

To be relevant, the information need not render the material fact more probable than not. It is a mistake to confuse relevance with sufficiency. Evidence at a trial comes in piece by piece. The entire case cannot be built all of a sudden: "A brick is not a wall."[11] You build a case brick by brick. Each piece of evidence, each brick, however, needs to have a legitimate influence on reason. The tendered evidence, to be relevant, must make the desired inference more probable than that inference would be if the evidence had not been led.[12]

There is a fundamental and unavoidable problem resident within the requirement that the evidence be relevant. When we ask the question whether the evidence tendered makes the proposition for which it is tendered any more likely than would be the case if the evidence was not introduced, the law of evidence does not furnish an answer. Relevance is not dictated by the law but by common sense and experience. The judge decides, based on his or her common sense and experience, whether the evidence has a legitimate influence on reason. Determinations of relevance will be informed by the judge's culture, gender, background, social origin and age. The pre-eminent question is whether the judge's common sense and experience are in fact common. Does his or her common sense and experience mirror that of the community? Is it common? Is it sensible? There may, in certain cases, be a requirement to inform the court, perhaps through expert evidence, about how the world really operates. The judge's intuition that fact X frequently accompanies fact Y, making X's presence relevant to Y's, may not accord with another's point of view. If this is noted, counsel may need to be provided with an opportunity to persuade the judge that his or her hunch is not correct and deserves to be rethought in light of another's experience.

Evidence is relevant if it has any tendency to make the proposition for which it is tendered more probable than that proposition would be without the evidence. For evidence to have any value there must be a premise, a generalization that one makes, allowing the inference to be made. Evidence that roses were in bloom, when tendered to prove that it was then springtime, has meaning only if we adopt the premise or generalization that roses usually bloom in the spring.[13] The tendency of evidence to prove a proposition, and

10 See *Morris v. R., supra*, note 8 at 11.
11 This famous phrase was coined by Professor Charles McCormick: see Kenneth S. Broun, ed., *McCormick on Evidence*, 6th ed. (St. Paul: West Publishing, 2006), s. 185, vol. 1 at 733.
12 See *R. v. Watson* (1996), 50 C.R. (4th) 245 at 257 (Ont. C.A.).
13 For this metaphor and the immediate subsequent analysis, we are indebted to David A. Binder & Paul Bergman, *Fact Investigation* (West Publishing, 1991).

hence its relevance, depends on the validity of the premise that links the evidence to the proposition. Sometimes the premise will be indisputable, sometimes always true, sometimes often true and sometimes only rarely true. But a premise there must be. When a proponent states that the evidence she proposes to offer is "clearly" relevant, it is fair to ask the proponent of the evidence to articulate for the court what premise she is relying on. Why is it clear? If she has no response, no premise, the evidence is irrelevant and must be excluded. If she articulates a premise, the opponent can debate with her the validity of the premise. On what experience does the proponent base her premise? Is there contrary experience? Is the premise based on myth? On unfair stereotypical thinking? Is the premise always true? Sometimes? Rarely? These latter parameters do not affect relevance since relevance has a very low threshold, but may affect the probative worth of the evidence that may cause rejection if the probative value is outweighed by other competing considerations. Approaching discussions of relevance in this way may yield a more intelligent discussion than the oftentimes typical exchange of bare conclusory opinions.

In a murder case, the Crown offers evidence that the accused had a motive to kill the victim. The Crown relies on the premise that persons with a motive to kill have a tendency to act on that motive. Since the accused had a motive it is more likely that the accused killed the victim. In this syllogistic reasoning the major premise can be analyzed. Motive is relevant to a material issue but how probative is it? Do persons with a motive frequently implement that motive? Is the premise always true? Usually true? Sometimes? Only rarely?

(c) Direct and Circumstantial Evidence and Relevance

At trial we seek to establish that certain facts occurred in the past. The evidence tendered to support the existence of a particular fact may be classified as either testimonial or circumstantial. With testimonial or direct evidence, the witness describes the material issue. He testifies to having witnessed the making of the contract, the devolution of the estate, the negligence of the driver's conduct, *etc.* The trier of fact is asked to infer from that testimony that the material facts occurred as the witness says. If the witness is regarded as credible, the inference is forthcoming. With circumstantial evidence, the witness professes no direct knowledge of the matter but describes other matters from which it is reasonable to conclude that the matter at issue did, in fact, occur in a certain way. If the evidence is circumstantial in nature the trier is first asked to infer that the testimonial evidence is reliable and, second, that from the circumstances thereby evidenced it is proper to infer that the material fact occurred.

A witness might testify that she saw the accused stab the victim. Counsel who called that witness wants to persuade the trier of fact that his proposition is to be preferred; that is, that the accused stabbed the victim. The trier listens to the witness, both in examination in chief and on cross and seeks to determine whether her statement is worthy of credit and the prosecution's proposition is to be accepted. The trier of fact asks whether it is right to infer from the witness's statement about the fact that the fact did indeed occur. The trier considers whether the witness is sincere: are there reasons to distrust her, resident in her biases? Was the witness seen as able to adequately perceive: what were the lighting conditions and how good was her eyesight? Is the witness able to accurately recall: what's her memory like with regard to other matters? Inferring from the witness's statement to the proposition to be established, *i.e.*, that the accused stabbed the victim, is a problem of relevance. Is there a rational connection? Is it reasonable to conclude from this evidence that the proposition sought to be established is true? But no one speaks of the problem in these terms. This sort of problem is normally spoken of as a problem of credibility. We are here dealing with direct evidence; the witness observed directly the material facts.

Suppose the witness testifies that she didn't see the accused stab the victim but she did see the victim emerge from a building bleeding profusely and that moments later she saw the accused emerge with a blood-stained knife in his grasp. Now we are dealing with circumstantial evidence. The witness has described certain circumstances that she has observed. This presents a true problem of relevance. Is the proposition to be established, that the accused stabbed the victim, advanced in a legitimate way by the evidence of seeing the victim bleeding profusely and the accused with a blood-stained knife in his grasp? Is it rational to use this evidence in determining that the accused stabbed the victim?

Notice that in the case of direct evidence there is but one source of error. The person who describes a stabbing that she witnessed might be mistaken or lying. The trier must decide whether the witness is sufficiently credible that he or she can conclude that the stabbing occurred as described. The witness who says she only saw certain circumstances, wounds to the victim's chest and a blood-stained knife in the hand of the accused, may also be mistaken or lying about those circumstances, but also, even if she's accurate in her description, the inference that the prosecutor wants the trier to draw may not be the correct one. That is why we say that circumstantial evidence has two sources of error: the assessment of credibility and the drawing of inferences. This leads some to conclude that circumstantial evidence is weaker than direct, but it would be a mistake to conclude that circumstantial evidence is always less reliable than direct. Frequently it is more reliable. It all depends on the facts of the particular case.

In a murder prosecution, the Crown introduces into evidence letters written by the accused confessing a great love for the victim's wife. The Crown says that these letters provide evidence of the accused's motive to kill. A Crown witness testifies that she saw the accused stab the victim. Which piece of evidence is stronger, more persuasive? The letters or the direct eye-witness testimony?

But suppose that during cross-examination of the eye-witness defence counsel is able to bring out that:

1. The opportunity to observe was momentary.
2. The room was dark.
3. The witness's eyesight was poor.
4. The witness had never seen the accused before.

Suppose also that the Crown, in addition to the love letters, leads circumstantial evidence that a knife capable of inflicting the stab wound was found in the accused's possession, that there were bloodstains on the accused's clothes matching the victim's blood-type and that the victim's prized pocket watch was found in the accused's dresser drawer. Which evidence is stronger? The value of the evidence is thus seen not to be dictated by the nature of the evidence. Direct or circumstantial, the evidence will carry the day if the trier is satisfied in the particular case that the evidence is sufficient.

(d) Prejudicial Evidence and Judicial Discretion

Even when evidence is relevant and material, the trial judge retains a discretion to exclude it. This discretion is used primarily in instances where the evidence is prejudicial: a trial judge should exclude when the prejudicial effect of the evidence outweighs its probative value. This formula applies to any evidence tendered by a criminal prosecutor or by either party in a civil case.[14] The Supreme Court of Canada has emphasized that the test is different when the evidence is being tendered by the defence in a criminal case. In that situation the test for admissibility is whether the prejudicial effect of the evidence *substantially* outweighs its probative value.[15]

To apply this balancing test, it is of course essential to understand what is meant by prejudicial effect and probative value. Probative value refers to the weight of the evidence, the strength of the rational connection between the evidence and the material fact to be established. Because we insist only on bare logical relevance, the probative value of relevant evidence admitted in Canadian trials varies greatly from evidence that carries trifling probative

---

14 *R. v. Seaboyer* (1991), 7 C.R. (4th) 117 (S.C.C.).
15 See *ibid.*; *R. v. Shearing* (2002), 2 C.R. (6th) 213 (S.C.C.).

value to evidence that is virtually determinative of the verdict. While there are no degrees of relevance, there are various degrees of probative value.

Prejudice is a more difficult concept, because one might be tempted to conclude that any evidence that weighs heavily against one party is prejudicial to that party. This is a mistake. Evidence can be damaging to a party's case, it can be incriminating or even damning, without being prejudicial. The evidence can properly be said to be prejudicial only if it operates *unfairly* against one party or distorts the fact-finding process. The unfairness associated with prejudicial evidence may occur in different ways. The trier of fact may:

1. exaggerate the probative value that the evidence deserves,
2. disregard the real issue in the case, or become confused as to what the real issues are, or
3. use the evidence for an improper purpose.

In any event, if the unfairness of the evidence outweighs its probative value, it deserves to be excluded.

Suppose there is a prosecution for murder. The defence is self-defence. The defence tenders evidence that the alleged victim was a person who frequently beat on people. If permitted, the defence will call many witnesses who will testify that they were brutalized by the alleged victim. The defence maintains this evidence is relevant as it tends to show that on the occasion under review the victim, acting in conformity with his character, was the aggressor. There is no rule of evidence banning evidence of character in such a case. But a trial judge might exercise the discretion to exclude, in a particular case, if the probative value of the evidence was outweighed by the possibility of prejudice to the proper outcome of the trial. The judge might decide that a jury, learning of the victim's character, might disregard the strong evidence against the accused, theorizing that the world was well-rid of such a despicable person.[16]

Draper v. Jacklyn[17] was an action for damages for personal injuries sustained in a motor vehicle accident. Two photographs of the plaintiff's face were admitted into evidence to help illustrate the testimony of a medical witness as to the condition of a scar at a time within five weeks of the accident. The photographs also showed two Kirschner pins, used to hold fractured bones in place, protruding from the plaintiff's face. The Court of Appeal decided the photographs should not have been admitted into evidence as they were inflammatory and could have distorted the minds of the jury as to the amount of damages to be assessed.[18] The Supreme Court

---

16 See *R. v. Scopelliti* (1981), 63 C.C.C. (2d) 481 (Ont. C.A.).

17 (1970), 9 D.L.R. (3d) 264 (S.C.C.).

18 [1968] 2 O.R. 683 (C.A.).

reversed. For the Court, it was a matter of probative value versus the possibility of prejudice. The Supreme Court recognized that it was a matter of judicial discretion and that the trial judge was in the better position to determine whether the photographs would inappropriately deflect that particular jury from the fact-finding process. According to the Court, an appellate court should be loath to interfere. The Court recognized that this discretion more regularly occurred in criminal cases but recognized its place in civil cases as well.

The trial judge's discretion to exclude evidence is well established in our law, but some questions remain unresolved about its scope. Occasionally a court suggests that trial judges have discretion to exclude unreliable evidence, either under the rubric of balancing prejudice against probative value or as a separate ground of exclusion.[19] But the weight of authority suggests that unreliability on its own does not affect the admissibility of evidence.[20] The Supreme Court has also recognized a discretion, rooted in the *Charter*, to exclude evidence in order to ensure that a criminal accused receives a fair trial.[21] The details of how and when that discretion should be exercised remain murky.

(e) Multiple Relevance

The same piece of evidence may be relevant to different matters. There may be a rule of evidence that excludes if the evidence is tendered for a certain purpose but the evidence may be received if tendered for another purpose. For example, suppose the accused is charged with fraud. The accused has a criminal record that includes convictions for obtaining money by false pretenses, perjury and sexual assault. Are those convictions relevant to the material issue? First, what is the material issue? The issue is whether or not he deliberately deceived another and thereby obtained a material benefit. Do the previous convictions make the proposition that he committed the fraud under review more probable than that proposition would be without the evidence of the previous convictions? What does your common sense indicate? Suppose the accused takes the witness stand and testifies that he didn't know that his representations were false. Are the previous convictions relevant to the credibility of the accused as a witness? Does your common sense and experience indicate that the accused's previous convictions rationally support the proposition that the accused may be lying when he

---

19 See *e.g. R. v. Humaid* (2006), 37 C.R. (6th) 347 at para. 57 (Ont. C.A.).

20 See *R. v. Buric* (1996), 48 C.R. (4th) 149 (Ont. C.A.), affirmed [1997] 1 S.C.R. 535; *R. v. Monteleone* (1987), 59 C.R. (3d) 97 (S.C.C.).

21 See *R. v. Harrer* (1995), 42 C.R. (4th) 269 (S.C.C.); *R. v. White* (1999), 24 C.R. (5th) 201 (S.C.C.).

denies the knowledge necessary to conviction? If the convictions are relevant to credibility they should be received. Suppose I now tell you that there is an exclusionary rule, *i.e.*, a rule that excludes relevant evidence, that forbids evidence of the bad character of an accused from being led for the purpose of persuading the trier of fact that the accused on the occasion under review acted in conformity with that character and committed the dastardly deed. What should the trial judge do? She might decide to admit for the one purpose, credibility, and exclude for the other, character. In that event she would give a limiting instruction to the jury that they are to use the evidence for only the one purpose. Or she might decide that in her particular case the limiting instruction would be futile, that the jury would use the evidence for the prohibited purpose and the accused would be unfairly prejudiced, and she might then decide to exclude the evidence altogether.[22]

(f) Conditional Relevance

Evidence at trial comes in piece by piece. The relevance of a single piece of evidence tendered at the beginning of a trial may not be manifest. In such a case, counsel will offer his undertaking that the relevance will later become apparent as other evidence is led. The judge, in her discretion, will admit the evidence conditionally on the later linking up. If the evidence necessary to fulfil the condition is not forthcoming, the trier will be instructed to disregard the earlier piece of evidence. In a proper case, there may need to be a mistrial declared.

(g) Specific Relevance Rules

While relevance is a matter of logic and there is no special legal test for relevance, certain factual situations so regularly occur that the law of evidence, applying the above general principles, has developed consistent approaches to these specific relevance problems. This section describes how some of these situations have been treated in the courts.

(i) *Post-offence Conduct*

In a criminal case, it is commonly understood that certain types of conduct by an accused after an offence has been committed can raise an

---

22 See *R. v. Corbett*, *supra*, note 8, discussed, *infra*, in Chapter 3, Witnesses, "Accused as Witness".

inference of guilt. An inference of guilt may be drawn from circumstantial evidence such as flight from the scene of a crime or from the jurisdiction, the fabrication of lies or the destruction of evidence relating to the offence in question. Evidence of such post-offence conduct is therefore commonly admitted as relevant to the material issue. However, in charging a jury, a trial judge must take care to ensure that the evidence is not misused. There is always a danger that a jury might leap from such evidence too quickly to a conclusion of guilt if not properly instructed. The probative worth of the incriminating circumstantial evidence may be tenuous in comparison to the possibility of prejudice resident in the jury giving the evidence more weight than it deserves. There may be other reasons accounting for the post-offence conduct.[23]

(ii) Subsequent Repairs and Settlement Offers

In a civil suit for damages, alleging negligence in the failure of the defendant to maintain his property in a safe condition, it is arguable that any repairs to the property made by the defendant subsequent to the accident are relevant to culpability. The fact of the subsequent repairs may indicate an awareness, a belief, in the defendant that the premises were unsafe at the time of the accident. From that belief it is rational to infer that in fact the premises were unsafe. Our courts used to exclude this evidence on the basis that receiving it might discourage property owners from properly maintaining their property. More recently, however, our courts have rejected this as a fallacious argument and have signalled a willingness to receive the same.[24]

If the defendant property owner in the above hypothetical offered to pay damages to the plaintiff to settle the controversy, such an offer might also be seen to be relevant to the issue of negligence. Again, the chain of reasoning is that such an offer indicated a belief in the defendant that he was negligent and from such a belief we could properly infer that he was in fact negligent. But, again, much would depend on the circumstances. Another explanation might be forthcoming: the defendant, a lifelong friend of his neighbour plaintiff, without any real belief in his own negligence, might have made the gesture out of feelings of friendship.[25] In such a case, the evidence would lack relevance. In any event, the courts might exclude such evidence, even if they concluded that there was relevance, on the basis that they want to encourage settlements to avoid congestion in the courts; if such

---

23 See *R. v. White* (1998), 16 C.R. (5th) 199 (S.C.C.).

24 See *Sandhu (Litigation Guardian of) v. Wellington Place Apartments* (2008), 291 D.L.R. (4th) 220 (Ont. C.A.); *Algoma Central Railway v. Herb Fraser & Associates Ltd.* (1988), 66 O.R. (2d) 330 (Div. Ct.).

25 *Walmsley v. Humenick*, [1954] 2 D.L.R. 232 (B.C. S.C.).

offers were routinely received in evidence they might not be as forthcoming.[26]

(iii) Liability Insurance

Is there relevance in a civil suit for negligence that the defendant was insured against liability? One could argue that if a person took out insurance against any liability flowing from his activities, such person might be less careful in carrying out those activities, as he is fully protected from loss, and from there infer that on the particular occasion under review he was negligent. Alternatively, one could argue that the probative worth of such evidence is tenuous and that being insured actually marks the person as one of those cautious and careful individuals who take all appropriate precautions against risk. Whatever view one takes of the relevance of evidence that the defendant was insured, such evidence also raises a possibility of prejudice. The concern is that a jury will be more likely to return a verdict that the defendant was negligent when they learn that the defendant will not personally have to pay any award and that damages will be payable by a large faceless corporation. In light of this concern, for many years Canadian courts upheld a rule that should any evidence be led from which a jury might reasonably conclude that the defendant is insured, the jury should be automatically discharged.[27] However, recognizing that insurance coverage is now very common and often compulsory, the Supreme Court of Canada has overturned the former rule.[28] The prejudicial effect of evidence that the defendant is insured must now be examined in each case, and the trial judge has discretion to remedy any prejudice by discharging the jury or simply offering an instruction.

(iv) Judicial Findings

Suppose a motor vehicle accident occurs, producing criminal and civil consequences. Suppose the driver of one of the vehicles is later convicted of criminal negligence in the operation of a motor vehicle following a plea of not guilty. Suppose the other driver now sues. Is the plaintiff entitled to prove the earlier conviction for the purpose of establishing the facts on which the conviction was based? Is it relevant? Suppose an accused is convicted of murdering his wife. The accused later sues to recover the proceeds of his deceased wife's estate. Can the estate resist his claims and

---

26 See Privilege for Without Prejudice Communications, *infra*, Chapter 6.
27 See *Bowhey v. Theakson*, [1951] S.C.R. 679.
28 *Hamstra (Guardian ad litem of) v. British Columbia Rugby Union*, [1997] 1 S.C.R. 1092.

prove the previous conviction as evidence that he was the author of the death and therefore cannot recover? Is it relevant?

Our courts have decided that previous convictions of a criminal offence are relevant and therefore receivable in a subsequent civil suit for the purpose of establishing the facts on which the conviction was based.[29] It is to be noted that the previous judicial finding is not conclusive on the point; it is simply seen to be relevant.[30]

Suppose in each of the above scenarios the accused had earlier pleaded guilty. Our courts have decided that a plea of guilty amounts to an admission and therefore evidences a belief in that person that he was guilty as charged; from that belief it is seen to be fair to infer that the person did do the things alleged.[31] Again, the plea is regarded as relevant and therefore receivable as evidence but it is not conclusive. Our courts recognize that there can be reasons for a plea other than a belief in guilt.

5. Character Evidence, Relevance and Judicial Discretion

A complex set of rules governs the admission of evidence about a person's character. These rules could have been explored later in this book, in the discussion of exclusionary rules. However, the character rules also illustrate many of the issues covered in this chapter, including relevance, prejudice, and judicial discretion. We will accordingly review the rules surrounding character here, with a view to shedding further light on these basic concepts.

(a) Habit

If a person is in the habit of acting in a particular way, that habit may be seen as circumstantial evidence which has relevance to how he acted on the occasion being litigated. It seems rational to conclude that a person would act in conformity with his habit. If the habit is of invariable regularity, the probative worth is high and the evidence deserves receipt. For example, in a homicide case where the defence claims the deceased was armed, the defence might well be entitled to lead evidence that the deceased always carried a gun.[32] If the habit is less ingrained, the trial judge will have to

---

29 *Demeter v. British Pacific Life Insurance Co.* (1983), 150 D.L.R. (3d) 249 (Ont. H.C.), affirmed (1984), 48 O.R. (2d) 266 (C.A.).

30 For statutory provisions authorizing the receipt of previous convictions in subsequent civil suits, see R.S.A. 2000, c. A-18, s. 26; R.S.B.C. 1996, c. 124, s. 71.

31 *English v. Richmond*, [1956] S.C.R. 383.

32 See *R. v. Watson* (1996), 50 C.R. (4th) 245 (Ont. C.A.).

determine admissibility by assessing its probative worth against the competing considerations of undue consumption of time, confusion of issues and prejudice to the proper outcome of the trial.

If a medical doctor always performs an operation in a particular way it seems sensible that he be able to testify that he performed the operation under review in that way even though he has no present knowledge of how the particular operation was performed. While there may be no direct evidence of how the operation was performed—the doctor may not be able to remember the particular operation—there would be circumstantial evidence in the form of invariable habit.[33] If, on the other hand, the doctor can only say that he's generally a careful person and he therefore probably performed the operation in a certain way, the judge may decide that his evidence concerning how the particular operation was performed is less than useful and exclude. The evidence that he's a careful person is relevant but so general in nature as to lack the necessary probative value when the competing considerations are taken into account.

Evidence of a person's invariable habit is broadly admissible in Canada. The exception to this rule is evidence of a discreditable habit of a criminal accused, which is treated as bad character evidence and is, as we will see, generally inadmissible.[34]

(b) Character Evidence Generally

A person's character, as evidenced by her conduct or reputation previous to the event being litigated, may be relevant in various ways. Most often, evidence of a person's character can help to ground an inference that the person acted in conformity with that character on the occasion under review.

In other cases, character may be relevant to a material issue without any need for the trier of fact to infer that the person acted in conformity with her previous conduct or reputation. For example, in a case of assault, a claim of self-defence might be founded on the accused's belief, based on his understanding of the victim's previous conduct or reputation, that the victim had a disposition towards violent behaviour; such a belief, if honestly held, could cause the accused to view the victim's conduct on the occasion under review with apprehension and so cause the accused to strike out at the victim. The chain of reasoning the proponent asks the trier of fact to follow in this case does not require any inference that the victim acted in conformity with his character. The evidence of character is led only for the

---

33 See, *e.g.*, *Belknap v. Meakes* (1989), 64 D.L.R. (4th) 452 (B.C. C.A.).

34 *R. v. B. (L.)* (1997), 9 C.R. (5th) 38 (Ont. C.A.).

purpose of persuading the trier of fact that the accused's belief was genuine. If such an honest belief is, by the substantive law, a material issue, then evidence of the victim's character is regarded as relevant thereto.

Occasionally, the character of a person is not just relevant to a fact in issue but rather is itself a material issue, an operative fact that dictates rights and liabilities. For example, in an action for defamation in which justification is pleaded, the plaintiff's reputation or character is the determining factor.

The above scenarios present few problems for the law of evidence. The special rules governing character evidence apply only in cases where evidence of character is offered to be used circumstantially; cases where the trier is asked to infer that an individual acted on the occasion under review in accordance with her character as shown by evidence of her reputation or of specific actions performed on other occasions.

The law regards character evidence as relevant to whether a person acted in a certain way on the occasion under review. Thus, the law has traditionally assumed that there is such a thing as a personality trait or character and that evidence of a person's character is rationally and legitimately connected to the proposition that he acted on a particular occasion in conformity with the same. Character evidence is viewed not as determinative of the issue but as having a legitimate influence on reason.[35] Many disagree with the law's basic assumptions in this area. For them, behaviour on a particular occasion is largely shaped not by the person's antecedents but by the specifics, by the context, of the occasion.[36] Much of what follows then, in discussing the law of evidence as to character, reflects a view of human nature that is debatable but is nonetheless reflected in our current law.

The common law of evidence concedes the relevance of character and focuses on when and how the same may be evidenced. Regarding character evidence as relevant does not, of course, guarantee receivability. It is important to remind oneself that character evidence is simply a particular form of circumstantial evidence. Evidence of a person's character is evidence of a circumstance from which we ask the trier of fact to infer that the person acted accordingly on the occasion being litigated. If the evidence is that the person always, invariably, acted in a certain way, the circumstantial evidence is very probative and deserves to be received. We label this as evidence of habit but see it for what it is: a piece of circumstantial evidence, more specific than evidence of the person's general character but differing only in degree and not in kind. Circumstantial evidence of invariable habit

---

35   See *R. v. Clarke* (1998), 18 C.R. (5th) 219 (Ont. C.A.).

36   See, *e.g.*, Miguel Angel Mendez, "California's New Law on Character Evidence" (1984) 31 U.C.L.A. L. Rev. 1003.

is very powerful. If the evidence is that the person normally acted in that way, the circumstantial evidence is less powerful. If the evidence is that she acted in that way occasionally, the court may have concerns that the time necessary to hear the evidence may not be justified given the low probative value. If the evidence is of the person's general character or personality trait, the court recognizes that, even though the evidence has relevance, its probative value may be outweighed by competing considerations. Even so-called "good people" sometimes do bad things and "bad people" can do good things. Plumbing the depths of their character may not be worth the time and trouble. Determining receivability is thus a matter for the trial judge's discretion: she must weigh probative value against the dangers of consumption of time, confusion of the issues and prejudice to the proper outcome of the trial.

(i) Character Evidence in Civil Cases

Generally speaking, the character of the plaintiff or defendant in a civil case is not receivable for the purpose of proving that the litigant acted in conformity therewith on the occasion under review.[37] The primary rationale for this rule is that permitting character evidence in civil cases would burden the litigants and the trial process itself with peripheral inquiries into the litigants' character.[38]

(ii) Character of the Accused

Evidence of character presents special problems in criminal cases. An accused can lead evidence of his good character for the purpose of persuading the trier of fact that he acted in conformity with that character on the occasion under review. Since such evidence is regarded as relevant, and there are no canons of exclusion, the evidence is receivable.[39] If, however, the accused puts his character in issue by leading evidence of good character, the prosecution is entitled to lead evidence to rebut the same to ensure that the trier of fact is not misled.[40]

The rule that when the accused puts character in issue, the prosecution may lead evidence of the accused's bad character represents an exception

---

37 See *Attorney General v. Radloff* (1854), 156 E.R. 366 at 371 (Exch.). But see "Similar Fact Evidence in Civil Cases" *infra*.

38 See, e.g., *Gentles v. Toronto (City) Non-Profit Housing Corp.*, [2006] O.J. No. 1013, 2006 CarswellOnt 1543 (Ont. S.C.J.).

39 See *R. v. Tarrant* (1981), 63 C.C.C. (2d) 385 at 388 (Ont. C.A.).

40 See, *e.g.*, s. 666 of the *Criminal Code*. And see generally *R. v. McNamara (No. 1)* (1981), 56 C.C.C. (2d) 193 at 352 (Ont. C.A.).

to a long-standing canon of exclusion. In general, the prosecution may not lead evidence of the accused's bad character for the purpose of persuading the trier that the accused acted in conformity with that character and did the deed alleged. The evidence is regarded as relevant but inadmissible because of the competing consideration of prejudice.[41] As explained above, prejudice does not mean that the evidence might increase the chances of conviction but rather that the evidence might be improperly used by the trier of fact. It is one thing for evidence to operate unfortunately for an accused but it is quite another matter for the evidence to operate unfairly. It is the possibility of unfairness that is the concern. The trier who learns of the accused's previous misconduct may view the accused as a bad person who either must be guilty of the instant offence or deserves punishment regardless of guilt or innocence on the charge at hand.

(iii) Manner of Proving Character of the Accused

Until the late nineteenth century, the normal technique of informing the trier of the accused's character, when evidence of character had been ruled admissible, was by the opinions of those who knew him, bolstered at times by their reports of his reputation. That practice was then reversed in the latter part of the nineteenth century to the current rule, whereby character witnesses testify solely to the person's reputation in the community for the character trait under review.[42] That community need not be the person's residential community; it may be the person's reputation among a circle of persons who are familiar with her, perhaps at her workplace.[43] This rule that character witnesses must testify to reputation applies to character witnesses other than the accused; the accused as a witness has greater scope testify to his or her own good character through opinion and reference to specific acts.[44]

(c) Similar Fact Evidence

A chain of reasoning through the accused's disposition to the event is often tenuous as people can change and dispositions can vary. The canon of exclusion erected by the law of evidence for bad character evidence tendered by the prosecution thus excludes material that is tenuous in nature.

---

41 See *R. v. Rowton* (1865), 10 Cox C.C. 25 at 38 (Eng. C.C.R.) and *Attorney General v. Hitchcock* (1847), 1 Exch. 91 (Eng. Exch.).

42 *R. v. Rowton, ibid.*

43 *R. v. Levasseur* (1987), 56 C.R. (3d) 335 (Alta. C.A.).

44 See *R. v. McNamara (No. 1), supra* note 40.

Such evidence has little probative worth and, when viewed against the possibility of prejudice, deserves exclusion. As we move, however, from evidence of an accused's general disposition to specific instances of the accused's prior discreditable conduct, the evidence will in some cases begin to acquire more force. In some circumstances, as when the accused's prior bad acts are very similar to the conduct under review, the evidence will acquire a degree of probative value that outweighs any potential prejudice. In such a case, though the evidence surely reflects poorly on the accused's character, the reason for the canon of exclusion disappears.

Consider a criminal case in which a young couple is accused of murdering an infant foster child and burying the body in their back yard. The accused claim the baby died by accident. Now suppose the prosecution proffered evidence that the bodies of several other babies were buried in the yards of the couple's former residences. Surely this evidence would raise a compelling inference that the child in question died as a result of foul play.[45] The evidence falls into the general category of bad character evidence, but it carries a probative value that weighs in favour of admission. And indeed, our courts have recognized that evidence of an accused's prior discreditable conduct sometimes carries a probative value that overcomes our concerns about prejudice. This recognition underpins the rules that operate to admit what is known as similar fact evidence.

(i) The Test in Criminal Cases

The jurisprudence surrounding similar fact evidence was for many years quite confusing. Our highest court has recently brought considerable clarity to the issue in *R. v. Handy*.[46] *Handy* confirms that, consistent with the general rule prohibiting bad character evidence against the accused, evidence of an accused's discreditable conduct other than the conduct that forms the subject matter of the charge is generally inadmissible. However, the Supreme Court carved out a narrow exception to the general rule: such similar fact evidence is admissible where its probative value outweighs the possibility of prejudice. The Court identified the forms of prejudice that might arise in this context as "moral prejudice" arising from the danger that the trier might conclude that the accused is a bad person and "reasoning prejudice" in the form of undue consumption of time, confusion of the issues and the risk that a jury might put too much weight on the similar facts. Finally, the Court recognized that a trier is permitted to reason through the accused's dem-

---

45 See *Makin v. Attorney General for New South Wales*, [1894] A.C. 57 (New South Wales P.C.).

46 (2002), 1 C.R. (6th) 203 (S.C.C.).

onstrated propensity or disposition, provided the same is not general but specific.[47]

While the admissibility of similar fact evidence always depends in the end on the balancing of probative value and prejudicial effect, our courts have articulated a special test that applies when similar fact evidence is relied upon to establish the accused's identity. Suppose an accused is charged with a murder but the Crown has no physical or testimonial evidence to link the accused to the crime scene. Instead, the Crown relies on evidence that the accused committed another murder in a similar way, at a similar location, with a similar victim, in a similar timeframe. Here, the Crown relies on evidence of the second murder not to show that the accused is the sort of person who would have committed the murder charged, but rather that the accused actually *is* the person who committed it. A high degree of similarity indeed would be required to warrant drawing this inference, in light of the tragic reality that murders bearing some resemblance to each other occur with some regularity. The Supreme Court has held that similar fact evidence going to identity should only be admitted when there is a "striking similarity", either in the form of a single extraordinary similarity or a series of significant ones, between the similar acts and the conduct charged.[48]

Whether similar fact evidence bears on identity or some other material issue, before allegedly similar facts can be considered as evidence in the case there must be seen to be a connection between the previous acts and the accused. If the previous acts cannot be tied to the accused, they have no relevance at all. Canadian courts have recognized this fact but have yet to clearly articulate an appropriate test. Should the prosecution have to establish beyond a reasonable doubt that the accused committed the earlier acts? On a balance of probabilities? To whose satisfaction? The judge, as a preliminary condition of admissibility? The jury, who decides everything at the end of the case?[49] The jurisprudence to date has paid little attention to this preliminary condition of admissibility. We can say, at least, that the trial judge must decide that there is some evidence capable of supporting a

---

47   See also Delisle, "Batte: Similar Fact Evidence Is a Matter of Propensity" (2000) 34 C.R. (5th) 240.

48   *R. v. Arp* (1998), 20 C.R. (5th) 1 (S.C.C.).

49   See generally David M. Tanovich, "Probative Value and the Issue of Proof in Similar Fact Evidence Cases" (1994), 23 C.R. (4th) 157. See *R. v. Ross* (1996), 48 C.R. (4th) 78 at para. 8 (Ont. Gen. Div.), *per* Salhany J., holding that the judge must "ensure that the allegations clearly establish that a criminal offence has been committed by the accused against that proposed witness."

finding that the accused was implicated in the other activities before the similar fact evidence can be considered for admission.[50]

Often, similar fact evidence comprises information about prior acts of the accused that are not otherwise before the court. Frequently, though, the prosecution seeks to have the evidence pertaining to each count on a multi-count indictment admitted as similar fact evidence on each of the other counts. In both cases, the test for admission laid out in *Handy* applies. Yet, Courts have recently begun to admit similar fact evidence more freely in cases involving multi-count indictments, particularly in trials by judge alone. It is argued that the test for admission is easier to meet in such cases: the potential prejudice associated with similar fact evidence is reduced when the evidence is before the trier in any event, and trial judges are less likely than juries to use the evidence for an improper purpose.[51]

The test for the reception or rejection of similar fact evidence in a criminal case is simple to articulate if we keep basic principles in mind. The trier who learns of the accused's previous misconduct may view the accused as a bad person who must be guilty or deserves punishment regardless of guilt. The law recognizes that reasoning through character can be dangerous as people can change and their dispositions can vary. The law then erects a canon of exclusion for character evidence which has little probative worth, when viewed against the possibility of prejudice. Where, however, evidence of the accused's prior bad acts has genuine probative worth that is not outweighed by considerations of prejudice, the reason for the canon of exclusion disappears and the similar fact evidence should be received. The application of the rule requires only that we measure probative worth against the possibility of prejudice. While the test is simple to articulate, the balancing of these competing considerations is one of the most difficult tasks facing a trial judge today.

(ii) Similar Fact Evidence in Civil Cases

There are far fewer reported civil cases involving the problem of similar facts than criminal cases. In those reported, the approach is usually essentially the same as in the criminal cases. The same underlying concerns are expressed. The defendant came to deal with one allegation of misconduct and it is not fair to call on him to defend all past allegations. He might be taken by surprise and he might be unfairly prejudiced in the eyes of the jury

---

50 *Sweitzer v. R.* (1982), 68 C.C.C. (2d) 193 (S.C.C.); and *R. v. Millar* (1989), 49 C.C.C. (3d) 193 (Ont. C.A.).

51 See, *e.g.*, *R. v. B. (R.T.)* (2009), 63 C.R. (6th) 197 (Ont. C.A.); *R. v. MacCormack* (2009), 241 C.C.C. (3d) 516 (Ont. C.A.). For criticism of the relaxed approached to admissibility in such cases, see Dufraimont, Annotation to *B. (R.T.)* (2009), 63 C.R. (6th) 198.

by evidence of his previous conduct. Again, a suitable answer lies in the discretion of the trial judge to weigh these competing considerations against probative value.[52]

The plaintiff sues for damages for injuries sustained from a fall on the defendant's premises. The plaintiff maintains that the fall was caused by the overly slick tile floor in the defendant's foyer. The defendant denies negligence on his part and maintains that the fall was caused by the plaintiff's own awkwardness. The defendant avers that he was unaware that the floor was slick. The plaintiff offers evidence that one, two, three or four others have fallen in the defendant's foyer. The number and the similarity of circumstances will affect probative value. The previous happenings could be relevant to whether the fall was caused by the slippery floor and could also be relevant to the issue of whether the defendant had notice of a dangerous condition on his property. The judge worries that if the jury hears of others being hurt on the defendant's premises they might be moved to award damages whether or not the jury was persuaded that there actually was negligence in the case being reviewed. The judge must exercise a discretion in determining whether to admit the evidence. Probative value must be balanced against prejudice and time, akin to the criminal law process. The judge might decide to admit the evidence for the purpose of establishing notice to the defendant but not on the issue of whether the injury was actually caused by a dangerous condition. Or the judge might decide to exclude altogether.

(d) Character of the Victim

As noted above, the previous character or conduct of a victim, if known to an accused, may have relevance to the actions of the accused, because that knowledge may have caused the accused to act as he did. Insofar as evidence of the victim's character is relied upon to support an inference about the accused's state of mind, it is not true character evidence: the evidence is not being used to support an inference that the victim acted in accordance with his character. Evidence of a victim's character could also be used as character evidence in this true sense. Information about the victim's disposition or prior acts, even though unknown to the accused at the time of the incident, may also have relevance as supporting an inference that the victim acted accordingly on the occasion under review. For example, previous acts of violence by the victim are receivable to show a disposition for violence in the victim and the jury may be invited to infer that the victim

---

52 See, *e.g.*, *G. (J.R.I.) v. Tyhurst* (2003), 226 D.L.R. (4th) 447 (B.C. C.A.); *Wall v. Horn Abbot Ltd.* (2006), 250 N.S.R. (2d) 200 (N.S. S.C.).

acted in conformity with that disposition on the occasion under review. That evidence could then support an accused's evidence that the victim acted on that particular occasion in a life-threatening manner.[53]

(i) The Potential for Prejudice

However, bad character evidence about a victim can raise issues of prejudice. The trier might conclude, as the result of such evidence, that the victim's worth as a person is suspect and, accordingly, they might not take their task of carefully analyzing the evidence as seriously as they should. The trial judge must carefully assess the probative value of the evidence of the victim's character and ensure that it outweighs the possibility of prejudice to the proper outcome of the trial.[54] Where admissible, evidence of the victim's character may be in the form of reputation or in the form of evidence of specific instances of previous conduct.

(ii) Character of the Victim in Sexual Assault Cases

There have long been special rules governing evidence of the character of the complainant in sexual assault cases. The position at common law was that evidence could be led: (1) of the alleged victim's general reputation and moral character, and (2) concerning sexual intercourse between herself and the accused on other occasions. No evidence could be called by the accused concerning sexual intercourse between the complainant and other men. The law regarded evidence of (1) and (2) as relevant to the material issue of consent but evidence of sexual intercourse between the complainant and other men as irrelevant to the issue of consent. The alleged victim, however, could be cross-examined about instances of sexual intercourse with persons other than the accused as the same was seen as relevant to credibility. If the alleged victim denied such activity she could not be contradicted because such contradictory evidence would be in violation of a rule of evidence which forbids the introduction of evidence of collateral facts; evidence which goes solely to credibility. At common law, the victim's reputation for promiscuity was also seen as relevant to her credibility as well as directly relevant to the issue of consent.[55]

In 1992, the *Criminal Code* was amended to provide as follows:

---

53 *R. v. Scopelliti, supra,* note 16; and *R. v. Yaeck* (1991), 10 C.R. (4th) 1 (Ont. C.A.).

54 See *R. v. Scopelliti, ibid.*

55 See *R. v. Krausz* (1973), 57 Cr. App. R. 466 (C.C.A.); and *R. v. Basken* (1974), 21 C.C.C. (2d) 321 (Sask. C.A.).

276. (1) In proceedings in respect of [sexual offences], evidence that the complainant has engaged in sexual activity, whether with the accused or with any other person, is not admissible to support an inference that, by reason of the sexual nature of that activity, the complainant

(a) is more likely to have consented to the sexual activity that forms the subject-matter of the charge; or
(b) is less worthy of belief.

(2) In proceedings in respect of an offence referred to in subsection (1), no evidence shall be adduced by or on behalf of the accused that the complainant has engaged in sexual activity other than the sexual activity that forms the subject-matter of the charge, whether with the accused or with any other person, unless the judge, provincial court judge or justice determines, ... that the evidence

(a) is of specific instances of sexual activity;
(b) is relevant to an issue at trial; and
(c) has significant probative value that is not substantially outweighed by the danger of prejudice to the proper administration of justice.

277. In proceedings in respect of [sexual offences], evidence of sexual reputation, whether general or specific, is not admissible for the purpose of challenging or supporting the credibility of the complainant.

The legislation also provided a detailed procedure for determining whether the evidence could be received under subsection (2).

On a trial of sexual assault, receiving evidence of the complainant's previous sexual history can invade the complainant's privacy and has the potential to prejudice the proper outcome of the trial. The trier may give the evidence exaggerated weight on the issue of consent. Alternatively, the trier might conclude, as the result of such evidence, that the complainant's worth as a person is suspect, and accordingly they might not take their task of carefully analyzing the evidence as seriously as they should; they might not see a conviction as important as it might be seen with respect to another victim. On the other hand, a blanket exclusion of such evidence could do an injustice as it could interfere with an accused's right to make full answer and defence; the accused's rights in this regard are guaranteed by the common law, and in Canada by the *Criminal Code*[56] and section 7 of the *Charter*.

To draw the appropriate line, which will ensure a fair trial and at the same time protect the legitimate interests of both the complainant and the accused, the evidentiary provisions enacted by the Canadian Parliament incorporate an overriding discretion in the trial judge to receive evidence of the complainant's previous sexual history when the trial judge determines that the probative value of the same is significant and outweighs the pos-

---

56   Sections 276(3)(a), 650(3) and 802(1).

sibility of prejudice to the proper administration of justice. Section 276(1) does prohibit the admission of evidence of the complainant's sexual history to support the inferences that, because of the sexual nature of her past activity, the complainant is either more likely to have consented or less worthy of belief. However, this prohibition does not interfere with the accused's right to call relevant evidence because these two inferences, which are known as the "twin myths," have no legitimate influence on reason.[57] So long as the inference from past to present behaviour does not rest on highly dubious beliefs about "women who do" and "women who don't", evidence of the complainant's previous sexual activity, with the accused or with another, will probably not be foreclosed by s. 276.[58] If the inference to be drawn from the evidence is regarded as rational and strong, the court will probably receive.

There is, of course, a fundamental and unavoidable problem resident in the determination of relevance as required by the legislation. As we've seen, it is the trial judge who needs to answer the question of whether the evidence of previous sexual history makes the proposition for which it is tendered any more likely than would be the case if the evidence was not introduced. It is for the trial judge, if the evidence is relevant, to determine how probative the evidence is in comparison to competing considerations. The law of evidence does not furnish an answer. Relevance is not dictated by the law but by common sense and experience. The judge decides, based on his or her common sense and experience. The pre-eminent question is whether the judge's common sense and experience in this area mirrors that of the community. While this problem is present in all determinations of relevance, the problem is seen to be particularly acute in sexual assault cases. This is because, historically, the law has accepted as relevant evidence in sexual assault cases material which is now seen to be clearly irrelevant. This area of the law has been particularly susceptible to the utilization of stereotypes in determinations of relevance.[59]

---

57 *R. v. Darrach* (2000), 36 C.R. (5th) 223 at paras. 32-33 (S.C.C.).

58 See, *e.g.*, *R. v. Temertzoglou* (2002), 11 C.R. (6th) 179 (Ont. S.C.J.); Delisle, "Adoption Sub-silentio, of the Paciocco Solution to Rape Shield Laws" (2001) 36 C.R. (5th) 254.

59 See Justice L'Heureux-Dubé in *R. v. Seaboyer*, [1991] 2 S.C.R. 577.

2

Manner of Proof

1. Introduction

It is rare that we can be certain regarding the existence of any past fact. In the courtroom we are in the hands of witnesses who seek to describe, often at a much later time, their earlier interpretation of the material events. If we required certainty in our judicial decision-making, decisions would be few and far between. Our procedural law, our law of evidence, accommodates this fact by providing the device of burdens of proof. A trier of fact is entitled to find for a party, though not certain that the facts occurred as alleged, if the trier is persuaded to a belief that the party's version is probably true, in civil cases, or is persuaded beyond a reasonable doubt, in criminal cases.

2. The Persuasive and the Evidential Burden of Proof

There are two legal burdens that need to be distinguished: the persuasive burden and the evidential burden. The former has to do with persuading the trier and the latter has to do with leading evidence concerning the matter. The law of evidence has nothing to do with the allocation of these burdens. The law of evidence does not determine responsibility regarding either the leading of evidence or regarding who should persuade whom. Rather, the law of pleadings and substantive law dictate the same. The law of evidence supplies the tools for the task but the policy decision of who will bear what burden is left to other disciplines. The following discusses the substance of the tools provided.

When a party has the persuasive burden with respect to a proposition concerning which the parties are at odds, we say that that party will lose the case if, at the end of the day, he hasn't persuaded the trier of fact to his point of view. If the plaintiff in a civil suit satisfies the jury that his view of the proposition is correct – that, for example, the defendant's negligence caused the plaintiff's damages – he wins. If, on the other hand, the jury concludes that the question of liability ought to be clearly answered in favour of the defendant, then the plaintiff loses. But, if the jury in a civil case is in a real state of doubt at the end of the case, the plaintiff has failed to satisfy his burden of proof and he loses.[1] The law demands that the plaintiff (or the prosecutor in a criminal case) persuade the trier to a real belief in his proposition. The persuasive burden is sometimes referred to as the legal, ultimate, major or primary burden.

The persuasive burden never shifts. The plaintiff or the prosecutor is saddled with the burden of proving guilt or liability at the outset of the case and this burden never leaves his or her shoulders. It is only discharged when the jury comes back in and says "We find for the plaintiff" or "Guilty, your honour." The persuasive burden is to be distinguished from the non-legal, tactical burden. A newcomer to the case asks a spectator how the case is going. The spectator says it's going pretty well for the plaintiff, or for the defendant, and that if the other side doesn't do something it will probably lose. The other side has the tactical burden. There is no legal consequence that flows from failure to discharge the tactical burden; it is simply that as a matter of tactics it would be wise to lead some evidence or risk failure.[2]

The evidential burden, a lesser burden than the persuasive, rests on any party who wants a certain proposition to be considered by the trier of fact. The proposition that the party sees as important will not be open for consideration by the trier of fact unless the trial judge determines there is some evidence in the case to make it a real issue. The party is not entitled to make submissions to the jury unless there is a basis for them in the evidence. Otherwise the decision would be speculative and not rational. The evidential burden is sometimes referred to as the minor or secondary burden.

The evidential burden, when resting on the shoulders of the plaintiff or prosecutor, is sometimes referred to as the duty of going forward or the duty of passing the judge. There is a legal effect if the plaintiff or prosecutor fails to discharge this burden. If the trial judge determines that there is insufficient evidence on which a properly instructed jury could reasonably conclude in favour of the plaintiff or prosecutor, the trial judge will not permit the trier to consider the case. Using the current jargon, the plaintiff in a civil case will be non-suited; in a criminal case, the trial judge will direct a verdict of acquittal for the accused.

The evidential burden resting on the shoulders of the defendant in a civil case or on the accused in a criminal case operates to foreclose consideration of a defence unless there is evidence in the case which gives the defence a foundation, known as an "air of reality." Suppose a criminal case. The prosecution and the defence have signalled to the trial judge that all the evidence they choose to lead in the case has been led. The trial judge asks

---

1 See generally *Abrath v. North Eastern Railway* (1883), 11 Q.B. 79 (C.A.), *per* Brett M.R.
2 See, *e.g.*, *Snell v. Farrell*, [1990] 2 S.C.R. 311 at 329.

the defence for assistance as to how she should charge the jury. It would be unthinkable for the defence to ask the judge to tell the jury that they might acquit if they found that the accused was drunk at the time of the incident and therefore incapable of forming the necessary intent, or that he is entitled to be acquitted if they find he was acting in self-defence, or that they might acquit if they find that there were grounds of duress excusing his actions, if there had been no evidence led in the case as to intoxication, self-defence or duress. A defence should not be put to the jury if a reasonable jury properly instructed would be unable to acquit on the basis of the evidence tendered in support of that defence. On the other hand, if a reasonable jury properly instructed could acquit on the basis of the evidence tendered with regard to that defence, then it must be put to the jury. It is for the trial judge to decide whether the evidence is sufficient to warrant putting a defence to a jury as this is a question of law alone. The trial judge needs to determine if there is an air of reality to the suggested defence.[3]

There is thus a two-step procedure that must be followed. First, the trial judge must review all the evidence and decide if it is sufficient to warrant putting the defence to the jury. The air of reality for a defence need not come from sources other than the accused but there must be something in the evidence, from the accused's testimony or elsewhere, that is capable of supporting the accused's or defendant's position.[4] If the accused or defendant fails to discharge this evidential burden, it would be irrational for the trier to consider the defence. When an evidentiary foundation does exist, however, the trial judge must move to the second step and put the defence to the jury, which in turn will weigh the evidence and decide whether the defence is made out. For most defences, which are known as "ordinary defences" and include self-defence, duress, alibi and accident, the Crown carries the persuasive burden and must disprove the defence beyond a reasonable doubt. For a few so-called "reverse onus defences," including mental disorder, the defence carries the persuasive burden and must establish the defence on a balance of probabilities.[5]

The U.K. case of *Woolmington* provides us with a good vehicle for seeing the distinction between the two burdens.[6] Reginald Woolmington was convicted of murdering his bride. Reggie testified. The shooting was admitted but Reginald said it was an accident. The trial judge told the jury that, once the killing was proved, a persuasive burden fell on the shoulders of the accused and the accused had to prove that the killing was an accident.

---

3 See *R. c. Cinous* (2002), 49 C.R. (5th) 209 at paras. 47-57 (S.C.C.).

4 *R. v. Osolin* (1993), 26 C.R. (4th) 1 (S.C.C.); *R. v. Park* (1995), 39 C.R. (4th) 287 (S.C.C.); *Cinous, ibid.* at para. 53.

5 *R. c. Fontaine* (2004), 18 C.R. (6th) 203 at paras. 53-56 (S.C.C.).

6 *Woolmington v. D.P.P.*, [1935] A.C. 462 (H.L.).

The accused had to satisfy the trier, had to persuade the trier, that his proposition of accidental death was the true version of what happened that day. The House of Lords said no. The Lords said that the prosecution had to prove both the killing and the requisite mental state of malice. The prosecution had to prove all of the material ingredients of the offence. Once the Crown had proved the killing there was evidence on which the jury might find guilt but they were not required to do so. There was no burden on the accused to prove his innocence, to prove the absence of a material ingredient. The accused was entitled to be acquitted at the end of the day if the trier of fact had a reasonable doubt concerning the existence of any material ingredient. His testimony concerning accident satisfied his evidential burden and, if the jury had a reasonable doubt as to whether the killing had been by accident, Woolmington deserved to be acquitted.

It is important to recognize that the imposition of the evidential burden regarding accident in *Woolmington* does not mean that the accused must himself testify, nor indeed call any evidence. It is enough for the accused to point out that there is evidence in the prosecution's case which will support the doubt. For example, there may have been a statement made to the police during the course of the investigation which was partly inculpatory and partly exculpatory: "I did it, but I was drunk." That statement when introduced by the Crown becomes evidence in the case and the defence might point to it and ask the judge to charge the jury to consider the possibility that, due to intoxication, the accused did not have the capacity to form the requisite intent.[7]

3. Facts Peculiarly Within the Knowledge of the Accused

We have said that the law of evidence does not allocate burdens of proof but that the same is done by the substantive law and the law of pleadings. However, our courts sometimes rely on a "doctrine" of evidence law that shifts the persuasive burden to the accused.

In an old English case, the accused was charged with having game in his possession.[8] The statute provided a number of exceptions and qualifications and the accused argued that before a conviction could be had the prosecution had to negative each. The Court decided that this would place an intolerable burden on the prosecution and, because the matter was a fact peculiarly within the knowledge of the accused, it lay with him to establish. In later cases, where the statute provided that it was an offence to do something without a licence, the courts decided that since the possession of

---

7 See *R. v. Latour*, [1951] S.C.R. 19 at 23.

8 *R. v. Turner* (1816), 105 E. R. 1026.

a licence was a fact peculiarly within the knowledge of the accused it was for him to establish.[9] All of this seems relatively sound. If a defendant in Ontario today is prosecuted for fishing without a licence, and there are many licence-issuing authorities within the province, it seems sensible that the accused prove his licence as it might be well nigh impossible for the prosecution to negative and it's quite a simple task for the accused. Even here, however, placing an evidential burden rather than a persuasive would be sufficient, although with licences it comes to pretty much the same thing.

The danger is that, if broadly applied, this principle could relieve the prosecution of its normal burden of proof and make a mockery of the presumption of innocence.[10] The principle has been applied to shift the persuasive burden to the accused in cases involving the provincial offence of careless driving and even the *Criminal Code* offence of dangerous driving; the driver bears the onus of explaining away his manner of driving, it is argued, since any innocent explanation lies particularly within his knowledge.[11] Similarly, on a charge of breaching occupational safety legislation, the doctrine has been used to place the onus on the accused to prove that the person who did the prohibited thing was not subject to the authority of the accused.[12] Given the variety of situations in which such reasoning might apply, the presumption of innocence could be seriously impaired if this doctrine is not narrowly confined. In a murder prosecution, where a killing by the accused was established, there could conceivably be a burden on the accused to establish that he did not intend to cause death, as nothing could be more peculiarly within the knowledge of the accused than whether or not he meant to cause death.

4. The Measure of the Burden of Persuasion

There is said to be a marked distinction between the degree of satisfaction that is necessary in order for the trier of fact to be persuaded in a civil case and that which is necessary in a criminal case. Traditionally we say that in a civil case the trier needs only to be persuaded on a balance of probabilities, by a preponderance of the evidence,[13] whereas in a criminal case the trier must be persuaded beyond a reasonable doubt.[14] One might wonder whether these standards of proof reflect the way these decisions are actually made. It seems plausible to consider that, instead, a trier is satisfied

---

9   See, *e.g.*, *John v. Humphreys*, [1955] 1 All E.R. 793.
10   *R. v. Billet* (1952), 105 C.C.C. 169 (B.C. S.C.).
11   *R. v. McIver*, [1965] 2 O.R. 475 (C.A.); *R. v. Peda* (1968), [1969] 1 O.R. 90 (C.A.).
12   *R. v. Strand Electric Ltd.*, [1969] 1 O.R. 190 (C.A.).
13   *Smith v. Smith*, [1952] 2 S.C.R. 312.
14   *Woolmington v. D.P.P.*, *supra*, note 6.

or not, has a belief in the proponent's position or does not. And the trier's necessary degree of satisfaction to achieve that belief may rest less on the characterization of the issue as civil or criminal than on the trier's awareness of the consequences that will flow from the decision. How much rides on the decision? Nevertheless, the formula of words, balance of probabilities or preponderance of the evidence in a civil case and beyond a reasonable doubt continues in force.

While our courts have long held that these standards apply consistently across cases, for many years there were suggestions in the jurisprudence that the application of the standard of proof should vary depending on the nature of the case. For example, in civil cases, it was suggested that a trier should scrutinize the evidence with greater care if there were serious allegations of wrongdoing.[15] The Supreme Court has recently clarified the law in this regard, holding that there is but one civil standard of proof in Canada: proof on a balance of probabilities.[16] The Court held that it would be inappropriate to recognize varying levels of scrutiny of the evidence for different types of cases. Instead, in all cases the evidence should be scrutinized with care and should be "clear, convincing and cogent" enough to meet the civil standard.[17]

Our highest Court has gone to even greater lengths to elucidate the criminal standard of proof. In *R. v. Lifchus*,[18] the Court held that the trial judge should explain to the jury that:

- the standard of proof beyond a reasonable doubt is inextricably intertwined with that principle fundamental to all criminal trials, the presumption of innocence;
- the burden of proof rests on the prosecution throughout the trial and never shifts to the accused;
- a reasonable doubt is not a doubt based upon sympathy or prejudice;
- rather, it is based upon reason and common sense;
- it is logically connected to the evidence or absence of evidence;
- it does not involve proof to an absolute certainty; it is not proof beyond *any* doubt nor is it an imaginary or frivolous doubt; and
- more is required than proof that the accused is probably guilty – a jury which concludes only that the accused is probably guilty must acquit.[19]

The Court also listed various explanations of the criminal standard that should not be used in charging the jury:

15 *Continental Insurance Co. v. Dalton Cartage Ltd.*, [1982] 1 S.C.R. 164 at 170.
16 *C. (R.) v. McDougall* sub nom. *F.H. v. McDougall* (2008), 61 C.R. (6th) 1 at para. 40 (S.C.C.).
17 *Ibid.* at paras. 45-46.
18 *R. v. Lifchus* (1997), 9 C.R. (5th) 1 (S.C.C.).
19 *Ibid.* at para. 36.

- describing the term "reasonable doubt" as an ordinary expression which has no special meaning in the criminal law context;
- inviting jurors to apply to the task before them the same standard of proof that they apply to important, or even the most important, decisions in their own lives;
- equating proof "beyond a reasonable doubt" to proof "to a moral certainty";
- qualifying the word "doubt" with adjectives other than "reasonable", such as "serious", "substantial" or "haunting", which may mislead the jury; and
- instructing jurors that they may convict if they are "sure" that the accused is guilty, before providing them with a proper definition as to the meaning of the words "beyond a reasonable doubt".[20]

The Court emphasized that the charge to the jury on reasonable doubt need not take any particular form of words, as long as it was consistent with these general principles. Since *Lifchus*, the Court has suggested that it can be useful to instruct the jury that, on the spectrum between absolute certainly and proof on a balance of probabilities, proof beyond a reasonable doubt falls much closer to the former.[21]

In determining guilt in a criminal case, in determining whether the trier is satisfied beyond a reasonable doubt, it is wrong, a reversible error for the judge to tell the trier to choose between the competing versions of events presented by the accused and the complainant.[22] To do so is to weaken the standard and to risk shifting the burden of proof to the accused. When the case comes down to a credibility contest between the accused and the complainant, the trier may be advised that if the evidence of the accused is believed he is entitled to an acquittal. If the testimony of the accused is not believed but the trier is left in a state of reasonable doubt by it, the accused is entitled to be acquitted. Even if the trier is not left in a state of doubt by the evidence of the accused, the trier must ask herself whether, on the basis of the evidence she does accept, she is convinced beyond a reasonable doubt of the accused's guilt.[23] In whatever form the trial judge charges the jury, it should be clear that the jury need not choose between two competing versions and that a finding that the accused lacks credibility does not amount to proof of guilt.[24]

---

20 *Ibid.* at para. 37.
21 *R. v. Starr* (2000), 36 C.R. (5th) 1 (S.C.C.).
22 See *R. v. Nadeau* (1984), 42 C.R. (3d) 305 (S.C.C.).
23 *R. v. W. (D.)* (1991), 3 C.R. (4th) 302 (S.C.C.); and *R. v. S. (W.D.)* (1994), 34 C.R. (4th) 1 (S.C.C.).
24 *R. v. S. (J.H.)*, [2008] 2 S.C.R. 152.

The requisite standard of proof is applicable at the end of the case and is to be applied only in answer to the question of whether on all the evidence the trier is satisfied or not. The standard is not to be applied to each piece of evidence that goes to make up the case. The function of the standard of proof is not the weighing of individual items of evidence but the determination of the ultimate issue.[25]

5. Circumstantial Cases and the Rule in *Hodge's Case*

This "rule" came to us in Canada as the result of our reading, or misreading, of an old English case.[26] In that case, the Court was dealing with a murder. The evidence against the accused was circumstantial in nature. In charging the jury, the trial judge told them that they could only find guilt if they were satisfied "not only that those circumstances were consistent with his having committed the act, but . . .also . . . that the facts were such as to be inconsistent with any other rational conclusion than that the prisoner was the guilty person." It now seems clear that this formula of words was not intended to lay down a new rule of law but rather simply to offer advice to the jury about how they might be satisfied beyond a reasonable doubt in cases where the evidence was circumstantial.[27] Nevertheless, it was viewed by our courts as raising the standard of proof in circumstantial evidence cases to a standard higher than beyond a reasonable doubt and the trial judge was obliged, as a matter of law, in such cases to utter this formula.[28] Thankfully our courts have now recognized the error of their ways and the *Hodge* formula is no longer an inexorable rule of law in Canada.[29]

The Supreme Court very recently confirmed that there is no legal requirement for any special instruction on circumstantial evidence.[30] According to the Court, the judge must impart the message that the jury must be satisfied beyond a reasonable doubt that guilt is the only rational inference to be drawn from the circumstantial evidence, but this message can be communicated in a variety of ways. It would seem that while judges need no longer recite the *Hodge* formula, the logic behind the formula remains.

---

25 See *R. v. Morin*, [1988] 2 S.C.R. 345.

26 *Hodge's Case* (1838), 168 E.R. 1136.

27 *R. v. McGreevy* (1972), [1973] 1 All E.R. 503 at 508-511 (H.L.).

28 See, *e.g.*, *R. v. Comba*, [1938] 3 D.L.R. 719 (S.C.C.).

29 *R. v. Cooper* (1977), 74 D.L.R. (3d) 731 at 746 (S.C.C.).

30 *R. v. Griffin*, (2009) 67 C.R. (6th) 1 (S.C.C.).

6. The Measure of the Evidential Burden

We noted above that the evidential burden resting on a defendant or an accused, in respect of a defence, requires that there be evidence in the case, led by plaintiff, prosecutor or accused, to lend an air of reality as to its existence. Now we examine the evidential burden carried by the Crown in a criminal case or by the plaintiff in a civil case.

The evidential burden on the plaintiff or Crown is sometimes referred to as the duty of passing the judge. The plaintiff or Crown must first persuade the judge as the trier of law that his or her case warrants consideration by the trier of fact, often a jury. It will eventually be for the jury to decide if they are satisfied on a balance of probabilities or beyond a reasonable doubt, but first the proponent must persuade the judge that there is sufficient evidence, which, if believed, would permit a jury to rationally conclude in favour of the plaintiff or the Crown. The judge's role is to confine the jury to act within the parameters of rationality. We don't want to interfere with the jury's ultimate task, but we want to ensure that the opponent is not called on to respond to the case unnecessarily.

The question for the judge is whether there is any evidence upon which a reasonable jury properly instructed *could* return a verdict of guilt or liability. Note the emphasis on the word "could". It will be for the jury to decide if they "would" decide in favour of the plaintiff or the prosecutor. It is for the judge to decide if they rationally *could*. When the trial judge does that assessment, should she incorporate the standard of proof? Should she say then, in a criminal case, "could the jury reasonably be satisfied beyond a reasonable doubt?" It seems logical to incorporate the standard, because the question of how a jury could rationally resolve a case depends on the standard of proof the jury will be obliged to apply. Nevertheless, the law was long unsettled on this point, with the bulk of the jurisprudence suggesting that the standard should not be incorporated.[31] The Supreme Court has now settled the issue in favour of incorporating the standard of proof into the evidential burden.[32]

In determining whether a trier of fact could rationally conclude in favour of the proponent of the case a trial judge should not assess the credibility of the proponent's witnesses.[33] In *R. v. Mezzo*,[34] the accused was charged with rape. The accused did not contest the fact that the victim had been raped. He took issue only with her identification of him as her assailant. At the

---

31　See, for example, *R. v. Syms* (1979), 47 C.C.C. (2d) 114 (Ont. C.A.); and *R. v. Sawrenko* (1971), 4 C.C.C. (2d) 338 (Y.T. C.A.), in which the Court split on the issue.

32　*Fontaine, supra* note 5 at para. 53 (S.C.C.).

33　*United States v. Sheppard* (1976), 30 C.C.C. (2d) 424 (S.C.C.).

34　(1985), 52 C.R. (3d) 113 (S.C.C.).

close of the Crown's case the trial judge, concerned as to the quality of the identification evidence, granted a motion for a directed verdict of acquittal. The Supreme Court held this to be error. According to the Court, the trial judge had disregarded the division of duties between a judge and a jury. It was for the judge to rule on questions of law and for the jury to decide questions of fact. Questions concerning credibility and the quality of the identification evidence were to be decided by the trier of fact.

More problematic is the question of whether a trial judge ruling on a motion for a directed verdict may weigh the evidence. In *Monteleone*,[35] the accused was charged with arson. The evidence was entirely circumstantial. The premises were owned by the accused. There was evidence to place him at the scene shortly before the fire started. At the close of the Crown's case, the trial judge acceded to a defence motion for a directed verdict of acquittal. The Supreme Court decided the trial judge had erred in considering the weight of the evidence, which the Court held a trial judge was prohibited from doing in a jury trial.

The Supreme Court's hard line stance on this issue has since been modified, however. In a unanimous decision in *R. v. Arcuri*,[36] the Court recognized a certain limited weighing function for the trial judge. That case dealt with the task of a judge on a preliminary inquiry determining whether there was sufficient evidence to commit an accused to stand his trial, but the test is recognized to be the same as the test on directed verdict application.[37] The Court in *Arcuri* noted that if the evidence for the prosecution was direct evidence concerning each and every element of the offence, the trial judge's function was very limited since she was not permitted to make any determinations as to credibility. However, if any of the elements of the offence were evidenced only by circumstantial evidence, there was a greater role for the trial judge. In such a case the judge needs to assess the legitimacy of the inferences necessary to guilt; the judge weighs the evidence, including any defence evidence, in the sense of assessing whether the evidence is reasonably capable of supporting the inferences the prosecution wants the jury to draw.

In a criminal matter, at the close of the prosecution's case, the accused may make an application for a directed verdict of acquittal. The trial judge is obliged to rule on that application when it is made.[38] In a civil case, the defendant at the close of the plaintiff's case may apply for a non-suit. On that application being made the trial judge will ask the defendant if he

---

35 *R. v. Monteleone* (1987), 59 C.R. (3d) 97 (S.C.C.).

36 (2001), 44 C.R. (5th) 213 (S.C.C.). See Delisle, "Limited Weighing of Circumstantial Evidence" (2001) 44 C.R. (5th) 227.

37 See, *e.g.*, *United States v. Sheppard*, *supra* note 33.

38 *R. v. Angelantoni* (1975), 31 C.R.N.S. 342 at 345 (Ont. C.A.).

intends to call any evidence. If the defendant says no, the trial judge is then assured that all the evidence is in and she will rule on the application. If the defendant says that he intends to lead evidence the trial judge will normally reserve her decision on the non-suit application until the defendant has led his evidence and take the defendant's evidence into account when reaching a decision on the non-suit application.[39]

7. Presumptions

To establish a material fact, a party may lead circumstantial evidence concerning the same hoping that the trier of fact will infer the material fact. By contrast, presumptions in the law of evidence are devices that effect a legal consequence whereby the trier is *required* to infer a presumed fact when other basic facts are proved, provided that the party against whom the presumption operates fails to do something prescribed by law. It bears emphasis that when a presumption operates, a legal result is compelled and not just permitted. It is one thing to say to a trier of fact that it is permissible to infer the material fact from certain circumstantial evidence; it is quite another, distinct thing to say that the trier must infer the material fact. Presumptions are statutorily or judicially directed to accommodate some extrinsic policy consideration.

(a) False Presumptions

The term "presumption" is legitimately used only when the matter presumed risks the possibility of rebuttal by the adversary doing something in response. A presumption is, by definition, rebuttable. It is not uncommon, however, to see our Legislature refer to "conclusive presumptions". For example "a place that is found to be equipped with a slot machine shall be conclusively presumed to be a common gaming house."[40] In truth this is not a presumptive device; rather it is a statement of substantive law. To minimize confusion stemming from the overuse of the term, it would be far better if the Legislature simply provided that "a place that is found to be equipped with a slot machine is a common gaming house." The effect is the same and much more straightforward.

Sometimes, what is simply a permissible inference is labelled a presumption. For example, it is sometimes said that a person is presumed to intend the natural consequences of his acts. This is error. To be consistent

---

39 *Ontario v. O.P.S.E.U.* (1990), 37 O.A.C. 218 (Div. Ct.); and *Bank of Montreal v. Horan* (1986), 54 O.R. (2d) 757 (H.C.).

40 *Criminal Code*, s. 198(2).

with the requirement that the prosecution has the burden of proving its case beyond a reasonable doubt, the jury needs to be advised that while they may infer an intention from the doing of an act there is no requirement that they must do so. They may, but there is no must about it.[41] It does not avoid criticism if such a so-called presumption is referred to as a presumption of fact as opposed to a presumption of law, or as a permissive presumption, although our jurisprudence does frequently use this misleading language.[42]

It is sometimes said that a person who is found in possession of goods that were recently stolen, in the absence of an explanation that might reasonably be true, is presumed to have stolen them or, at least, to have known that the goods were stolen. Indeed sometimes a court will even refer to the operation of this so-called presumption as the "doctrine of recent possession". There is no presumption in such cases, much less a doctrine. What is permitted is an inference. A trier may, but is not obliged to, infer from the facts proved that the accused was the thief or knew of the goods' stolen character.[43] This is simply the operation of common sense as opposed to the operation of law. The prosecution on a charge of possession of stolen goods needs to prove that the accused was in possession of said goods and that the accused knew of their stolen nature. Suppose the prosecution leads evidence that the accused was found in possession of goods which were stolen 30 minutes earlier. The accused offered no explanation then or at trial. The fact that the goods were recently stolen is circumstantial evidence from which it seems reasonable, an exercise in common sense, in the absence of any explanation forthcoming from the accused, to infer that the accused knew the goods were stolen.

In the name of clarity of thought, presumptive language should be reserved for those evidentiary devices that mandate a result if the party against whom the presumption operates fails either to lead evidence to the contrary or to prove the contrary. The task assigned to the opponent varies depending on the language that created the presumption.

(b) True Presumptions

True presumptions mandate a finding, produce a legal consequence, but only if the opponent does not do as the legislation or the common law provides. Sometimes legislation will provide that the opponent has an evidential burden and failure to satisfy the same will demand that the trier find

---

41   See *R. v. Ortt*, [1969] 1 O.R. 461 at 463 (C.A.); *R. v. Steane*, [1947] 1 K.B. 997 at 1004; and *Hosegood v. Hosegood* (1950), 66 T.L.R. 735 at 738 (C.A.).

42   See, *e.g.*, *R. v. Oakes* (1986), 50 C.R. (3d) 1 (S.C.C.).

43   *R. v. Kowlyk* (1988), 65 C.R. (3d) 97 (S.C.C.); *R. v. Graham* (1972), 7 C.C.C. (2d) 93 (S.C.C.); *R. v. Choquette* (2007), 228 O.A.C. 352 (C.A.).

the presumed fact to exist. Evidential burdens arising from presumptions operate somewhat differently from the evidential burden that rests on any party seeking to raise an issue. Instead of being required to point to evidence to put a matter in issue, in the context of a presumption the evidential burden requires the party to bring forth evidence or have an issue decided against her by operation of the presumption. The effect, however, is the same: if the evidential burden is not discharged, its bearer will have the matter decided against her.

For example, the *Criminal Code* provides that it is an offence to break and enter a place with the intention of committing an indictable offence therein. The Code also provides that in the prosecution of such a case, where the prosecution leads evidence that the accused broke and entered, that, in the absence of evidence to the contrary, is proof of an intention to commit an indictable offence therein.[44] The Code thus creates a presumption and the language of this statutory provision, "in the absence of evidence to the contrary", casts an evidential burden on the accused. If there is no evidence indicating a contrary intention, then the trier is mandated to conclude that there was an intention to commit an indictable offence in the place which was broken into. There is no may about it; it is a must.[45] In the civil context, our courts decided that a will was to be presumed to be made by a person with testamentary capacity. If there was evidence to the contrary, the effect of the presumption was lost and the proponent of the will would be obliged to prove testamentary capacity positively. This common law presumption cast an evidential burden on the opponent of the will.[46]

Sometimes the legislation creating a presumptive device will cast a persuasive burden on the accused. For example, the *Criminal Code* provides that in a prosecution for having the care or control of a motor vehicle while impaired, where it is proved that the accused occupied the seat ordinarily occupied by the driver, the trier will be obliged to find that the accused had care and control unless the accused establishes that he did not occupy the seat for the purpose of setting the vehicle in motion.[47] In such a case, even though the accused's testimony raised a reasonable doubt in the mind of the trier of fact as to whether the accused had care and control of the vehicle, the trier must convict if the accused did not satisfy his persuasive burden, if he failed to "establish", failed to persuade the trier to that effect.[48] When a persuasive burden is imposed on an accused in a criminal case, the burden is satisfied if the accused persuades the trier on a balance of probabilities;

---

44 R.S.C, 1985, c. C-46, s. 348(2).

45 See *R. v. Proudlock* (1979), 5 C.R. (3d) 21 (S.C.C.).

46 *Robins v. National Trust*, [1927] A.C. 515 at 519; and *Smith v. Nevins*, [1925] S.C.R. 619 at 638.

47 Section 258(1)(*a*).

48 *R. v. Appleby* (1971), 3 C.C.C. (2d) 354 (S.C.C.).

the accused never has to prove anything beyond a reasonable doubt.[49] In a civil case, our courts decided that there was a presumption of legitimacy for children born in lawful wedlock and the same was not to be displaced save by persuading the trier to the contrary.[50]

(c) Presumptions and The Charter

Section 11(d) of the Charter[51] provides that "[a]ny person charged with an offence has the right to be presumed innocent until proven guilty according to law." Presumptions that operate to shift the burden of proof to the accused run counter to this Charter guarantee.

In *Oakes*,[52] the Supreme Court considered the constitutionality of such a reverse onus provision. The accused had been charged with possession of a narcotic for the purpose of trafficking. The *Narcotic Control Act* provided that in such a prosecution the trial was to proceed as if it were a prosecution for simple possession. At the conclusion of the first stage, the Court was to make a finding as to whether the accused was in fact in possession. If the accused was found to be in possession, the Act provided that he was to be given the opportunity of establishing that he was not in possession for the purpose of trafficking. If the accused failed to establish this then he would be convicted of the much more serious offence of possession for the purpose of trafficking.[53] Thus, with respect to the proof of a material ingredient of the crime, the purpose of the possession, the accused, and not the prosecution, had the persuasive burden. All were in agreement that whenever a statutory provision placed a persuasive burden on an accused it would be satisfied by proof on a balance of probabilities and would not require proof beyond a reasonable doubt. The Court decided that the provision of the *Narcotic Control Act* was in violation of s. 11(d) of the Charter and announced the applicable test. If a provision cast a burden on the accused of disproving an essential element of an offence, making a conviction possible despite the existence of a reasonable doubt concerning a material ingredient, that provision would be a violation of s. 11(d). In a later case, the Court explained that there would be a violation whether the legislative provision had to do with an essential element, a collateral factor, an excuse or a defence; the characterization of the factor with respect to which the accused has a burden does not affect the analysis of the presumption of innocence.

---

49   See *R. v. Oakes, supra*, note 42.
50   *Welstead v. Brown* (1951), [1952] 1 D.L.R. 465 (S.C.C.).
51   *Canadian Charter of Rights and Freedoms*, Part I of the *Constitution Act, 1982*, being Schedule B to the *Canada Act 1982* (U.K.), 1982, c. 11.
52   *R. v. Oakes, supra*, note 42.
53   *Narcotic Control Act*, R.S.C. 1985, c. N-1, s. 8, as rep. by S.C. 1996, c. 19, s. 94.

Whenever legislation places a persuasive burden on the accused that could permit the accused to be convicted despite the existence of a reasonable doubt about guilt, that provision violates s. 11(d) and must be struck down unless it is saved by s. 1 of the Charter.[54]

After finding a violation of s. 11(d) in *Oakes*, then, the Court looked to s. 1 to see whether this violation could be justified. Section 1 of the Charter provides:

> The *Canadian Charter of Rights and Freedoms* guarantees the rights and freedoms set out in it subject only to such reasonable limits prescribed by law as can be demonstrably justified in a free and democratic society.

The violation in the *Oakes* case was prescribed by law, by s. 8 of the *Narcotic Control Act*. Therefore the violation could be considered under s. 1.

The Court announced what has become known as the "*Oakes* test" as the normal means for s. 1 analysis. First it is the party who seeks to uphold the provision under s. 1 who has the onus of proving that the provision is reasonable and demonstrably justified. The onus is on the balance of probabilities but the degree of probability needed to justify overriding a Charter right will be very high.[55] To be upheld as a reasonable limit under s. 1 of the Charter, a law must satisfy two criteria. First, the objective the measures are designed to serve must be sufficiently important to warrant overriding a constitutional right or freedom. The objective must, at a minimum, relate to concerns that are pressing and substantial. Care must be taken in this first step not to overstate the legislative objective. Stating the objective too broadly could exaggerate its importance and compromise the s. 1 analysis.[56] For example, in *Fisher*,[57] the accused was an employee of the government. He was charged under the *Criminal Code* with accepting a benefit without the written consent of the head of his branch. The Code cast a persuasive burden on the accused to prove he had the necessary consents.[58] The Crown, seeking to justify a violation of s. 11(d), argued that the objective of the impugned provision was to preserve the integrity and the appearance of integrity of the public service. The Court decided this was too broad a description of the objective. It was the objective of the reverse onus clause

---

54 *R. v. Whyte* (1988), 64 C.R. (3d) 123 (S.C.C.).

55 This heightened onus in the Charter context was specifically mentioned by the Supreme Court in *C. (R.) v. McDougall, supra* note 16 at para. 29, and therefore will likely remain unaffected by the holding in that case that the civil standard of proof is unvarying and the scrutiny of the evidence should not be affected by the type of case.

56 *RJR-MacDonald Inc. v. Canada (Attorney General)* (1995), 100 C.C.C. (3d) 449 (S.C.C.), *per* McLachlin J.

57 *R. v. Fisher* (1994), 17 O.R. (3d) 295 (C.A.), leave to appeal to S.C.C. refused (1995), 35 C.R. (4th) 401 (S.C.C.).

58 Section 121(1)(c).

contained in the section, rather than the objective of the whole of the section, that should be the focus of a s. 1 Charter analysis. The reverse onus clause itself must have an underlying objective which is sufficiently important to warrant overriding s. 11(d).

Second, the means chosen to achieve the objective must be seen to be proportional to the task. This second criterion has three components. First, the means chosen must be rationally connected to the objective. Second, the means chosen should impair the right or freedom as little as possible. This requirement is sometimes stated to be as little as reasonably possible, or as little as possible while remaining as effective, but the courts have not been entirely consistent in this area.[59] Finally, there must be a proportionality between the effects of the measures which are responsible for limiting the right or freedom and the objective which has been identified as important.

In the result in the *Oakes* case, the Court decided that the reverse onus provision under review could not be saved by s. 1 as the provision was not internally rational. Possession of narcotics, regardless of amount, could not be said to rationally support an inference that the person was in possession for the purpose of trafficking. The Court refused to read limitations into the legislation to make it internally rational, though later courts have taken to reading into or reading down legislation to make it consistent with the Charter.[60] Since *Oakes*, various provisions that place a persuasive burden on the accused, including reverse onus defences, have been upheld as reasonable limits on the accused's s. 11(d) rights.[61]

Presumptions that place an evidential burden on the accused have also been seen to impair the accused's presumption of innocence.[62] For example, the *Criminal Code* provides that evidence that a person lives with a prostitute is, in the absence of evidence to the contrary, proof that the person lives on the avails of prostitution.[63] The language chosen for this presumptive device

---

59 See, *e.g.*, *R. v. Chaulk*, [1990] 3 S.C.R. 1303; and *R. v. Wholesale Travel Group Inc.*, [1991] 3 S.C.R. 154.

60 See, *e.g.*, *R. v. Fisher*, *supra*, note 57, where the Court decided to delete the offensive words "the proof of which lies on him" and *R. v. Laba* (1994), 34 C.R. (4th) 360 (S.C.C.), where the Court redrafted the section to conform to the Charter. In *Laba*, the Court said there was no need for the provision to be internally rational; this statement is at odds with other Supreme Court decisions: see Delisle, "Confusion on Evidentiary Burdens" (1994), 34 C.R. (4th) 402. See also *R. v. Curtis* (1998), 14 C.R. (5th) 328 (Ont. C.A.) where the court simply deleted the phrase that reversed the onus, "the proof of which lies upon him." Compare Delisle, "Stone: Judicial Activism Gone Awry to Presume Guilt" (1999) 24 C.R. (5th) 91.

61 See, *e.g.*, *Chaulk*, *supra* note 59, in which the Supreme Court relied on s. 1 to uphold the reverse onus on the defence of insanity or mental disorder.

62 *R. v. Boyle* (1983), 5 C.C.C. (3d) 193 (Ont. C.A.); *R. v. Downey* (1992), 13 C.R. (4th) 129 (S.C.C.).

63 Section 212(3).

places an evidential burden on the accused. A conviction is mandated if there is no evidence to the contrary even if there is no positive evidence as to the material ingredient of the offence that the accused actually did live on the avails. Our Supreme Court decided that this violated s. 11(d) on the basis, per *Oakes,* that a conviction was mandated though there could be a reasonable doubt as to a material ingredient.[64] One might ask whether this guide, suitable when considering a statutory provision which imposes a persuasive burden, is also suitable when testing an evidential burden. If there was evidence led to the contrary the presumptive device would be spent and there would not be a conviction required. If there was no evidence led to the contrary, arguably there would be no basis for a *reasonable* doubt.[65]

8. Judicial Notice

We do not prove by evidence, indeed we cannot prove by evidence, all the facts that are necessary to a judicial decision. Judges frequently rely on propositions not in evidence by taking judicial notice.

(a) Noticing Facts

The general rule is that judges may notice facts that are indisputable. Suppose a civil suit for damages sustained in a motor vehicle accident. The defendant describes his speed and his handling of the car. He maintains that the accident was unavoidable as he was unable to bring his vehicle to a stop in time to avoid the plaintiff's vehicle. The plaintiff maintains that the defendant was negligent in that he was driving too fast for the conditions of the road. The evidence indicates that it was raining at the time of the accident. To resolve the issue of negligence, do we need evidence that rain makes road surfaces wet, that the coefficient of friction between asphalt and tires is thereby reduced, that such fact is well-known to all drivers and that careful drivers lower their speed in such conditions? Such matters are so well-known in the community as to be indisputable. This material need not be proved in accordance with the normal rules of evidence. This knowledge is assumed to be already possessed by the judge and the party who has the burden of proof on the issue may simply call on the judge to judicially notice those facts which are necessary to determine the question.

---

64 *R. v. Downey, supra,* note 62.
65 See R. Delisle, "When Do Evidential Burdens Violate Section 11(d)?" (1992), 13 C.R. (4th) 161.

The judge may not herself have the requisite knowledge and may need to be informed. Dictionaries, atlases and the like are ready to hand and may be freely consulted. Thus, our highest Court has recognized that judges may notice facts that are:

> (1) so notorious or generally accepted as not to be the subject of debate among reasonable persons; or (2) capable of immediate and accurate demonstration by resort to readily accessible sources of indisputable accuracy[.][66]

A strict standard for judicial notice is embodied in these dual criteria, which have become known as the "Morgan criteria" because they emerge from the writings of Professor Edmund Morgan.[67] In the leading case of *R. v. Spence*, the Supreme Court described the Morgan criteria as the "gold standard" for judicial notice and reaffirmed that facts meeting these criteria will be noticed.[68]

However, the Court further held that some facts can be judicially noticed even if they do not meet the strict Morgan criteria. Here the Court relied on the distinction, well-established in the cases and the literature, between "adjudicative," "legislative" and "social" facts. Adjudicative facts are facts personal to the immediate parties before the court; they have to do with the what, where, when and how of the matter being litigated. Details about the crime scene, for example, would be adjudicative facts in a criminal case. Legislative facts are the legal policy considerations used by a court in interpreting legislation or developing the law. In *Oakes*, for instance, the Supreme Court considered legislative facts when it referred to domestic and international policy documents on the issue of drug trafficking.[69] Finally, social facts emerge from social science research that provides a structure or context for analyzing the factual issues at trial. Examples of social facts include the insights courts have taken from the social sciences in their approach to evidence about the timing of disclosures by sexual assault complainants.[70] The most important distinction to bear in mind is the divide between adjudicative facts on the one hand and non-adjudicative, social and legislative facts on the other. Courts are more free to take judicial notice of the latter than the former.

According to *Spence*, adjudicative facts can only be noticed if they meet the strict Morgan criteria. Legislative and social facts, by contrast, can in some circumstances be judicially noticed even if they do not meet this gold standard. The closer these non-adjudicative facts come to the dispositive

---

66   *R. v. Find* (2001), 42 C.R. (5th) 1 at para. 48 (S.C.C.).
67   See *R. v. Spence* (2005), 33 C.R. (6th) 1; Edmund M. Morgan, "Judicial Notice" (1943-1944) 57 Harv. L. Rev. 269.
68   *Spence, ibid.* at para. 61.
69   *R. v. Oakes, supra,* note 42.
70   See, *e.g., R. v. D. (D.)* (2000), 36 C.R. (5th) 261 (S.C.C.).

issue in the case, the more difficult it will be to take judicial notice. Ultimately, a court should only take judicial notice if the fact is one that reasonable people informed on the topic would consider to be beyond reasonable dispute for the purpose for which it is to be used.

The limits on judicial notice reflect a concern about fairness to the parties within the adversary process. Once a fact has been judicially noticed, it a conclusively held to be true for the purposes of the proceeding and the opposing party has no opportunity to challenge it.[71] Clearly this procedure departs from our normal expectations of the adversary process, in which each party can challenge the other's factual claims through cross-examination and the calling of witnesses. Given this departure from adversary norms, one can understand why judicial notice is limited to facts that are in some sense indisputable. The more disputed the fact, and the closer it falls to the centre of the controversy, the greater would be the sense of unfairness to the party against whose interests judicial notice of fact is taken.[72] These fairness concerns are compounded when a court remains silent about its intention to use judicial notice; the parties are left to guess at the judge's appreciation of the applicable facts and may miss the opportunity to assist the court by displaying contrary data to support a competing view. Consequently, when a court plans to take judicial notice of a fact that is or may be disputed, fairness often dictates that the judge give notice and the parties be given a chance to present information and argument on the issue.[73] Often there are respectable competing schools of thought as to whether the matter should be judicially noticed or proved by evidence in the normal way.[74]

An interesting question arose in *Zundel*.[75] The accused was charged with publishing statements that he knew to be false and likely to cause mischief to the public interest. He had published a pamphlet "Did Six Million Really Die?" The Crown then asked the judge to judicially notice the fact of the Holocaust as notorious. The trial judge refused and the Court of Appeal agreed. The Court decided that to judicially notice the Holocaust would have necessitated the judge telling the jury that they must find the Holocaust to have occurred and this would have been prejudicial to the accused as it would have influenced the drawing of the inference concerning the accused's knowledge of the falsity of the pamphlet. The reader might

---

71 *Spence, supra* note 67 at para. 55.

72 See, *e.g., R. v. Peter Paul* (1998), 18 C.R. (5th) 360 (N.B. C.A.).

73 Compare *Moge v. Moge*, [1992] 3 S.C.R. 813 and *Cronk v. Canadian General Insurance Co.* (1995), 25 O.R. (3d) 505 (C.A.).

74 See Delisle, "The Dangers of Unrestricted Judicial Notice" (1998) 12 C.R. (5th) 209; and *R. v. P. (S.D.)* (1995), 98 C.C.C. (3d) 83 (Ont. C.A.), in which the Ontario Court of Appeal split over whether the trial judge erred in taking judicial notice, based on an unspecified body of "literature", that child witnesses have difficulty remembering dates.

75 *R. v. Zundel* (1987), 56 C.R. (3d) 1 (Ont. C.A.).

ask whether taking judicial notice would have unfairly prejudiced the accused.[76]

Reported cases illustrate the variety of facts that are commonly noticed by our judges, dispensing with the need for formal proof. Our courts have decided, for example, that it is not necessary to prove that Victoria is in British Columbia,[77] that L.S.D. can be a mind destroying drug,[78] that big horn sheep are mountain sheep,[79] or that "O.D.'d" means overdosed on a drug.[80] More controversially, courts have taken judicial notice of the prevalence of racism against minority groups in permitting prospective jurors to be challenged for cause of the basis of racial bias.[81]

(b) Noticing Facts the Judge Personally Knows

It is one thing for a judge to judicially notice things which are generally known and another for a judge to notice facts that have been proved before her in other cases. The latter is forbidden by our courts.[82] The adversary system dictates that the parties present the evidence and the trier should only notice things commonly known. If the judge has information about the case before her, not shared by others, she should disregard the same or take the witness stand and be cross-examined as to whether her belief is accurate! Nevertheless, the line may be difficult to draw. For example, suppose an expert witness testifies before Judge A on Monday that it is not uncommon for a victim of sexual assault to recant an earlier complaint.[83] Judge A takes that evidence into account in assessing the credibility of the complainant before her who did recant her accusation. Must she hear evidence again on Tuesday to similar effect? On Wednesday? Suppose she takes it into account and an appellate court decides she was right to take it into account. At some point in time the evidence passes the stage of necessary testimony into the realm of judicial notice and from there into the domain of *stare decisis*.[84]

---

76 For criticism of the Court's approach see Delisle, Annotation to *Zundel* (1987), 56 C.R. (3d) 94.

77 *R. v. Kuhn* (1970), 1 C.C.C. (2d) 132 (B.C. Co. Ct.).

78 *R. v. Shaw* (1977), 36 C.R.N.S. 358 (Ont. C.A.).

79 *R. v. Quinn* (1975), 27 C.C.C. (2d) 543 (Alta. S.C.).

80 *R. v. MacAulay* (1975), 25 C.C.C. (2d) 1 (N.B. C.A.).

81 See *R. v. Parks* (1993), 24 C.R. (4th) 81 (Ont. C.A.); *R. v. Williams* (1998), 15 C.R. (5th) 227 (S.C.C.); *R. v. Koh* (1998), 21 C.R. (5th) 188 (Ont. C.A.).

82 *R. v. Holmes* (1922), 70 D.L.R. 851 (Alta. S.C.); *R. v. Dickson* (1973), 5 N.S.R. (2d) 240 (S.C. (A.D.)); and *R. v. Potts* (1982), 26 C.R. (3d) 252 (Ont. C.A.).

83 See *R. v. J. (F.E.)* (1990), 74 C.R. (3d) 269 (Ont. C.A.).

84 See *U.S. v. Lopez*, 328 F.Supp. 1077 (E.D.N.Y. 1971), *per* Weinstein J.

(c) Noticing Law

A judge is presumed to know the domestic law of the jurisdiction in which she presides – the domestic common and statutory law. If it is not ready to mind she is bound to acquire it. Information concerning the domestic law is not led by the parties through evidence though the parties may direct the judge to what they believe is the applicable law. There are statutory provisions requiring the judge to notice federal and provincial legislation.[85] The judge is not restricted to information from the parties and, frequently, while having reserved her decision, she will inform herself as to the law. Should she be in error an appellate court is there to correct. If it is the final appellate tribunal discovering or creating the law we must accept its discovery as accurate. Delegated legislation like municipal by-laws is sometimes seen not to possess the requisite notoriety or accessibility for judicial notice and may need to be proved as a fact.[86]

9. Real Evidence

Aside from testimonial evidence, the trier might be informed by real evidence. Rather than having a witness describe the gun that was used, the gun itself might be placed into evidence. Rather than describing the intersection where the car accident occurred, the court may go to the scene and examine the intersection itself. The trier does not rely on what a witness has said; the trier essentially becomes the witness.[87] The kinds of real evidence are infinitely variable and here we will discuss only a few of them, as well as some general principles applicable to all.

(a) Authentication

To be receivable, real evidence must, of course, be relevant and it will only be relevant to the matters in issue if the item offered into evidence is

---

85 See, *e.g.*, *Canada Evidence Act*, R.S.C. 1985, c. C-5, ss. 17 and 18. For provincial and territorial legislative provisions mandating judicial notice of statutes, see: R.S.A. 2000, c. A-18, s. 32; R.S.B.C. 1996, c. 124, s. 24; C.C.S.M., c. E150, ss. 29 and 30; R.S.N.B. 1973, c. E-11, s. 70; R.S.N.L. 1990, c. E-16, s. 26; R.S.N.W.T. 1988, c. E-8, s. 38; R.S.N.S. 1989, c. 154, s. 3(3); S.O. 2006, c. 21, Sch. F, s. 13; R.S.P.E.I. 1988, c. E-11, s. 21; S.S. 2006, c. E-11.2, s. 40; and R.S.Y. 2002, c. 78, s. 30.

86 See, for example, *MacLeod v. Yong* (1999), 67 B.C.L.R. (3d) 355 (C.A.); *Grand Central Ottawa Ltd. v. Ottawa (City)* (1997), 39 O.R. (3d) 47 (Prov. Div.); *R. v. Snelling*, [1952] O.W.N. 214 (H.C.). But compare *R. v. Smith* (1988), [1988] O.J. No. 2551 (Ont. Prov. Ct. (Crim. Div.)).

87 *R. v. Palmer* (1994), 1994 CarswellOnt 2732, [1994] O.J. No. 105 at para. 33 (Ont. Gen. Div.).

identified as genuine. The item must be authenticated to be what it is represented to be and the connection to the issues before the court made out. For example, in a prosecution for assault causing bodily harm, a blood stained shirt offered in evidence is not relevant to the matter in issue, that harm was visited on the victim, unless it is identified as having been worn by the victim on the evening in question. A witness must testify that this is the shirt. There are functions here for both the judge and the jury. The judge must be satisfied that there is sufficient evidence introduced to permit a rational finding by the jury that the item is as claimed. The jury will, later in their deliberations, weigh the evidence supposedly identifying the item, and determine whether the item is in fact authentic.[88]

(b) Photographs

A picture, as we know, can be worth a thousand words. A photograph then is a common form of real evidence. The photograph may be a still photograph or a series of photos; in other words the same principles will be applicable to a still shot as are applicable to a video recording. In *Schaffner*,[89] the accused was charged with theft of moneys from the liquor store. He had been employed as a clerk. The management had noticed inordinately high shortages. They decided to use video surveillance. Attached to the video-cassette recorder were a tape stacker and a time/date generator that would imprint directly on each videotape the date and the time it was taken. There was no operator present during the filming; the procedure was automatic. During the *voir dire,* the investigating officer showed and commented upon four tapes depicting irregularities on the part of the accused in conjunction with the detailed cash register tape for each day under study. He was able to identify the accused and pointed out four separate irregularities in the handling of cash by the accused. On appeal from conviction, the Court stated that a photograph is admissible in evidence if it accurately represents the facts, is not tendered with the intention to mislead and is verified on oath by any person who is capable of attesting that the photograph has these necessary qualities. The photographer who took the pictures need not be called and there need not be an eye-witness to the matter recorded. In the result in *Schaffner*, the Court was satisfied that the tapes were properly authenticated and admitted into evidence.[90] In short, to be admissible, pho-tographs must be relevant, material, accurate, fair and authentic; and of course, even when these requirements are met the trial judge retains a

---

88   See, *e.g.*, *R. v. Parsons* (1977), 37 C.C.C. (2d) 497 (Ont. C.A.).

89   *R. v. Schaffner* (1988), 44 C.C.C. (3d) 507 (N.S. C.A.).

90   Compare *R. v. Nikolovski* (1996), 3 C.R. (5th) 362 (S.C.C.) with respect to a video where the victim cannot identify the accused but the trial judge can.

discretion to exclude photographs whose prejudicial effect outweighs their probative value.[91]

(c) Documents

The most common form of real evidence is a document. The authenticity of the tendered document may be established in a variety of ways. The party tendering may call the suggested writer, may call someone who saw the document being made, may have a witness compare the handwriting in the document with writing known by the witness to be that of the suggested writer,[92] may call experts in handwriting or experts in typefaces, and so on.

There are some documents so frequently encountered in litigation that the common law developed special rules of self-authentication. If a document is over 30 years old, there are no circumstances indicating fraud, and it is produced from a place where its custody would be natural, the circumstances call for it to be presumed authentic.[93] If a letter is received, purportedly signed by "Smith", the law will presume the letter to be authentic if it was received in response to an earlier letter addressed to Smith. The reply indicates knowledge in the signer which, relying on the habitual accuracy of the mails, could only have come from the earlier letter addressed to Smith.[94] The legislation is also filled with statutory provisions to aid in the authentication of government documents and judicial records.[95]

(d) The Best Evidence Rule

There was, before the detailed development of our rules of evidence, a broad rule at common law known as the best evidence rule. The rule had exclusionary and inclusionary aspects. If it was shown that there was better

---

91 *R. v. Teerhuis-Moar* (2009), 237 Man. R. (2d) 26 at para. 66 (Q.B.). See also *R. v. S. (J.)* (2008), 236 C.C.C. (3d) 486 (Ont. S.C.J.).

92 See, *e.g.*, s. 8 of the *Canada Evidence Act*. For similar provincial and territorial provisions, see: R.S.N.L. 1990, c. E-16, s. 25; R.S.N.W.T. 1988, c. E-8, s. 58; R.S.N.S. 1989, c. 154, s. 41; R.S.O. 1990, c. E.23, s. 57; and R.S.P.E.I. 1988, c. E-11, s. 20.

93 *Montgomery v. Graham* (1871), 31 U.C.Q.B. 57 (Ont. Q.B.); *Canada (Minister of Citizenship & Immigration) v. Fast* (2003), 240 F.T.R. 161 at paras. 26-28 (F.C.); *Delgamuukw v. British Columbia* (1989), 38 B.C.L.R. (2d) 165 (S.C.).

94 See *Stevenson v. Dandy*, [1920] 2 W.W.R. 643 at 661 (Alta. S.C. (A.D.)).

95 See, *e.g.*, *Canada Evidence*, ss. 19 to 23. For similar provincial and territorial provisions, see: R.S.A. 2000, c. A-18, ss. 27-31; R.S.B.C. 1996, c. 124, ss. 25-27; C.C.S.M., c. E150, ss. 34 and 38; R.S.N.B. 1973, c. E-11, ss. 72-75, 77; R.S.N.L. 1990, c. E-16, ss. 20, 21; R.S.N.W.T. 1988, c. E-8, ss. 39, 49; R.S.N.S. 1989, c. 154, ss. 3-10; R.S.O. 1990, c. E.23, ss. 24-27; R.S.P.E.I. 1988, c. E-11, s. 22; S.S. 2006, c. E-11.2, ss. 41, 47; R.S.Y. 2002, c. 78, ss. 31, 41.

evidence available than that being tendered the tendered evidence would be rejected. If it was shown that the evidence being tendered was the very best available then it deserved receipt. As the rules of evidence developed, little remained of the rule and what does remain might better be called the documentary originals rule.[96] The current rule requires production of the original document when it is available.[97] A copy is admissible when the proponent of the evidence can satisfy the court that the original has been lost or destroyed or is in the possession of another and cannot be obtained. Also, certain statutory provisions have been enacted to provide for the introduction of copies when to produce the original would cause great inconvenience.[98]

The documentary originals rule was born at a time when copies of documents were made by hand and the possibility of error in the copying was real. Today, insistence on the rule is often waived.

(e) Views

If it is physically impossible to bring the real evidence into a courtroom, the courtroom may have to go to the evidence and take a view. There is statutory authority for the same.[99] Taking a view is disruptive of normal court proceedings and it will be up to the discretion of the trial judge who will assess the importance of the evidence against the disruption that will occur. The courts appear to be divided as to whether the view is only a device for better understanding the evidence adduced in the courtroom or whether the view is evidence in and of itself that may contradict evidence given in the courtroom. The better position is the latter.[100] The former position confuses what is real evidence with what is sometimes referred to as demonstrative evidence. Demonstrative evidence – charts, models and the like – comprises tools to assist the trier in understanding the evidence.

---

96   See *Garton v. Hunter*, [1969] 1 All E.R. 451 at 453 (C.A.).

97   *R. v. Betterest Vinyl Manufacturing Ltd.* (1989), 52 C.C.C. (3d) 441 at 447-48 (B.C. C.A.).

98   See, *e.g.*, *Canada Evidence Act*, ss. 29 to 31. For similar provincial and territorial provisions, see: R.S.A. 2000, c. A-21, s. 33; R.S.B.C. 1996, c. 124, ss. 33-35; C.C.S.M., c. E150, ss. 35-37; R.S.N.B. 1973, c. E-11, ss. 36-43; R.S.N.L. 1990, c. E-16, ss. 27, 29; R.S.N.W.T. 1988, c. E-8, ss. 39, 45, 51; R.S.N.S. 1989, c. 154, ss. 12-22; R.S.O. 1990, c. E.23, ss. 28-33; R.S.P.E.l. 1988, c. E-11, ss. 27-30; S.S. 2006, c. E-11.2, ss. 43-47; R.S.Y. 2002, c. 78, ss. 32-37.

99   See, *e.g.*, s. 652 of the *Criminal Code* and the *Ontario Rules of Civil Procedure*, R. 52.05.

100   See *Buckingham v. Daily News Ltd.*, [1956] 2 All E.R. 904 at 914 (C.A.), *per* Lord Denning; *Meyers v. Manitoba* (1960), 26 D.L.R. (2d) 550 (Man. C.A.); and *G & J Parking Lot Maintenance Ltd. v. Oland Construction Co.* (1978), 16 A.R. 293 (S.C. (T.D.)).

Real evidence, whether tendered as an object within the courtroom or viewed outside is not a helpful aid but rather is evidence itself. Nevertheless, there is appellate authority to the contrary.[101]

---

101 See *Chambers v. Murphy*, [1953] 2 D.L.R. 705 (Ont. C.A.); *Triple A Investments Ltd. v. Adams Brothers Ltd.* (1985), 56 Nfld. & P.E.I.R. 272 (Nfld. C.A.); and *Swadron v. North York (City)* (1985), 8 O.A.C. 204 (Div. Ct.).

3

Witnesses

1. Introduction

The testimonial qualifications of a witness are measured according to that witness's ability to observe, to recall her observation, and to accurately communicate her recollection to the trier of fact. The witness's ability to communicate has two aspects: the intellectual ability to understand questions and to give intelligent answers, and the moral responsibility to speak the truth. Each of these qualifications provides fertile ground for the cross-examiner to explore, for the benefit of the trier of fact, the credibility and reliability and hence the worth of the testimony. Were you able to see? Do you now properly remember? What do you mean by those words? Do you hate my client?

The early common law erected rules which completely forbade testimony from certain classes of individuals who were regarded as incapable of exercising the normal powers of observation, recollection and communication. For these individuals, the safeguard of cross-examination was seen as insufficient to the task of insuring credibility and reliability. Therefore, they were ruled incompetent as witnesses. Later, the law refined its approach and decided that, rather than approaching these witnesses as classes and rejecting them wholesale, it was preferable to examine the credentials of each particular individual being tendered as a witness. If the person was found to be competent, any deficiencies in testimonial qualifications would affect the weight to be given to the testimony rather than its admissibility. Under the modern approach, then, the great majority of proposed witnesses are competent, in the sense that they are permitted to testify. Moreover, in general, competent witnesses are also compellable: they can be forced to testify *sub poena*, under penalty of law.

Factors affecting a witness's competence can be organic, within the witness's own being, or emotional, as the result of a personal relationship with the matter being litigated or the parties thereto.

2. Organic Incapacity and the Oath

Early on, the common law insisted that all testimony be given on oath. This requirement led to the disqualification of numerous potential witnesses who were unable or unwilling to take an oath, including people with intellectual disabilities, children, and those with conscientious objections.

(a) Mental Incapacity

Initially a witness who was mentally ill was regarded as incompetent to take the witness stand. The courts came to recognize that this put the person who was mentally ill in a particularly vulnerable position. In *Hill*,[1] the accused was an attendant at a mental institution. He was charged with the manslaughter of one of the patients. The chief prosecution witness was another patient. It was objected that he was incompetent because of his mental illness. The precedents at the time were in conflict over whether there should be a blanket rule of inadmissibility. Instead of excluding him entirely the Court decided it would be better for the trial judge to conduct an examination of the particular individual whose mental capacity was questioned to determine whether the individual, though mentally ill, was nevertheless sufficiently aware of his moral responsibility to speak the truth in the courtroom and intellectually able to observe, recollect and communicate. There were seen to be two aspects to his competence: one moral and one intellectual. There were seen to be two possible sources of error: the witness might be unable to adequately appreciate the moral obligation of speaking the truth or the witness might not have the mental ability to accurately perceive and fully understand what he or she has seen or to properly remember or communicate the same. Although the witness in *Hill* had described his awareness of the consequences of a false oath—eternal damnation—the bulk of the evidence led on his testimonial qualifications concerned his ability to accurately observe, recollect and rationally communicate. Evidence was given that the witness did suffer the delusion that spirits spoke to him, but he was also described as having a good memory and a good ability to give an accurate account of events observed. It was decided that the trial judge was right in swearing the witness.

The common law on a witness's mental capacity is now embodied in statute. Section 16 of the *Canada Evidence Act* governs the testimonial competence of adults with mental illnesses and intellectual disabilities:

---

1   *R. v. Hill* (1851), 169 E.R. 495 (C.C.C.R.).

16. (1) If a proposed witness is a person fourteen years of age or older whose mental capacity is challenged, the court shall, before permitting the person to give evidence, conduct an inquiry to determine

  (a) whether the person understands the nature of an oath or a solemn affirmation; and
  (b) whether the person is able to communicate the evidence.

(2) A person referred to in subsection (1) who understands the nature of an oath or a solemn affirmation and is able to communicate the evidence shall testify under oath or solemn affirmation.

(3) A person referred to in subsection (1) who does not understand the nature of an oath or a solemn affirmation but is able to communicate the evidence may, notwithstanding any provision of any Act requiring an oath or a solemn affirmation, testify on promising to tell the truth.

(4) A person referred to in subsection (1) who neither understands the nature of an oath or a solemn affirmation nor is able to communicate the evidence shall not testify.

(5) A party who challenges the mental capacity of a proposed witness of fourteen years of age or more has the burden of satisfying the court that there is an issue as to the capacity of the proposed witness to testify under an oath or a solemn affirmation.[2]

Under this section, proposed adult witnesses whose mental capacity is challenged fall into three categories: those who may give sworn testimony, those who may only testify unsworn, and those who may not testify at all. Individuals who are incapable of communicating the evidence fall into the latter category. Capacity to communicate the evidence entails the abilities to perceive and remember events as they actually occurred, and to understand and respond to questions intelligibly.[3]

When deciding whether the witness should testify sworn, the legislation makes it clear that the judge must inquire into the proposed witness's understanding of the oath or affirmation. Awareness of God is not essential, but to qualify to testify sworn the witness must appreciate the solemnity of the occasion and the added responsibility to tell the truth in court after taking an oath over and above the ordinary duty to tell the truth in normal social conduct.[4] Although on its face the legislation does not require it, the courts have decided that an analogous inquiry into the moral aspect of the witness's capacity should be conducted even before the witness is allowed to testify

---

2 *Canada Evidence Act*, R.S.C. 1985, c. C-5.

3 *R. v. Farley* (1995), 40 C.R. (4th) 190 (Ont. C.A.); *R. v. Marquard* (1993), 25 C.R. (4th) 1 (S.C.C.).

4 *R. v. Fletcher* (1982), 1 C.C.C. (3d) 370 (Ont. C.A.), and *R. v. Khan* (1990), 59 C.C.C. (3d) 92 (S.C.C.).

unsworn. In order to make the promise to tell the truth meaningful, the judge should determine that the proposed witness understands the duty to speak the truth in everyday social conduct, and a witness who lacks this under-standing should not be allowed to testify even unsworn.[5] These inquiries into witnesses' moral understanding can be problematic, because individ-uals with cognitive limitations can often give valuable testimony by de-scribing past events even if they have trouble answering questions about abstract notions like oaths, promises, duties and truth.[6]

Notice that under s. 16 the capacity of an adult witness is presumed. That capacity can be challenged and the challenger will have the onus of introducing evidence to raise the issue of incapacity. Then the party ten-dering the witness will have the burden of proving that the witness is competent.[7] The challenge regarding mental capacity should be taken at the outset and not after the witness has testified.[8] It would be wrong for counsel to sit in the bushes and wait to see whether the witness helps or hurts his case. If the witness's incompetency only becomes manifest later the evi-dence might be stricken or the jury cautioned regarding its weight.[9] The competency *voir dire* should take place in the presence of the jury, the theory being that the jury will then be better able to evaluate the worth of what a witness has to say if he is allowed to speak.[10] Normally the proposed witness should take the stand during the *voir dire*, so that the judge may observe and question the individual rather than relying on experts' opinions about the individual's competence.[11] Ultimately, the judge determines com-petence to speak and the jury determines credibility.

(b) Immaturity

The law governing child witnesses has changed dramatically in recent years. Early on a child could only be competent to testify if an examination revealed that he or she possessed sufficient knowledge of the nature and

---

5   *Farley, supra* note 3.
6   See the transcript of the judge's questioning of an intellectually disabled man in *Farley, ibid.*
7   *R. v. Hawke* (1975), 22 C.C.C. (2d) 19 at 27 (Ont. C.A.).
8   *R. v. Steinberg*, [1931] O.R. 222 at 257 (C.A.) and *R. v. Hawke, ibid.*
9   See the difficult case of *R. v. Thurlow* (1994), 34 C.R. (4th) 53 (Ont. Gen. Div.) where the court had to deal with a witness who admitted to having at least six different person-alities.
10 See, *e.g., Toohey v. Metropolitan Police Commissioner*, [1965] 1 All E.R. 506 at 512 (H.L.): "[T]here would not be the inconvenience of having to exclude the jury, since the dispute would be for their use and their instruction."
11 *R. v. Parrott* (2001), 39 C.R. (5th) 255 (S.C.C.).

consequences of an oath.[12] If the child was ruled incapable of taking an oath there was no way for her information to come before the court. In the nineteenth century the legislature recognized that children were at risk particularly with respect to sexual assault. Initially with respect to prosecutions for such assaults, and later expanded to all legal proceedings, the legislatures decided that a child, though ruled not competent to take an oath, could give evidence unsworn provided the child possessed sufficient intelligence to justify reception of the evidence and understood the duty of speaking the truth.[13]

Although permitting some children to testify unsworn allowed more young people to participate in the justice system, the law remained essentially mistrustful of child witnesses. For example, while the general rule is that the trier may rely on the evidence of a single witness, the unsworn evidence of children was subject to a corroboration requirement: it could not be relied upon without confirmatory evidence from another source.[14] By 1992, this corroboration requirement had been removed and the Supreme Court of Canada declared that the law had moved beyond the idea that children's evidence was inherently unreliable.[15] As we will see, the law has since evolved even further in the direction of openness to children's evidence.

Until very recently, child witnesses were presumed incompetent to testify. Aside from that presumption of incompetence, child witnesses were treated exactly as adults whose mental capacity is challenged are treated today under s. 16 of the *Canada Evidence Act*, discussed above. That is, child witnesses could give evidence sworn or unsworn, depending on the judge's assessment of their level of understanding of the oath or the duty to tell the truth. They could not testify at all if they could not demonstrate an understanding of the duty to speak the truth, or if they were unable to communicate the evidence. Sworn testimony was seen to have greater value than unsworn testimony, which meant that children's evidence was frequently discounted.[16] Provincial and territorial legislation maintains a distinction between the sworn and unsworn evidence of children,[17] but the federal scene has changed.

---

12 *R. v. Brasier* (1779), 168 E.R. 202 (C.C.R.).

13 See, *e.g.*, *Canada Evidence Act*, R.S.C. 1970, c. E-10, s. 16(1).

14 See, *e.g.*, *Canada Evidence Act*, R.S.C. 1970, c. E-10, s. 16(2).

15 *R. v. W. (R.)* (1992), 13 C.R. (4th) 257 (S.C.C.).

16 Nick Bala, Katherine Duvall-Antonacopoulos, R.C.L. Lindsay & Victoria Talwar, "Bill C-2: A New Law for Canada's Child Witnesses" (2006), 32 C.R. (6th) 48 at 57-58.

17 See, *e.g.*, R.S.A. 2000, c. A-18, s. 19(1); R.S.B.C. 1996, c. 124, s. 5; R.S.N.S. 1989, c. 154, s. 63(1); R.S.O. 1990, c. E.23, s. 18.1.

In 2006, s. 16.1 of the *Canada Evidence Act* came into effect and many of the old rules and assumptions about child witnesses were discarded. The new section provides:

16.1 (1) A person under fourteen years of age is presumed to have the capacity to testify.

(2) A proposed witness under fourteen years of age shall not take an oath or make a solemn affirmation despite a provision of any Act that requires an oath or a solemn affirmation.

(3) The evidence of a proposed witness under fourteen years of age shall be received if they are able to understand and respond to questions.

(4) A party who challenges the capacity of a proposed witness under fourteen years of age has the burden of satisfying the court that there is an issue as to the capacity of the proposed witness to understand and respond to questions.

(5) If the court is satisfied that there is an issue as to the capacity of a proposed witness under fourteen years of age to understand and respond to questions, it shall, before permitting them to give evidence, conduct an inquiry to determine whether they are able to understand and respond to questions.

(6) The court shall, before permitting a proposed witness under fourteen years of age to give evidence, require them to promise to tell the truth.

(7) No proposed witness under fourteen years of age shall be asked any questions regarding their understanding of the nature of the promise to tell the truth for the purpose of determining whether their evidence shall be received by the court.

(8) For greater certainty, if the evidence of a witness under fourteen years of age is received by the court, it shall have the same effect as if it were taken under oath.[18]

This section abolishes the presumption of incapacity and establishes a presumption that children are competent to testify. It also eliminates the distinction between sworn and unsworn testimony of children, requiring all witness under 14 years of age to testify unsworn on a promise to tell the truth. Contrary to prior practice, such testimony is not to be discounted because it is unsworn; unsworn children's testimony is to have the same effect as if it had been given on oath. Finally, the section puts an end to the practice of questioning children about their understanding the oath and the promise to tell the truth. Rather, under the new law, the judge need only be satisfied that the proposed child witness can understand and respond to questions.

---

18   *Canada Evidence Act*, R.S.C. 1985, c. C-5.

Notice that the statute says that where a child witness's capacity is in issue "the court . . . shall . . . conduct an inquiry" into the matter. This language remains unchanged from the prior legislation, and it seems likely that certain features of the competency inquiry will persist under the new law. For example, while often it is the judge who asks the questions of the child, the courts have recognized that the Crown, who is less of a stranger to the child, may be the better questioner. Just because the court is to conduct the inquiry does not necessarily mean that the court must actually ask the questions.[19] Under the former law, a practice developed of inquiring into the child's ability to communicate by asking questions about a past event that was not in issue, such as a birthday. This approach seems equally appropriate in the context of a s. 16.1 inquiry into the child's ability to understand and respond to questions.[20]

The changes in s. 16.1 reflect insights from empirical research into child witnesses. The research has revealed that children's ability to answer questions about the meaning of abstract concept like truth, lie and promise bears no relation to whether they will in fact tell the truth.[21] Contrary to the view sometimes expressed in the courts that the promise to tell the truth would be an empty formalism without an inquiry into the proposed witness's moral understanding,[22] the research suggests that children who promise to tell the truth are more likely to do so, even if they cannot answer abstract questions about the meaning of that promise.[23]

The new regime under s. 16.1 has been challenged on the basis that the presumption of testimonial capacity and the process of allowing child witnesses to testify unsworn without the traditional inquiry into their moral understanding interferes with the accused's Charter right to a fair trial. So far these constitutional challenges have been unsuccessful, and the Supreme Court of Canada will consider the issue shortly.[24] There is reason to hope that the Supreme Court will affirm the lower court decisions upholding the law, which represents a measured and empirically-grounded attempt to facilitate children's participation in the justice system without eroding the rights of the accused.[25] Indeed, the changes in s. 16.1 form a part of a larger, salutary trend toward openness to children's evidence. In the same spirit, legislators have recently allowed for the admission of video-recorded evi-

---

19 See, *e.g.*, *R. v. Peterson* (1996), 47 C.R. (4th) 161 (Ont. C.A.), leave to appeal refused [1996] 3 S.C.R. xii.

20 See Bala *et al.*, *supra*, note 16 at 56-57.

21 *Ibid.* at 58.

22 See *Farley*, *supra*, note 3.

23 See Bala *et al.*, *supra*, note 16 at 55.

24 *R. v. S. (J.)* (2008), 61 C.R. (6th) 282 (B.C. C.A.), leave to appeal to S.C.C. [2008] S.C.C.A. No. 542; *R. v. Persaud* [2007] O.J. No. 432 (Ont. S.C.J.).

25 See Dufraimont, Annotation to *R. v. S. (J.)* (2008), 61 C.R. (6th) 284.

dence of children and made it easier for child witnesses to testify live behind a screen, through closed circuit television, or with the aid of a support person.[26]

(c) The Oath and the Affirmation

At common law, it was decided fairly early on that anyone could take an oath provided they believed in a God and future rewards and punishments. The oath need not be a Christian oath.[27] The form of the oath is not prescribed by law. Nothing is said about its form in the *Canada Evidence Act*. The Ontario *Evidence Act* does provide a form of oath involving holding the Old or New Testament but also provides that should the witness object to such form any form may be followed that binds the conscience.[28] By definition, an "oath" is calling on God to witness that a person is going to tell the truth and involves a recognition that God will either reward or punish the person in this world or the next. Our courts have said, however, that belief in God is not required, and a witness may take an oath if he understands the added responsibility of telling the truth in the courtroom. In *Fletcher*,[29] the Court recognized that as society has changed over the years the oath for many has lost its spiritual and religious significance. Nonetheless, the sense of moral obligation, of binding one's conscience, will suffice for a witness to take an oath.

At common law, some people who did believe in God were excluded as witnesses. For example, the Quakers thought it wrong to call on God to witness their temporal matters. Legislation was enacted to accommodate them. The *Canada Evidence Act* provides:

> 14. (1) A person may, instead of taking an oath, make the following solemn affirmation:
>
> I solemnly affirm that the evidence to be given by me shall be the truth, the whole truth and nothing but the truth.

---

26 See, *e.g.*, *Evidence Act*, R.S.O. 1990, c. E.23, ss. 18.3, 18.4, 18.5; *Criminal Code*, R.S.C, 1985, c. C-46, ss. 486.1, 486.2, 715.1; *R. v. L. (D.O.)* (1993), 25 C.R. (4th) 285 (S.C.C.); *R. v. Levogiannis* (1993), 25 C.R. (4th) 325 (S.C.C.).

27 *Omychund v. Barker* (1744), 26 E.R. 15 (C.A.).

28 R.S.O. 1990, c. E.23, s. 16. To like effect, see C.C.S.M., c. E150, ss. 14 and 15; R.S.N.B. 1973, c. E-11, s. 13; R.S.N.W.T. 1988, c. E-8, s. 21; R.S.Y. 2002, c. 78, s. 19; on a bible or with uplifted hand: R.S.A. 2000, c. A-18, ss. 14-16; oath with an uplifted hand: R.S.B.C. 1996, c. 124, s. 22. No form of oath is prescribed in Saskatchewan, Nova Scotia, Newfoundland or Prince Edward Island.

29 *R. v. Fletcher*, *supra*, note 4.

(2) Where a person makes a solemn affirmation in accordance with subsection (1), his evidence shall be taken and have the same effect as if taken under oath.

As an example of provincial legislation, the Ontario *Evidence Act* provides:

17.—(1) Where a person objects to being sworn from conscientious scruples, or on the ground of his or her religious belief, or on the ground that the taking of an oath would have no binding effect on the person's conscience, he or she may, in lieu of taking an oath, make an affirmation or declaration that is of the same force and effect as if the person had taken an oath in the usual form.[30]

It seems sensible for counsel calling a witness to advise that witness, in advance of the proceedings, of his options. Indeed it is sensible for counsel, knowing her witness's preferences, to announce the same to the court as the witness proceeds to the stand so that the witness does not himself have to take on that obligation. The witness is normally strange to the setting and may find it difficult to announce his preference in a crowded courtroom.

3. Emotional Incapacity

At common law, persons who were seen to be interested in the outcome of a piece of litigation were regarded as incompetent to be witnesses. A rather blunt tool to be sure, but the law decided that such persons were so suspect that they should not be heard at all. This disqualification therefore meant that the parties to a matter, the plaintiff and the defendant in a civil trial, and the accused in a criminal trial, were not competent as witnesses. The law also saw the spouses of the parties to be similarly interested and spouses as well were regarded as incompetent.

There was one exception regarding spouses. The law early recognized that a spouse was vulnerable to abuse that might never be prosecuted if the spouse was incompetent to speak and therefore the common law provided that a spouse could testify against her spouse if she was the subject of his abuse.[31] This exception has been preserved by legislation.[32] In fact, there is authority indicating that in such a case the spouse is also a compellable witness at the instance of the prosecution.[33] Our courts have reasoned that

---

30 For similar provisions in other provinces, see: R.S.A. 2000, c. A-18, s. 17; R.S.B.C. 1996, c. 124, s. 20; C.C.S.M., c. E150, s. 16; R.S.N.B. 1973, c. E-11, s. 14; R.S.N.W.T. 1988, c. E-8, s. 23; R.S.N.S. 1989, c. 154, s. 62; R.S.P.E.I. 1988, c. E-11, s. 13; S.S. 2006, c. E-11.2, s. 25; and R.S.Y. 2002, c. 78, s. 21.

31 See *Lord Audley's Trial* (1631), 3 Howell's State Trials 401 (H.L.).

32 Section 4(5) of the *Canada Evidence Act*.

33 *R. v. McGinty* (1986), 52 C.R. (3d) 161 (Y.T. C.A.).

in a case of spousal abuse it is not just the spouse who is interested in a successful prosecution—society also has an interest. Such crimes are common, the consequences frequently grave and, since these crimes are usually committed in the privacy of the home, they are often impossible to prosecute unless the victim testifies.

Reforming legislation came about in the nineteenth century. In civil cases, parties and their spouses were rendered competent as witnesses and their interest was left to impact solely on the weight to be given to their testimony. For example, the Ontario *Evidence Act* provides:

> 8.(1) The parties to an action and the persons on whose behalf it is brought, instituted, opposed or defended are, except as hereinafter otherwise provided, competent and compellable to give evidence on behalf of themselves or of any of the parties, and the husbands and wives of such parties and persons are, except as hereinafter otherwise provided, competent and compellable to give evidence on behalf of any of the parties.[34]

In the criminal context, the accused was rendered a competent witness in Canada in 1893. The *Canada Evidence Act* provides that the accused and his spouse are competent witnesses for the defence:

> 4. (1) Every person charged with an offence, and, except as otherwise provided in this section, the wife or husband, as the case may be, of the person so charged, is a competent witness for the defence, whether the person so charged is charged solely or jointly with any other person.

It has been suggested that a spouse who is competent to testify for the defence by virtue of s. 4(1) may also be compelled to testify for the defence, but the Supreme Court has declined to finally decide the issue.[35]

In general, neither the accused nor his spouse are competent witnesses for the Crown. With respect to the accused this rule is absolute: the accused in a criminal case can never be called as a witness by the prosecution. Whether or not he takes the witness stand is solely up to him. This lack of competence in the accused is rooted in the privilege against self-incrimination. The spouse's lack of competence, by contrast, is rooted in the notion that it is wrong for the courts to disrupt marital harmony by having one spouse testify against the interests of the other. Recognizing this as the basis for their lack of competence our courts have decided that where there is no marital harmony to disrupt, where the spouses though married are irrecon-

---

34 See also R.S.A. 2000, c. A-18, s. 4; R.S.B.C. 1996, c. 124, s. 7; C.C.S.M., c. E150, s. 4; R.S.N.B. 1973, c. E-11, s. 3; R.S.N.L. 1990, c. E-16, s. 2; R.S.N.W.T. 1988, c. E-8, s. 3; R.S.N.S. 1989, c. 154, s. 45; R.S.P.E.I. 1988, c. E-11, ss. 2, 3 and 4; and R.S.Y. 2002, c. 78, s. 3.

35 See *R. v. Couture* (2007), 47 C.R. (6th) 1 at para. 40 (S.C.C.); *R. v. Amway of Canada Ltd./Amway du Canada Ltée*, [1989] 1 S.C.R. 21; *R. v. Gosselin* (1903), 33 S.C.R. 255.

cilably separated, a spouse may testify.[36] The federal legislation also provides for a number of exceptions to the general common law rule of spousal incompetence. In addition to preserving the exception for abused spouses noted above, the *Canada Evidence Act* makes the accused's spouse competent and compellable with respect to certain crimes, largely sexual offences,[37] and with respect to various violent crimes where the victim is under the age of 14 years.[38]

It is worth noting that these common law and statutory spousal incompetency rules apply only to legally married spouses and not to unmarried cohabitants. This differential treatment has the potential to raise equality concerns under the Charter.[39] With its mix of common law and statutory components, the current law on spousal incompetency has been criticized as too complex, unprincipled and potentially arbitrary.[40] However, the Supreme Court has indicated that any major changes to the law should be left to Parliament.[41]

4. Manner of Questioning

The principal source of information at a trial is oral testimony elicited out of the mouths of witnesses called by the parties. The fact that the witnesses were chosen by the parties, and that they may have been prepared by the parties as to how to give their evidence, led to different rules regarding the manner of questioning depending on who puts the questions.

The witness's description of the incident under review is first elicited by the party who called him. This process is called examination-in-chief or direct examination. At the conclusion of the direct examination, the adversary is allowed to ask questions of the witness. The adversary is then able to elicit other data concerning the incident which might be favourable to her position. The adversary is also able to put questions to the witness concerning his powers of perception and memory, to demand explicitness in his communication and to explore his sincerity. These questions are designed to challenge the accuracy of the witness's description of the incident. This process is known as cross-examination. Notice that there are two

---

36 *R. v. Salituro*, [1991] 3 S.C.R. 654.

37 Section 4(2) of the *Canada Evidence Act*.

38 Section 4(4) of the *Canada Evidence Act*.

39 In *R. v. Masterson* (2009), 245 C.C.C. (3d) 400, the Ontario Superior Court of Justice ruled that s. 4 of the *Canada Evidence Act* violates the equality guarantee in s. 15 of the Charter because it denies a benefit to common law spouses that is offered to legally married spouses. The Court determined that the appropriate remedy was to read common law spouses into s. 4 of the Act.

40 See, *e.g.*, Lee Stuesser, "Abolish Spousal Incompetency" (2007), 47 C.R. (6th) 49.

41 See *Couture, supra* note 35 at para. 47.

purposes in cross-examining: to gain additional information from the witness that the adversary neglected to bring out and to attack the worth of the evidence that was elicited. After cross-examination, the witness may be re-examined by the party who called him and given an opportunity to explain or amplify answers given on cross-examination. Further opportunities to cross-examine and re-examine, all at the discretion of the trial judge, are possible.

(a) Leading Questions

Speaking generally, the party who calls a witness should not ask the witness leading questions. A leading question is one which suggests the answer. The reason for the prohibition is obvious. There is a concern that since the party has chosen to call this witness, the witness favours that party and will readily agree to any suggestions put in the form of questions. This concern is amplified by the fact that counsel will have gone over the witness's evidence in advance of the trial and the witness will understand what answers are preferable. The trier of fact deserves the evidence of the witness as opposed to the evidence of the lawyer who is putting the questions and therefore suggestive questions must be avoided.

Like all rules of evidence this rule should not be applied if the reason for the rule does not exist. In determining whether a question suggests an answer, much will depend on the character, mood and bias of the witness, and the manner and inflection of the questioner, all matters particularly suited to the exercise of discretion by the trial judge. If the matter being pursued is a preliminary matter, such as identifying the witness and his means of knowledge, leading questions are not only permitted but are also the sign of a good advocate who has chosen not to waste the court's time. If it is necessary to identify for the witness the particular matter that the examiner wishes to explore, leading questions may be necessary and are therefore permitted. If it is necessary to refresh the witness's memory or if there is an apparent problem with the witness due to age, education, language or mental capacity, the trial judge will relax the rule and permit leading questions as the reason for the prohibition will be seen to not exist. If the witness appears clearly hostile to the examiner's position, clearly not ready to adopt any suggestion of the questioner, the examiner will ask the trial judge for a declaration of hostility and then leading questions will be permitted. Finally, apart from these specific situations, the trial judge has discretion to permit leading questions on direct where necessary in the interests of justice.[42]

---

42   *R. v. Rose* (2001), 42 C.R. (5th) 183 (Ont. C.A.).

While leading questions are generally prohibited when counsel is examining in chief, they are permitted in cross-examination. Indeed, leading questions are the hallmark of cross-examination. The advocate uses leading questions to achieve the dual purposes of cross-examination: eliciting additional information and challenging specific parts of the witness's testimony. The opportunity to cross-examine opposing witnesses in this way is thought to aid in the discovery of truth and represents a cornerstone of trial fairness in the adversary system. Indeed, for the criminal accused, the right to cross-examine receives constitutional protection under ss. 7 and 11(d) of the Charter.[43] A trial judge has discretion to restrain a cross-examination that is irrelevant, repetitive, unduly prejudicial or abusive to the witness, but the scope of permissible cross-examination remains very broad.[44] The Supreme Court has even held that a cross-examiner may put suggestions to the witness for which there is no evidence, provided that the questioner has a good faith basis for the suggestion. This good faith basis may be rooted in reasonable inference, experience or even the cross-examiner's intuition.[45]

From the above analysis it might appear logical that if the opposing witness actually favours the position of the cross-examiner, the trial judge should have the power to restrain the questioner from asking leading questions. Again we want the evidence of the witness and not the evidence of the questioner. Although apparently logical, the cases suggest that a trial judge may not limit cross-examination in this way. Rather, the weight to be given to the answers in such a situation will be affected.[46] Apart from leading questions, there is also a prohibition against what might be called misleading questions. It is wrong for counsel to phrase a question so as to assume within it the truth of some fact which remains controverted between the parties as the witness may be unfairly misled. The classic example is "When did you stop beating your wife?"

(b) Refreshing Memory

While ethical considerations forbid placing a story in the mouth of a prospective witness, there appear to be few restrictions on the methods used to refresh a witness's memory prior to the trial. The Supreme Court recently ruled inadmissible evidence of memories recovered through hypnosis.[47] But other means of refreshing a witness's memory pre-trial have generally been

---

43 *Canadian Charter of Rights and Freedoms*, Part I of the *Constitution Act, 1982*, being Schedule B to the *Canada Act 1982* (U.K.), 1982, c. 11.

44 *R. v. Lyttle* (2004), 17 C.R. (6th) 1 (S.C.C.).

45 *Ibid.*

46 See, *e.g.*, *R. v. McLaughlin* (1974), 2 O.R. (2d) 514 (C.A.).

47 *R. v. Trochym* (2007), 43 C.R. (6th) 217 (S.C.C.).

permitted, including allowing the witness to read her own notes or an earlier statement given to police.[48] Where a witness refreshes her memory from her notes before coming to court, the opposing counsel should have the opportunity to see the same for the purpose of possible impeachment.[49]

A witness in the stand may profess a lack of memory concerning the incident. That witness may then be shown notes concerning the incident made at an earlier time and, on seeing the notes, two things are possible. The witness, on seeing the notes, might profess a present memory concerning the matter. We have all had the experience of failing to remember a matter but on being reminded of something associated with the matter having the memory released thereby. The triggering device might be a note, a song, or a picture. In most cases that concern us, the trigger will be a note. In such a case, we have a true case of refreshment of memory and the witness will be permitted to testify, in accordance with that memory, concerning the event. We employ a piece of jargon and say that this is a case of present memory revived. On the other hand, on seeing the notes the witness might say that the notes do not revive his memory concerning the incident but that he remembers making the notes, remembers that the notes were made contemporaneously with the incident or at a time shortly thereafter when the events were fresh in his mind, and that the notes accurately record the incident. The witness who now has no present memory of the matter is prepared to vouch for the accuracy of the earlier description. In this situation, the so-called refreshment of memory is actually a case of past recollection recorded.[50]

Both phenomena are often referred to as refreshing the memory of the witness. This is unfortunate, because only in the case of present memory revived is the witness's memory actually refreshed. In a case of past recollection recorded it is the earlier note that is speaking. The earlier out-of-court statement is received as evidence of its truth as an exception to the hearsay rule.[51] In this instance it is the out-of-court statement that is the evidence and deserves to be received.[52] To guarantee reliability we insist that the statement be one made by the witness and accurately recorded at

---

48   See *R. v. B. (K.G.)* (1998), 125 C.C.C. (3d) 61 (Ont. C.A.). See also *R. v. Allen (No. 2)* (1979), 46 C.C.C. (2d) 477 (Ont. H.C.) regarding the use of sodium amytol to release repressed memories.

49   See, *e.g.*, *R. v. Monfils*, [1972] 1 O.R. 11 at 11-13 (C.A.); *Cornerstone Co-operative Homes Inc. v. Spilchuk* (2004), 72 O.R. (3d) 103 (SCJ.). But see *R. v. Kerenko* (1964), [1965] 3 C.C.C. 52 (Man. C.A.); *Shearer v. Hood*, (2008), [2008] M.J. No. 434, 2008 MBQB 317 (Q.B.).

50   These phrases were coined by Professor John Henry Wigmore: see 3 Wigmore, *Evidence* (Chadbourn Rev. 1970), s. 735. They have been adopted by Canadian courts: see, *e.g.*, *R. v. Wilks* (2005), 35 C.R. (6th) 172 (Man. C.A.).

51   See *R. v. Meddoui* (1991), 61 C.C.C. (3d) 345 (Alta. C.A.).

52   See, *e.g.*, *R. v. Richardson* (2003), 174 O.A.C. 390 (C.A.).

the time of the incident. Those requirements are appropriate in a case of past recollection recorded. They operate to ensure accuracy of recording and of memory. The adversary is unable to test the witness's present memory in cross-examination and there need to be other assurances. If, on the other hand, we have a true case of the memory being refreshed, the evidence is the testimony of the witness and not the note earlier made. The witness is thereby open for cross-examination as to whether he actually does have a present memory and to be questioned regarding the accuracy of his present memory. This is not a case of hearsay. The requirements of contemporaneity and that the notes be made by the witness deserve, in such a situation, to be relaxed.[53]

When a witness uses notes to refresh memory the adversary is also entitled to look at the notes and to ask questions of the witness concerning them. Were the notes made by the witness himself or were they made in collaboration with others? Why are there seeming interlineations? Erasures? What of the other notes which seem to qualify the witness's evidence?

(c) Examination by the Court and the Order of Witnesses

In a civil case, the court has no power to call witnesses. Who will be called as a witness is a decision for the parties.[54] The court may call a witness in a criminal case when doing so is necessary to discover the truth or in the interests of justice, but this discretion should rarely be exercised.[55] In criminal cases, society has its own interest in gaining the truth. In civil trials, while truth is important, justice in the sense that both litigants feel satisfied that their dispute, framed and processed by them, was properly settled, is paramount.

The prosecution is not entitled to split its case and therefore cannot call further witnesses after the defence has closed its case unless the matter has arisen *ex improviso, i.e.,* unless it is a matter that human ingenuity could not have foreseen.[56] This limitation is also applicable to the judge who normally may not call witnesses after the defence has closed its case.[57]

Both in civil and in criminal cases, the court has the right to ask questions of the witnesses to clarify matters. In exercising this right the court

---

53 See, *e.g., R. v. Bengert (No. 5)*, [1979] 1 W.W.R. 472 (B.C. S.C.), affirmed (sub nom. *R. v. Bengert (No. 11)*) (1980), 53 C.C.C. (2d) 481 at 522 (B.C. C.A.).

54 See *Re Fraser* (1912), 26 O.L.R. 508 at 521 (C.A.); and *Fowler v. Fowler*, [1949] O.W.N. 244 (C.A.).

55 *R. v. Finta* (1994), 28 C.R. (4th) 265 at paras. 295-96 (S.C.C.).

56 See, e.g., *R. v. John* (1985), 49 C.R. (3d) 57 (S.C.C.); *R. v. Anderson* (2009), 448 A.R. 165 (C.A.); *R. v. Dalen* (2008), 240 C.C.C. (3d) 557 (B.C. C.A.).

57 *Finta, supra* note 55 at para. 296.

should be cautious as it does not know as much about the case as the parties and interference can have the opposite effect to that intended.[58]

While the judge in a criminal case has no control over the order in which the accused calls his witnesses,[59] many provinces have enacted in rules of court governing civil cases a power in the court to require that the party be examined before other witnesses on his behalf.[60] These rules also provide power in the court to order the exclusion of prospective witnesses until they are required to give evidence. In criminal cases, there is inherent power in the court, to ensure a fair trial, to order the exclusion of witnesses. Since the accused has the right to be present during the whole of his trial he cannot be the subject of such an order. At one time it was understood that if an accused was going to testify he should testify first. That is no longer a requirement but if he does not testify first and so gains the advantage of listening to his witnesses being examined and cross-examined before himself going into the witness box, he risks a comment being made as to his credibility.[61]

5. Impeachment of a Witness

Aside from weakening a witness's description of a matter by cross-examination, the adversary is permitted to impeach the credibility of a witness by other evidence. This may be done by showing that the witness on another occasion made a statement concerning the matter which is inconsistent with her present testimony, by evidencing a bias in the witness which would cause the witness to be inaccurate, by extrinsic evidence attacking the character of the witness, or by leading evidence attacking the capacity of the witness to observe, remember or communicate.

(a) Prior Inconsistent Statements

A trier of fact is entitled to accept all, part or none of a witness's evidence. Contradiction on one aspect of the testimony will be taken into account when assessing the credibility of the witness in other aspects; if the witness is seen to be in error on one point, she is seen to be at least capable of error on other points. If counsel can establish that the witness on another

---

58 See *Jones v. National Coal Board*, [1957] 2 Q.B. 55 at 63 (C.A.); and *R. v. Rhodes* (1981), 59 C.C.C. (2d) 426 (B.C. C.A.).

59 *R. v. Smuk* (1971), 3 C.C.C. (2d) 457 (B.C. C.A.); and *R. v. Angelantoni* (1975), 31 C.R.N.S. 342 (Ont. C.A.).

60 See, *e.g., Ontario Rules of Civil Procedure*, R. 52.06(2).

61 But see *R. v. P. (T.L.)* (1996), 193 A.R. 146 (C.A.).

occasion made a statement which is inconsistent with her present testimony she has displayed a capacity to err as both statements cannot be correct. Counsel might then ask the witness "When were you lying? Then or now?"

(b) Collateral Facts Limitation

Counsel may be able to elicit the earlier inconsistent statement out of the mouth of the witness during cross-examination. If the witness does not admit making an earlier statement inconsistent with her present testimony, counsel may have to independently prove the same. If that method of contradiction proved necessary the common law developed a limitation.

The common law was concerned that independent proof of a previous inconsistent statement carried with it certain problems. First, there was the amount of time to be taken in such an exercise. Second, there was concern that the trier of fact could be led away from the main issue before it and become confused. Third, it was seen to be unfair to a witness who came to court to testify concerning a particular matter to be confronted with inconsistencies about other matters. The common law came up with a rule called the collateral facts rule. It is simple to state: while a witness may be asked all manner of questions impacting on credibility, she may not be contradicted by independent proof if the matter is collateral. If the matter is collateral the cross-examiner must accept the answer given.[62]

While the rule is easy to articulate, the determination of exactly what is collateral has proved to be difficult. Some would ask whether the matter would be independently provable whether or not the question was put on cross-examination. If the answer is yes then the matter is not collateral. Any independently provable matter has relevance to the material issues being litigated or to a testimonial factor affecting the witness and is therefore not collateral. A variant on this would be to ask whether the matter had meaning apart from the contradiction *simpliciter.* If yes, then the matter is not collateral. For example, evidence showing that the witness has a bias against the cross-examiner's party goes to the capacity of the witness to accurately describe the matters in issue, and is therefore not collateral.

The wisest approach might be to define collateral in terms of the reason for the rule. If the matter was seen as having great probative value either regarding the material issues or the credibility of the witness, if the introduction of the evidence would not confuse or mislead the trier, if proof would not consume too much time, and if it would not be unfair to the witness to bring extrinsic evidence, then the matter should not be regarded

---

62   *R. v. Krause* (1986), 54 C.R. (3d) 294 (S.C.C.).

as collateral. In other words, if the matter is important it's not collateral. If it's unimportant it's collateral.[63]

(c) Procedure for Using Prior Inconsistent Statements

The legislatures have enacted procedures for impeaching a witness by a previous inconsistent statement. For example, the *Canada Evidence Act* provides:

> 10. (1) On any trial a witness may be cross-examined as to previous statements that the witness made in writing, or that have been reduced to writing, or recorded on audio tape or video tape or otherwise, relative to the subject-matter of the case, without the writing being shown to the witness or the witness being given the opportunity to listen to the audio tape or view the video tape or otherwise take cognizance of the statements, but, if it is intended to contradict the witness, the witness' attention must, before the contradictory proof can be given, be called to those parts of the statement that are to be used for the purpose of so contradicting the witness, and the judge, at any time during the trial, may require the production of the writing or tape or other medium for inspection, and thereupon make such use of it for the purposes of the trial as the judge thinks fit.

> . . .

> 11. Where a witness, on cross-examination as to a former statement made by him relative to the subject-matter of the case and inconsistent with his present testimony, does not distinctly admit that he did make the statement, proof may be given that he did in fact make it, but before that proof can be given the circumstances of the supposed statement, sufficient to designate the particular occasion, shall be mentioned to the witness, and he shall be asked whether or not he did make the statement.[64]

Section 10 has to do with written statements and s. 11 with oral statements. The legislation incorporates the common law collateral facts rule by saying the earlier statement has to be "relative to the subject-matter of the case" before it can be proved. The statute provides that counsel in cross-examination is allowed to ask questions concerning the earlier statement, and if in writing without first showing the witness the statement, but that if counsel intends to independently prove the statement the witness must first

---

63 See Irving Younger, *The Art of Cross-Examination* (1974) ABA Monograph Series at 15.

64 For provincial and territorial counterparts, see: R.S.A. 2000, c. A-18, ss. 22, 23; R.S.B.C. 1996, c. 124, ss. 13, 14; C.C.S.M., c. E150, ss. 20 and 21; R.S.N.B. 1973, c. E-11, ss. 18 and 19; R.S.N.L. 1990, c. E-16, ss. 10-12; R.S.N.W.T. 1988, c. E-8, ss. 27, 28; R.S.N.S. 1989, c. 154, ss. 56 and 57; R.S.O. 1990, c. E.23, ss. 20 and 21; R.S.P.E.l. 1988, c. E-11, ss. 16 and 17; S.S. 2006, c. E-11.2, s. 19; and R.S.Y. 2002, c. 78, ss. 25 and 26.

be reminded of the circumstances of the earlier statement and how it is suggested that there is a contradiction. This provides the witness the opportunity to explain or accept the earlier statement. This process is economical since if the witness accepts that she did make the earlier statement it obviates the need for independent proof. It is also a case of simply being fair to the witness and allowing her to offer, if she can, an explanation.

(d) Impeaching One's Own Witness

There is thought to be something wrong in a counsel calling a person as a witness and then, if the evidence is not as favourable as expected, attacking the witness's credibility. There is thought to be a danger that the witness would then be at the mercy of counsel. But suppose, in preparation for trial, counsel interviews a prospective witness, that witness says he is prepared to describe the incident in a favourable way, counsel calls the witness and the witness surprises counsel and describes the matter in a completely different way. If counsel is not permitted to impeach the witness by proving the previous inconsistent statement we have counsel at the mercy of the witness. The Legislature has effected a compromise.

For criminal cases, the *Canada Evidence Act* provides:

> 9. (1) A party producing a witness shall not be allowed to impeach his credit by general evidence of bad character, but if the witness, in the opinion of the court, proves adverse, the party may contradict him by other evidence, or, by leave of the court, may prove that the witness made at other times a statement inconsistent with his present testimony, but before the last mentioned proof can be given the circumstances of the supposed statement, sufficient to designate the particular occasion, shall be mentioned to the witness, and he shall be asked whether or not he did make the statement.

> (2) Where the party producing a witness alleges that the witness made at other times a statement in writing, reduced to writing, or recorded on audio tape or video tape or otherwise, inconsistent with the witness' present testimony, the court may, without proof that the witness is adverse, grant leave to that party to cross-examine the witness as to the statement and the court may consider the cross-examination in determining whether in the opinion of the court the witness is adverse.

The legislation continues the prohibition against adducing general evidence of bad character. The legislation seems to provide that a ruling of adversity is necessary before a party can lead evidence that contradicts his previous witness but this is recognized by all as a blunder in legislative drafting and there is no such requirement.[65] There is such a requirement

---

65 *Greenough v. Eccles* (1859), 141 E.R. 315 at 321.

before a party will be permitted to prove a previous inconsistent statement of his own witness. The legislation provides that if the judge decides that the witness is adverse to the party calling him the party can impeach by proving the previous statement. Once the previous statement has been proved cross-examination can be had thereon. The cases conflict on the meaning of "adverse": while some courts have held that adverse means hostile in demeanour, the prevailing view seems to be that adversity simply means opposed in interest.[66] A hostile witness in the traditional sense – one who is belligerent and uncooperative toward the party who called him – may, under the common law, be cross-examined at large by that party.[67] Some courts have held that a witness who is adverse within the meaning of s. 9(1) can also be cross-examined at large, while others have concluded that a witness who is merely adverse but not hostile may only be then cross-examined on the subject of the prior inconsistent statement.[68]

Section 9(2) was introduced in 1969 to facilitate the finding of adversity. The cross-examination mentioned was designed to take place in the absence of the jury; it was to help the judge decide whether the witness was adverse and the party permitted to prove the earlier statement under s. 9(1). When it came to be judicially interpreted, however, it was decided that s. 9(2) was not just a preface to s. 9(1) but rather was a device unto itself providing a separate mode of impeachment that does not require a declaration of adversity: the cross-examination spoken of in s. 9(2) will take place in front of the jury if the judge determines that the previous statement was in fact inconsistent with the witness's present testimony. In *Milgaard*,[69] the Court announced the proper procedure when counsel wishes to make an application under s. 9(2): advise the court of the intention to make an application. The jury retires. Counsel produces the statement for the trial judge to read. The trial judge determines whether in fact there is an inconsistency between the statement and the evidence the witness has given. If there is no inconsistency, that's the end of the matter. If there is an inconsistency counsel is called on to prove the statement. Counsel can produce it to the witness and have the witness admit having made the statement or, if the witness does not admit it, counsel can provide the necessary proof by other evidence. Once the statement is proved, counsel for the opposing party has the right to cross-examine as to the circumstances under which the statement was made and the right to call evidence as to factors relevant to obtaining the

---

66 The leading case is *Hanes v. Wawanesa Mutual Insurance Co.* (1961), [1963] 1 C.C.C. 176 (Ont. C.A.). But see *R. v. McIntyre*, [1963] 2 C.C.C. 380 (N.S. S.C.).

67 See, *e.g.*, *R. v. S.W.S.*, [2005] O.T.C. 1004 (S.C.J.). But see *R. v. Malik* (2003), 194 C.C.C. (3d) 572 (B.C. S.C.).

68 See *R. v. Vivar*, [2004] O.T.C. 5 (S.C.J.).

69 *R. v. Milgaard* (1971), 2 C.C.C. (2d) 206 (Sask. C.A.). The *Milgaard* view was specifically approved in *R. v. Rouse* (1978), 42 C.C.C. (2d) 481 (S.C.C.).

statement for the purpose of attempting to show that the cross-examination that is the object of the s. 9(2) application should not be permitted. The trial judge should then decide whether or not she will permit the cross-examination and, if so, the jury is recalled. The cross-examination provided for in the section will be in the presence of the jury. If the trial judge then decides and declares that the witness is adverse, s. 9(1) comes into play and the statement may be proved to the jury. The trial judge may, as the result of the cross-examination, also declare that the witness is hostile and permit cross-examination at large.[70]

In civil cases, of course, the provincial legislation applies. All provinces and territories have legislation to the same effect as s. 9(1) of the *Canada Evidence Act* without the s. 9(2) provision.[71] The procedure for impeachment of one's own witness in civil cases is seemingly simpler than is the case with criminal prosecutions.

(e) Bias

Witnesses are no longer barred from testifying solely because they are interested in the outcome.[72] Feelings for or against a party, though causing the witness's testimony to be less than impartial, are not grounds for exclusion. Rather they are fruitful areas for counsel to explore for impeachment purposes. Since such feelings betray emotional partiality which may impair the witness's testimonial qualifications, evidence of the same is not collateral and counsel is entitled not only to explore those feelings on cross-examination but also to prove them should the witness deny them. If counsel intends to impeach the witness by evidence of bias counsel is obliged to first put the question to the witness. Again it's a matter of economy and fairness. If the witness is asked about the possibility of bias and admits it, there is no need to take up the court's time with independent proof. Also, it is fairer to ask the witness in the stand so that he might perhaps explain the appearance of bias than to surprise him afterward when he has no opportunity to respond.[73]

---

70 See Michael E. Webster, "Cross-examination on a Finding of Adversity" (1995), 38 C.R. (4th) 35.

71 R.S.A. 2000, s. A-18, s. 25; R.S.B.C. 1996, c. 124, s. 16; C.C.S.M., c. E150, s. 19; R.S.N.B. 1973, c. E-11, s. 17; R.S.N.L. 1990, c. E-16, s. 10; R.S.N.W.T. 1988, c. E-8, s. 30; R.S.N.S. 1989, c. 154, s. 55; R.S.O. 1990, c. E.23, s. 23; R.S.P.E.I. 1988, c. E-11, s. 15; S.S. 2006, c. E-11.2, s. 19(6)-19(8); and R.S.Y. 2002, c. 78, s. 29.

72 See *R. v. Dikah* (1994), 31 C.R. (4th) 105 (Ont. C.A.), affirmed [1994] 3 S.C.R. 1020.

73 See *Attorney General v. Hitchcock* (1847), 154 E.R. 38 (Exch. Ct.); and *General Films Ltd. v. McElroy*, [1939] 4 D.L.R. 543 at 549 (Sask. C.A.).

(f) Character of the Witness

Although it is very uncommon, it is permissible to call a witness to testify concerning another witness's character for truth-telling. The witness may testify to the other witness's bad reputation for veracity and might even be allowed testify to her opinion that she, the impeaching witness, would not believe the other witness on his oath. This entitlement is from another age and its limited use to be appreciated.[74] A trial judge, of course, has discretion to disallow these questions where their prejudicial effect outweighs their probative value. In the exercise of this discretion, the inquiry into the character witness's opinion of the other witness's oath will generally be disallowed, while the questions about the other witness's reputation for veracity are likely to be permitted.[75]

The common law has long held that independent proof of specific acts of a person impacting on that person's character for veracity was not receivable. The witness might be asked about these matters in cross-examination but it was regarded as necessary to exclude independent proof of the same to avoid undue consumption of time, confusing the issues and out of considerations of fairness to the witness. This is the collateral facts rule.[76]

The common law, however, provided that should the previous actions of the witness have resulted in a criminal conviction the same could be proved as the competing dangers were very much minimized. The previous judgment of conviction was conclusive, didn't need to be litigated and was quick to prove. Persons who had been convicted of an infamous crime were not competent as witnesses until the middle of the nineteenth century. When they were made competent, legislation was enacted paralleling the common law, permitting questions to the witness about previous convictions and independent proof should the witness deny them. In Canada, our legislatures have copied this legislation. For example, the *Canada Evidence Act* provides:

> 12. (1) A witness may be questioned as to whether the witness has been convicted of any offence, excluding any offence designated as a contravention under the *Contraventions Act*, but including such an offence where the conviction was entered after a trial on an indictment.
>
> (1.1) If the witness either denies the fact or refuses to answer, the opposite party may prove the conviction.

---

74 See *Masztalar v. Wiens* (1992), 2 C.P.C. (3d) 294 (B.C. C.A.).

75 *R. v. Clarke* (1998), 18 C.R. (5th) 219 (Ont. C.A.).

76 Discussed, *supra*, Collateral Facts Limitation.

(g) Accused as Witness

Section 12 on its face makes no distinction between the accused and other witnesses, and an accused who testifies may be impeached by reference to his criminal record. Obviously, an accused who chooses to become a witness risks far more from this type of questioning than does the ordinary witness. The questions and independent proof should he deny the previous convictions are, in theory at least, solely referable to the accused/witness's credibility. But the trier of fact may use the evidence of the previous convictions as proof that the accused is the sort of person who would commit the act alleged. That use is, of course, prohibited.[77] In a jury trial, the judge must instruct the jury that the criminal record evidence can only be used to assess the accused's credibility and not his character. This limiting instruction may well be futile, particularly if the previous convictions are for activity similar to that being prosecuted.

The Supreme Court decided in *R. v. Corbett*[78] that s. 12 is subject to judicial discretion and if the trial judge decides that the probative value of the criminal record evidence on the issue of credibility is outweighed by the possibility of prejudice to the accused, evidence of the previous convictions should be excluded. An accused who seeks to have such evidence excluded must bring what is known as a *Corbett* application, which should be decided at the close of the Crown's case, before the accused must choose whether to testify.[79] Such an application may result in the admission of the accused's criminal record, the exclusion of the entire record, or even editing of the record to remove its more prejudicial elements.[80]

Factors that are relevant in assessing the probative value or potential prejudice of the accused's criminal record include the nature of the previous conviction and its proximity in time to the present charge. Acts of deceit, dishonesty and fraud reflect adversely on a person's credibility and honesty, while acts of violence which may result from a combative nature, and reflect on the person's propensity for violence, generally have little bearing on veracity. The more similar the offence to which the previous conviction relates to the conduct for which the accused is on trial, the greater the possibility of prejudice produced by its admission. The more distant in time the less probative value in the previous conviction. If there was a deliberate attack upon the credibility of a Crown witness it may be necessary to permit cross-examination of the accused to ensure the jury is not presented with a

---

77 See Chapter 1, Character of the Accused.

78 (1988), 64 C.R. (3d) 1 (S.C.C.).

79 *R. v. Underwood* (1998), 12 C.R. (5th) 241 (S.C.C.).

80 On editing the accused's criminal record, see for example *R. v. Madrusan* (2005), 35 C.R. (6th) 220 (B.C. C.A.).

distorted picture but, of course, this should only be done when it would render the trial more, and not less, fair. While there is broad agreement about the factors to be considered, the courts' exercise of the discretion recognized in *Corbett* has been uneven and many, if not most, trial judges permit an accused who testifies to be confronted with his entire record.[81]

Our courts have also decided that while witnesses generally are open to cross-examination at large as to their credit, the vulnerable position of the accused means that this cross-examination should be limited with respect to an accused. Thus, aside from questions regarding previous convictions, an accused should not be cross-examined for impeachment purposes with regard to previous misconduct or discreditable associations unrelated to the charge.[82]

(h) Primary Witness in Prosecutions of Sexual Assault

At common law, when the alleged victim testified in a rape prosecution, she could be cross-examined not only concerning the material facts but also as to her character as this was seen to reflect on her credibility. In this she was treated as any other witness. If the questions had relevance solely to her credibility, she could not be contradicted in her answers as this would offend the collateral facts rule.

The common law decided that unchasteness was relevant to credibility. Therefore she could be asked about previous sexual intercourse with the accused and with others. If asked about previous sexual intercourse with persons other than the accused, the law regarded such questions as solely referable to credibility and she could not be contradicted if she denied the same. One can imagine, however, how a jury might react simply to the questions being put. If the questions were about previous sexual intercourse with the accused and the witness denied the same, evidence could be led as the common law regarded evidence of a previous sexual relationship with the accused as relevant not just to credibility but also to whether the alleged victim had consented on the occasion under review and therefore independent proof of the same did not offend the collateral facts rule. The common law also decided that she could be asked about her reputation as a prostitute or for promiscuity; these questions were also regarded as not collateral and independent proof could be led with respect to them.

These common law rules have been swept away by rape shield laws restricting the use that can be made of the sexual history of the complainant

---

81 See, *e.g.*, *R. v. Saroya* (1992), 18 C.R. (4th) 198 (Ont. Gen. Div.), affirmed (1994), 76 O.A.C. 25 (C.A.). But see *R. v. McFadyen* (2002), 2 C.R. (6th) 344 (Ont. C.A.).

82 *R. v. Davison* (1974), 20 C.C.C. (2d) 424 (Ont. C.A.). See also *R. v. Lee* (2005), 205 O.A.C. 155 (C.A.). But see *R. v. R. (J.W.)* (2007), 246 B.C.A.C. 196 (C.A.) .

in sexual offence cases. This sexual history evidence is now generally inadmissible, under ss. 276-277 of the *Criminal Code*, even on the issue of the complainant's credibility as a witness. These provisions are discussed in greater detail in Chapter 1.[83]

(i) Defects in the Capacity of a Witness

The cross-examiner is always entitled to attempt impeachment by questioning the witness's general capacity to observe, recollect and communicate, and his particular ability in the case under review. "Witness, you say that you were able to see the accident from a distance of 50 metres. When was the last time you had your eyes checked?" Sometimes the witness will confess the possibility of error as the result of certain incapacities. If the witness denies the possibility, counsel may want to lead extrinsic evidence to contradict. There are no hard and fast rules. The judge will decide, in her discretion, whether the probative value of the extrinsic evidence, outlined by counsel, outweighs competing considerations of time, confusion of the issues and fairness to the witness.

When a witness, because of a physical or mental defect, is not capable of giving an accurate account concerning the incident, a medical expert will be permitted to testify to this fact. An optometrist who is able to say that the witness's eyesight is so defective that he couldn't possibly have seen the incident from his position at the time will be allowed to speak and thus impeach the witness. So, too, a psychiatrist will be allowed to testify that because of the witness's mental disability his description of the matter is suspect.[84]

6. Supporting a Witness's Credibility

Speaking generally, evidence in support of a witness's credibility is not receivable, unless and until the witness's credibility has been attacked. It is not irrelevance that dictates rejection but rather superfluity. Until there has been an attack on the witness's credibility it is assumed that the witness is credible and it is not worth the consumption of time to lead evidence in support. Therefore, a witness will normally not be allowed to testify that another witness is a truthful person or ought to be believed. Similarly, previous consistent statements of a witness are generally inadmissible because they are seen to be superfluous. At times the courts will say that evidence of a previous statement consistent with the witness's present tes-

---

83 See Chapter 1, Character of the Victim in Sexual Assault Cases.
84 *Toohey*, *supra* note 10; and *R. v. Dietrich* (1970), 1 C.C.C. (2d) 49 (Ont. C.A.).

timony is excluded because it is self-serving and there is a danger that the witness manufactured evidence for himself by making the earlier statement. But the better explanation is superfluity. As with any rule of evidence, there are seen to be exceptions. The so-called exceptions might better be seen as instances when the rule does not apply because the basis of the rule doesn't exist. Nevertheless for ease of reference we will here consider them as exceptions.

(a) To Rebut the Allegation of Recent Fabrication

If a witness's account of events is challenged as being a recent invention, it is not superfluous to lead evidence to rebut that suggestion by showing that at an earlier time the witness made a statement consistent with her present testimony. The exception operates when the trial judge in her discretion judges that there has been a suggestion that the witness has recently made up the story. The allegation need not be express but may also arise implicitly from the whole circumstances of the case and the conduct of the trial.[85] At times the court might emphasize the requirement that the alleged invention needs to have been recent. Recentness in this context should not be interpreted strictly; all that is required is an allegation that the witness adopted the false story at some point after the events in question occurred, for example after a motive to fabricate arose.[86] However, an allegation that the witness's story has been fabricated from day one is not sufficient to trigger the exception.[87] The Supreme Court has held that when a prior consistent statement is admitted under this exception, the trier's use of the statement is limited to rebutting the allegation of recent fabrication. Consistent with the hearsay rule, the prior consistent statement remains inadmissible as proof of the truth of its contents.[88]

(b) Prior Identification

When a witness at trial is asked to identify a person in the courtroom, the circumstances surrounding that identification may seriously weaken the weight that will be given to it by the trier of fact. When the eyewitness says that the person in the dock, sitting between two constables, is the person who did the dastardly deed, the trier might theorize that the witness is not giving his present recollection of the incident but rather that the witness is

---

85 *R. v. Giraldi* (1975), 28 C.C.C. (2d) 248 (B.C. C.A.).

86 See *R. v. Stirling* (2008), 54 C.R. (6th) 228 at paras. 5-7 (S.C.C.).

87 *R. v. Pangilinan* (1987), 60 C.R. (3d) 188 (B.C. C.A.).

88 *Stirling*, *supra* note 86 at para. 7.

concluding from the accused's location in the courtroom that the police have arrested the proper person. Since the circumstances surrounding the witness's in-court statement of identification cast doubt on its validity, and the witness's original identification of the accused from a police line-up or otherwise is normally much more probative of the perpetrator's identity, evidence of the previous identification is not superfluous and therefore is receivable.[89]

(c) Recent Complaint

The common law decided that a complaint by a victim of sexual assault, if made at the first reasonable opportunity after the assault, was receivable in evidence. The reason, again, was that such a complaint was not regarded as superfluous. It was thought that if a woman was sexually assaulted it would be a very natural thing to complain about it. A failure to do so would be seen to contradict her allegation. If nothing was said at trial about a complaint being made then the trier might assume there was none and the credibility of the complainant would be adversely affected. Accordingly, if there was a complaint, evidence of the fact of the complaint and its details could be led to counter this assumption.[90] If there was no complaint, the judge was required to instruct the jury that the lack of complaint could raise an inference that the allegation was untrue. More recently it has been recognized that adverse inferences from a failure to complain are unfounded as there are many reasons why a victim of sexual assault will not report the assault at the first opportunity. In 1983, the *Criminal Code* was amended to provide "S. 275. The rules relating to evidence of recent complaint [in sexual assault cases] are hereby abrogated."

The section is ambiguous: it might limit the admissibility of evidence of the timing of a complaint, the right of counsel or the judge to comment on any delay, or the inferences that can be drawn from such delay. It seems to be commonly understood that the defence can still cross-examine the complainant on the issue of delayed complaint, but that the Crown can no longer introduce evidence of a recent complaint unless defence challenges the complainant's credibility on the basis of a failure to complain.[91] The Supreme Court has held that no presumptive adverse inference arises from delayed complaint, and "the timing of the complaint is simply one circumstance to consider in the factual mosaic of a particular case."[92] Consistent with this guidance, courts have approved instructions that invite juries

---

89 See *R. v. Christie*, [1914] A.C. 545 at 551 (H.L.).

90 *R. v. Lillyman*, [1896] 2 Q.B. 167 (C.C.C.R.).

91 *R. v. O'Connor* (1995), 100 C.C.C. (3d) 285 (Ont. C.A.).

92 *R. v. D. (D.)* (2000), 36 C.R. (5th) 261 (S.C.C.).

consider the presence or absence of an early complaint as part of the circumstances relevant to assessing the complainant's credibility.[93] The courts have also emphasized that where evidence of recent complaint is admissible to rebut a defence allegation that complaint was delayed, these prior consistent statements cannot be relied upon for the truth of their contents.[94]

(d) Narrative

There are times when the unfolding of the story for the trier of fact requires that the trier understand that statements were made which caused certain action. For example, evidence might be admitted that a child complainant reported sexual abuse to her mother, who brought the matter to the attention of police.[95] Receiving evidence of such statements is commonly referred to as admitting the evidence as part of the narrative. The Supreme Court has recently confirmed that prior consistent statements can be admitted as part of the narrative to help the trier of fact understand how events unfolded surrounding the allegation, which in turn bears on the assessment of the complainant's credibility.[96] The probative value of the statement in this context is said to lie in the fact that it was made and not in its content.[97] Thus, as in the case of the other exceptions, a prior consistent statement admitted under the narrative exception is not admissible as proof of the truth of the allegation, and a jury must be so instructed.[98] Unfortunately, this instruction may be more confusing than helpful, because in practice it can be difficult to sort out the permissible and impermissible uses of a prior consistent statement.[99]

(e) Expert Evidence

Traditionally, our courts took the view that, while an expert could testify to impeach credibility, it was wrong to permit an expert to testify in support. It was frequently said that to do so was to revert to the middle ages concept of oath-helping.[100] In the last quarter century, however, many Canadian

---

93   See *R. v. Cole* (2006), 211 O.A.C. 295 (C.A.); *R. v. J.G.B.* (2002), 4 C.R. (6th) 150 (Ont. C.A.).

94   See, *e.g.*, *R. v. Garon* (2009), 240 C.C.C. (3d) 516 (Ont. C.A.).

95   See *R. v. Jones* (1988), 44 C.C.C. (3d) 248 (Ont. C.A.).

96   See *R. c. Dinardo* (2008), 57 C.R. (6th) 48 (S.C.C.).

97   See, *e.g.*, *R. v. Curto* (2008), 54 C.R. (6th) 237 (Ont. C.A.).

98   See *Curto, ibid.*; *Dinardo, supra* note 96; *R. v. Ay* (1994), 93 C.C.C. (3d) 456 (B.C. C.A.).

99   Dufraimont, "*R. v. Dinardo*: Troubling Issues Regarding Prior Consistent Statements" (2008), 57 C.R. (6th) 76.

100   See, *e.g.*, *R. v. Kyselka* (1962), 133 C.C.C. 103 (Ont. C.A.).

courts have admitted evidence from experts on child sexual abuse to help the trier of fact assess the complainant's credibility. Often these experts have been allowed to explain that behaviours that might seem to damage the complainant's credibility—pre-trial recantations of the allegations for example—are common behaviours among sexually abused children and are therefore not inconsistent with the truth of the allegations.[101] While such expert evidence on human behaviour has been admitted to provide context for assessing credibility, the law is clear that the expert witness may not testify to an opinion that a particular witness is truthful.[102]

In *R. v. D. (D.)*,[103] the Supreme Court held that a witness should not have been able to testify that delayed disclosure of the allegation was consistent with its truth. Instead of admitting expert evidence, the trial judge should simply have instructed the jury that victims behave in different ways and that, standing alone, delays in disclosing abuse allegations say nothing about the complainant's credibility.[104] *D. (D.)* has discouraged the practice of admitting expert evidence on the credibility of child sexual abuse complainants, but there is authority suggesting that such evidence can still be admitted as long as it addresses more than the simple issue of delay.[105]

7. Corroboration

Historically, ecclesiastical and civil law systems of proof provided that a verdict could not be had on the strength of one witness's testimony. For most issues, two witnesses were required. In addition, particular witnesses, because of their station in life, would be assigned a fractional value. The common law generally resisted this quantitative method and a single witness was, and continues to be, sufficient to prove most allegations. There were, and are, exceptions.

(a) Perjury

In a prosecution for perjury in the common law courts, one witness was not sufficient unless there was other evidence which corroborated the witness in a material particular that implicated the accused. This requirement was a historical accident. Perjury had been prosecuted in the Court of Star

---

101 See *R. v. J. (F.E.)* (1990), 74 C.R. (3d) 269 (Ont. C.A.); *R. v. C. (R.A.)* (1990), 57 C.C.C. (3d) 522 (B.C. C.A.); *R. v. T. (S.)* (1986), 55 C.R. (3d) 321 (Ont. C.A.).

102 *Marquard, supra,* note 3.

103 *Supra,* note 92.

104 *Ibid.* at para. 59.

105 *R. v. Talbot* (2002), 1 C.R. (6th) 396 (Ont. C.A.).

Chamber which had followed ecclesiastical procedures. When that Court was abolished in 1641 and perjury was taken over by the common law courts, the long-established procedure was incorporated. That practice, requiring corroboration in a perjury prosecution, found its way into our *Criminal Code:*

> 133. No person shall be convicted of an offence [of perjury] on the evidence of only one witness unless the evidence of that witness is corroborated in a material particular by evidence that implicates the accused.

(b) Treason

A statute enacted in England in 1547 required two witnesses for a treason prosecution. It was said that this was necessary protection against allegations of fictitious conspiracies. The *Criminal Code* continues the requirement:

> 47. (3) No person shall be convicted of high treason or treason on the evidence of only one witness, unless the evidence of that witness is corroborated in a material particular by evidence that implicates the accused.

(c) Accomplices and Other Unsavoury Witnesses

The common law has long recognized that the evidence of accomplices may be suspect. A witness who was an accomplice of the accused might be purchasing immunity from prosecution by giving evidence for the prosecution against his former partner. This motive should be taken into account in assessing the worth of the witness's testimony. These concerns about accomplice testimony gave rise to a common law rule requiring the judge to instruct the jury that it was unsafe to convict on the evidence of the accomplice unless the evidence was *corroborated.* Unfortunately, the law requiring such an instruction in each case involving accomplice testimony, and the magic formula of words demanded, became unduly and unnecessarily complex.

The Supreme Court eliminated this corroboration rule in *R. v. Vetrovec,*[106] holding that there was no special category for accomplices. Instead of pigeon-holing witnesses into categories and reciting a ritualistic formula of words, the Court decided that judges should instruct juries about the credibility of individual witnesses in a manner appropriate to the circumstances. Where a particularly disreputable or unsavoury witness testifies for the Crown, the Court explained that it might be appropriate for the judges

---

106 (1982), 67 C.C.C. (2d) 1 (S.C.C.).

to deliver a "clear and sharp" warning to the jury about the risks of adopting the witness's unconfirmed testimony. The decision whether to offer such a "*Vetrovec* warning" and the content of the warning normally lie within the discretion of the trial judge, but the credibility problems of some unsavoury witnesses are so pronounced that a *Vetrovec* warning will be required as a matter of law.[107]

The Supreme Court has recently laid out a flexible framework to guide judges in crafting *Vetrovec* warnings.[108] Although the content of such warnings will vary, in general the trial judge should draw the jury's attention to the testimony that requires special scrutiny, explain why the special scrutiny is warranted, caution the jury that it is dangerous to convict on the unconfirmed evidence (though they may do so if they are satisfied that it is true), and urge the jury to look for evidence from another source confirming that the unsavoury witness is truthful about the accused's guilt.[109]

Although there are no formal categories of witnesses requiring special warnings, the unsavoury Crown witnesses about whom such warnings are regularly offered include accomplices and those with long criminal histories. And because perjured testimony from jailhouse informants has played a well-documented role in wrongful convictions,[110] a clear and sharp *Vetrovec* warning is normally required where a jailhouse informant's testimony forms an important part of the prosecution's case.[111]

(d) Primary Witnesses in Sexual Assault Cases

For generations our courts expressed concern over the worth of a complainant's testimony in prosecutions for sexual assault. It was said that such an accusation was easily made and hard to defend,[112] and that sexual cases were particularly subject to the danger of false charges.[113] The common law began to insist on the same type of warning about the evidence of complainants in sexual assault cases as it had respecting the evidence of accomplices. These attitudes found their way into our *Criminal Code*. In cases of rape, attempted rape, sexual intercourse with a female under 16 and indecent assault, s. 142 formerly required trial judges to warn juries that it would be

---

107 See, *e.g.*, *R. v. Bevan* (1993), 21 C.R. (4th) 277 (S.C.C.).

108 *R. v. Khela* (2009), 62 C.R. (6th) 197 (S.C.C.).

109 *Ibid.* at para. 37.

110 See Federal, Provincial and Territorial (FPT) Heads of Prosecutions Committee Working Group on the Prevention of Miscarriages of Justice, *Report on the Prevention of Miscarriages of Justice* (Ottawa: Department of Justice, 2004).

111 See, *e.g.*, *R. v. Brooks* (2000), 30 C.R. (5th) 201 at para. 130 (S.C.C.), *per* Binnie J., concurring.

112 Sir Matthew Hale, *Pleas of the Crown* (1680) at 633.

113 Glanville Williams, "Corroboration", [1962] Crim. L. Rev. 662.

unsafe to convict on the uncorroborated testimony of a female complainant. Section 139 provided that with respect to certain sexual offences a conviction could not be had unless there was corroboration. In these instances a warning was not sufficient; a conviction was barred. These provisions have now been repealed but it is debatable whether the attitudes toward the evidence of complainants have changed. Legislation can only do so much.[114]

(e) Unsworn Evidence of Children

The *Canada Evidence Act* and the *Criminal Code* had, until recently, provisions mandating corroboration if the evidence of a child was given unsworn. Indeed, even if the evidence was given sworn, the law appeared to require that a warning be given to the jury about the frailties of children's evidence.[115] Several provinces and territories maintain corroboration requirements for unsworn children's evidence,[116] but others have eliminated them.[117] As we saw earlier, the *Canada Evidence Act* now specifies that all children's evidence must be given unsworn, and that this unsworn evidence has the same effect as if it were given on oath. Under this regime, no warning should now be given about the fact that the testimony of the child is unsworn.

Notwithstanding the amendments to the *Canada Evidence Act*, it remains possible that a trial judge might find it appropriate to caution the jury about the credibility of a particular child witness. A child's evidence should be treated with caution where such caution is merited in the circumstances of the case. The Supreme Court has held that it is wrong to apply negative stereotypes to the evidence of children generally, or to view children's evidence as inherently unreliable.[118] Each child witness should be approached as an individual. We cannot expect child witnesses to perform in the same manner as adults. This does not mean that the courts should subject their testimony to a lower level of scrutiny for reliability. While courts have become more accepting of children's evidence, it would be wrong to adopt an undiscriminating attitude toward the evidence of children while holding adults to higher standards.[119]

---

114 See e.g. *R. v. S. (F.)* (1997), 116 C.C.C. (3d) 435 (Ont. C.A.).
115 See *R. v. Horsburgh*, [1968] 2 C.C.C. 288 (S.C.C.).
116 See R.S.A. 2000, c. A-18, s. 19(2); R.S.N.W.T. 1988, c. E-8, s. 19; R.S.N.S. 1989, c. 154, s. 63(2); R.S.Y. 2002, c. 78, s. 17.
117 See R.S.N.L. 1990, c. E-16, s. 18.1; R.S.O. 1990, c. E-23, s. 18.2.
118 *W. (R.) supra*, note 15.
119 *Ibid.*

4

Hearsay

1. Introduction

Common law courts disapproved of hearsay evidence with increasing frequency throughout the seventeenth and eighteenth centuries. By the end of the eighteenth century, this disapproval hardened into an exclusionary rule in both civil and criminal practice.[1] By then the adversary system had become established. The parties had taken control over who would be called as witnesses. It made sense that a witness called by one party should be open for testing for worth by questions from the opposing party. Thus came into being the notion of cross-examination which is peculiar to the common law tradition. With that development the hearsay rule could not be far behind. The law of hearsay is predicated on the thought that the adversary should have the right to test by cross-examination the reliability of any description of the material event.[2] If the person with knowledge of that event is not present in the witness stand, the adversary is frustrated. The conduct of a fair trial in the adversary system requires that the person with knowledge relate the story in open court.

The description of a past event by any witness has resident within it the possibility of error due to four dangers. First, the witness's description may be defective because the witness did not perceive the event accurately. Second, the witness when describing the event may not have then correctly remembered his earlier observation of the event. Third, the witness in describing the event may have been ambiguous or misleading in the language he chose. Fourth, the witness may have been insincere and deliberately wished to mislead. To have the witness's story related by another is regarded as unfair. That other cannot describe why the description of the event is accurate as he is unable to answer any questions from the adversary concerning its accuracy. The adversary cannot test whether the person who actually witnessed the event had able powers of perception, whether that

---

1 John H. Langbein, *The Origins of Adversary Criminal Trial* (New York: Oxford University Press, 2003) at 242.

2 See *R. v. Khelawon* (2006), 42 C.R. (6th) 1 at para. 35 (S.C.C.).

person's description of the event was rendered at a time when the event was fresh in that person's memory, whether the words used to describe the incident are properly understood in the sense that the person intended and whether the person who observed the event was motivated to give a true rendition. Those possibilities, those dangers, cannot be explored unless the witness himself is in the witness stand. These are the "hearsay dangers": defects in perception, memory, sincerity and communication.[3]

Another, distinct, reason for insisting on the presence in the courtroom of the person with actual knowledge has to do with the jury's capacity to adequately assess the worth of the description. The jury, the trier of fact, will be more assured of accuracy in their decision if the description of the event is given in open court by the person with knowledge and not through an intermediary. The presence in the courtroom of the person with the knowledge will enhance trustworthiness. The witness who speaks in open court takes an oath and knows that he is subject to a perjury prosecution should he lie. The witness who speaks in open court is encouraged to speak honestly without exaggeration by the solemnity of the occasion and by the presence of the party against whose interests he speaks. The witness, if in open court, will be open to examination as to his demeanour, his manner of speaking, and the trier of fact will therefore be better able to evaluate his credibility.

And so we say that it is not right for a witness to relate what he or she has *heard* another *say*. The *hearsay* rule refers to testimony relating statements that a witness has heard another make about the matter. That is prohibited. It does not signify, though an intelligent argument could otherwise be maintained, that the person who observed the event must be *here* to *say* what happened. The rule is the *hearsay* rule and not the *heresay* rule.

2. Identifying Hearsay

Not all out-of-court statements are deserving of the label hearsay. The principal reasons for excluding hearsay evidence are the lack of the protective safeguards of oath and cross-examination, safeguards which are only necessary when the value of the evidence depends on the credibility of the asserter.[4] If the value of the out-of-court statement rests not on the credibility of the asserter, but has value resident solely in the fact that the statement was made, there can be no hearsay objection to the introduction of such a statement.

---

3 Edmund M. Morgan, "Hearsay Dangers and the Application of the Hearsay Concept" (1948) 62 Harv. Law Rev. 177.

4 See Edward W. Cleary, ed., *McCormick on Evidence*, 2d ed. (St. Paul: West Publishing, 1972), s. 246, at 584.

A sues B for failure to deliver lumber in accordance with their contract. B defends, denying the existence of any contract. A calls X to testify that he heard B unequivocally and unambiguously agreeing to deliver lumber to A on a certain date for a certain price. Clearly this is not hearsay. We care not whether B was sincere in expressing his intention to accept the terms. The legal consequences of a valid contract are produced by the fact that B spoke the words. The value of the words does not rest on the credibility of the out-of-court asserter. B's out-of-court statement is not hearsay.

Similarly, proof of statements constituting defamation would not offend the hearsay rule. The plaintiff who complains that he was defamed by the defendant's out-of-court statement and seeks to prove that the defendant made the statement is obviously not attempting to prove the truth asserted within the statements. The evidentiary value of the statement resides solely in the fact that the statement was made.

Words accompanying actions can affect the legal character of those actions and evidence of such out-of-court statements may not be hearsay. Consider the statement, "I give this land to you for your use and for the use of your heirs." If the substantive law of property characterizes such a trans-action as a gift when the donor's intention is manifested by words, then the value of the statement rests solely in the fact that the statement was made.

When the defence claims that the police investigation of a crime was inadequate, the Crown may be entitled to lead evidence of what the police were told by various sources during their investigation and how they followed up on those leads. Although the cases label this kind of evidence "investigative hearsay", it is clear that such evidence can only be admitted for the non-hearsay purpose of establishing the narrative of the investigation. The evidentiary value of the statements lies in the fact that they were made to police in the course of their investigation.[5] Similarly, the accused who seeks to rely on the defence of provocation is able to relate for the court what another said to him that caused him to react in the manner in which he did. The list of situations of relevant non-hearsay statements, and their variety, is limitless, and their identification is only eased when the purpose of the hearsay rule is kept in the forefront. The hearsay rule is designed to protect the adversary against the admission of evidence which cannot be tested by the adversary as to its worth.

Identifying whether an out-of-court statement is hearsay or not is seen by many as a difficult exercise and various formulae of words have been used for the purpose. One popular formula, which as we will see was recently approved by the Supreme Court, is to ask whether the statement is being tendered for its truth or tendered for the fact that the statement was made.

---

5 See *R. v. Van* (2009), 65 C.R. (6th) 193 (S.C.C.); *R. v. Dhillon* (2002), 5 C.R. (6th) 317 (Ont. C.A.).

Although this is a fair description, the formula frequently produces circum-locutions that confound. It is not unusual for counsel to seek an end run around the hearsay rule by insisting that she is not tendering the evidence for the purpose of establishing its truth but rather only for the purpose of establishing that the statement was in fact made. When counsel offers this in justification, the adversary should ask the proponent of the evidence to precisely articulate the relevance in the case resident in the fact that the statement was made. It will often be seen that the only relevance that can be found will reside in accepting the speaker's belief concerning an external event as accurate; the statement will be seen to be of value only if we assume its truth. The statement on close analysis will often be seen to be hearsay.

An example might assist. Dante is charged with the robbery of Harold. When Dante was arrested, he was taken to a detention centre and booked in. Investigating Officer King has testified that the victim Harold gave him a list of the serial numbers of the bills taken from him in the robbery. Harold had made the list just before the robbery. King went to the detention centre and, on examining the booking sheet, observed that when Dante was booked in certain personal effects were taken from him. He asked to see those effects. He was given an envelope which had the name "Dante" written thereon. In the envelope were found two bills with serial numbers matching numbers on the list provided by Harold. Harold is prepared to testify, refreshing his memory from the list that he prepared, that these two bills were part of the money taken from him during the robbery. Dante attacks the evidence as hearsay. The Crown argues that the evidence is not hearsay. The Crown argues that the name "Dante" on the envelope is not an out-of-court statement being tendered for the purpose of proving its truth. It is evidence only that the statement was in fact made. The fact that the statement was made is a piece of original circumstantial evidence from which the trier of fact can infer that the two bills were in Dante's possession when he was arrested. This is quite an attractive argument, at least on the surface, and might be accepted.[6] But analyze the situation. How is the fact that the name "Dante" appears on the envelope relevant to the issue? Someone, probably the booking officer, wrote the name "Dante" on the envelope. The fact of the name appearing, the fact that the statement was made, only has relevance if we accept that the writer was accurate when he identified these effects as belonging to Dante. If the booking officer had written on the envelope "I found the contents of this envelope on the person of Dante when he arrived at the booking office" all would quickly see that this was a hearsay statement. The worth of the statement depended on the credibility of the out-of-court asserter, the booking officer, and the adversary, Dante, was prevented from

---

6 For judicial acceptance of such an argument, see *R. v. Bastien* (1968), 20 C.C.C. (2d) 562 (B.C. Co. Ct.).

challenging, through cross-examination, the worth of the out-of-court statement.[7]

A better analytical technique for determining whether a statement is hearsay would be framed in terms of the underlying concern of the rule. As with the proper application of all rules of evidence, it is wise to always keep in mind the purpose of the rule. Given the basis for the hearsay rule—the adversary's inability to cross-examine the person with knowledge of the event—we can then construct an analytical tool for identifying hearsay. If there are relevant, meaningful questions that the adversary might wish to ask of the person who made the out-of-court statement, then the out-of-court statement is hearsay; if there are no meaningful questions that can be put, the statement is not hearsay. To properly identify whether or not an out-of-court statement is hearsay keep in mind the reason for the rule.

A classic example of the problem of identification, taken from the cases, might assist in a better understanding of this technique. In *Subramaniam*,[8] the accused had been convicted of unlawfully possessing ammunition thereby assisting the terrorist enemy. He was sentenced to death. His defence had been duress and he had sought to relate conversations he had had with the terrorists who had threatened him. The terrorists had, according to the accused, told him that he would be shot if he didn't help them. The Trial Court ruled this evidence was hearsay, and not admissible unless the terrorists were called. On appeal this was held to be error. The appellate Court noted that evidence of a statement made to a witness by a person who is not himself called as a witness is hearsay and inadmissible only when the object of the evidence was to establish the truth of what was contained in the statement. The Court recognized that in this case the fact that the statement was made, quite apart from its truth, was relevant in considering the mental state and conduct of the accused to whom the statement was made. The trier of fact would not be misled, nor the adversary prejudiced, by the absence from the witness stand of the terrorist-declarant. Using the suggested method of identifying whether or not an out-of-court statement is hearsay, ask yourself whether there are any meaningful questions that the adversary, the prosecution, might want to put to the out-of-court terrorist-declarant. If the terrorist were called as a witness, what questions would the adversary ask? Could the adversary ask the terrorist if he was sincere when he threatened the accused? If he intended to communicate a threat? Surely those questions would be properly objected to as immaterial since the issue before the Court was not the terrorist's state of mind but rather the accused's. Since it was the fact of the statement having been made that was relevant, since there

---

7   For judicial recognition that this is the proper analysis, see *R. v. Lal* (1979), 51 C.C.C. (2d) 336 (B.C. C.A.).

8   *Subramaniam v. Public Prosecutor*, [1956] 1 W.L.R. 965 (Malaya P.C.).

were no meaningful questions that the adversary could put, the adversary would be protected and trustworthiness assured by allowing the accused to testify; the accused is on oath and may be cross-examined regarding his sincerity, perception and memory concerning whether the statement was in fact made and whether he was in fear as a result.[9]

Recently in *R. v. Khelawon*,[10] the Supreme Court defined hearsay in terms consistent with the above analysis. According to the Court, the two "essential defining features of hearsay are. . .(1) the fact that the statement is adduced to prove the truth of its contents and (2) the absence of a contemporaneous opportunity to cross-examine the declarant."

Given this focus on the opportunity to cross-examine *contemporaneously* with the making of the statement, the Supreme Court explained that an out-of-court statement tendered for the truth of its contents is hearsay even if the declarant, the maker of the out-of-court statement, appears as a witness in the trial.[11] When a witness repeats or adopts a prior out-of-court statement, the statement made in court constitutes original evidence, subject to adversarial testing, and there is no problem of hearsay. But if a witness in the stand has no memory of the events described, or offers a version of events that conflicts with an earlier version offered by her, a party may seek to have that witness's out-of-court statements about the event taken as evidence of what really happened. Here there is a hearsay problem, because the out-of-court statements are indeed being relied on for their truth. One might be tempted to say that this is not hearsay because the declarant is before the trier of fact, under oath and subject to cross-examination. But consider whether the adversary can really meaningful questions to test the reliability of the out-of-court statements. If the adversary had been able to cross-examine the declarant contemporaneously with the making of the statements, there would have been a real opportunity to probe the declarant's perception, memory, narration and sincerity: did you have a good view of events? how reliable is your memory of the events now? However, since the witness either cannot remember the events or disavows her earlier statements about them, cross-examination is likely to reveal little about the reliability of those statements. The adversary cannot meaningfully test the reliability of the out-of-court statements; they are hearsay.

---

9   Even experts in the law of evidence can be fooled; see the contrasting opinions of Justices Sopinka and McLachlin in *R. v. Dipietro* (1993), (sub nom. *R. v. Evans*) 25 C.R. (4th) 46 (S.C.C.).

10   *Supra*, note 2, at para. 35.

11   *Khelawon, ibid.* at paras. 37-41.

3. Implied Assertions

Out-of-court statements can be made otherwise than by words. A nod of the head can communicate assent as readily as the spoken word "yes"; pointing to a suspect can be as communicative as the statement "that is the man". Actions which are intended by the actor to be assertions are therefore as capable of attracting hearsay analysis as verbal utterances.

But what of implied assertions? What of conduct which was not intended by the actor to be assertive of anything but from which an onlooker might draw an inference regarding the actor's beliefs? Should we subject such conduct to hearsay requirements? An example might assist. A ship was lost at sea. All hands were lost. In a civil suit brought against an insurance company the claim is resisted on the basis that the ship was not seaworthy when it sailed. The plaintiff wants to introduce into evidence the fact that before the ship sailed the captain examined the vessel. He then sailed off in it with his family. The plaintiff says this is circumstantial evidence from which the trier can infer that the ship was seaworthy. The defendant insurance company maintains that the conduct of the sea captain amounts to an implied assertion by the captain that he regarded the vessel as seaworthy and his conduct only has meaning in the case if we accept the captain's belief as accurate. The defendant argues that if the captain had said, prior to his departure, "I regard this ship as seaworthy", all would agree such a statement would be labelled hearsay and the fact the assertion is implied rather than express should make no difference. The defendant says he will be prejudiced if the evidence is received because he will be unable to cross-examine the captain. How should a judge rule?

The problem has confounded law students, lawyers and judges for generations. It is perhaps a blessing that the problem is so seldom recognized. But now and then it rears its ugly head. The English case of *R. v. Kearley*[12] provides classic, logical reasoning, but, some might say, an absurd result. In *Kearley*, the police had raided the accused's flat. They found drugs but not in sufficient quantities to justify an inference that the accused was a dealer. The accused was taken down to the station. Over the next few hours, in the accused's absence, the police took telephone calls asking for the accused and asking to buy drugs; there were also seven callers at the door similarly interested. At his trial on charges of possession with intent to supply, the Crown called the police officers to testify to the phone calls and the visitors received. The defence unsuccessfully objected that this evidence was hearsay. The accused was convicted and his appeal dismissed. The House of Lords, however, allowed the accused's appeal. The Lords were divided. The majority ruled the evidence was hearsay and inadmissible.

---

12 [1992] 2 All E. R. 345.

The minority cried out that "laymen would say the law is an ass"[13] but the majority replied that "a common sense approach is not necessarily a reliable guide in a criminal trial".[14] Canadian courts have dealt with several similar cases, and the prevailing view in this country is that the evidence is not hearsay.[15]

4. The Principled Approach to Hearsay

While identifying a piece of evidence as hearsay can be challenging, it is by no means the end of the matter. To be sure, the hearsay rule has always been and continues to be a general exclusionary rule.[16] But the hearsay analysis is complex and a piece of hearsay evidence may or may not be admissible in a given case.

Until about 30 years ago, the hearsay rule was understood as a rigid exclusionary rule with a number of established exceptions for various types of evidence, such as dying declarations and co-conspirator statements. Hearsay could not be admitted unless it fit into one of the traditional exceptions, and it was not open to the courts to create new ones.[17] Depending on who was counting, the number of exceptions ranged from 22 to 28 and each had its own individual parameters. Professor Wigmore, looking back at all these exceptions, sought a theory to explain them and to bring some coherence to the list. Generally speaking, he came up with the thought that usually there were grounds of necessity and circumstantial guarantees of trustworthiness underlying the exceptions. Building on Professor Wigmore's insight, Canadian courts have recognized that hearsay evidence should be admitted even when it does not fit within a traditional exception, as long as the hearsay is both necessary and reliable. This new emphasis on necessity and reliability marks a fundamental shift in Canadian evidence law from an analysis based on rigid categorical exceptions to what has become known as the principled approach to hearsay.

The Supreme Court of Canada cast off the shackles of the past in the groundbreaking decision of *Khan*.[18] That decision was later characterized by the Court as "the triumph of a principled analysis over a set of ossified

---

13 *Ibid., per* Lord Griffiths at 348.

14 *Ibid., per* Lord Oliver at 370.

15 See, *e.g.*, *R. v. Edwards* (1994), 34 C.R. (4th) 113 (Ont. C.A.), affirmed (1996), 45 C.R. (4th) 307 (S.C.C.); *R. v. Bui* (2003), 18 C.R. (6th) 371 (B.C. C.A.).

16 See *Khelawon, supra*, note 2 at para. 34.

17 See *Myers v. Director of Public Prosecutions*, [1965] A.C. 1001 (H.L.).

18 *R. v. Khan* (1990), 79 C.R. (3d) 1 (S.C.C.). See also *Ares v. Venner*, [1970] S.C.R. 608 in which the Court had earlier embraced a principled approach to hearsay in the civil context.

judicially created categories."[19] *Khan* was a sexual assault case, in which the infant complainant described the criminal act to her mother shortly after it occurred. The child was not permitted to testify at trial, and the issue was whether her mother would be permitted to testify as to the statement made to her. The Court decided the statement did not fit within a recognized exception but announced that it could be received if the trial judge found grounds of necessity and guarantees of trustworthiness in the circumstances surrounding the making of the out-of-court statement. Since *Khan*, the Supreme Court has developed this principled approach in a series of important hearsay cases.[20]

(a) Rules and Principles

Before delving further into the details of the principled approach, it is worth pausing to consider the implications of replacing strict rules with general principles. Rigid exclusionary rules tend to be both over- and under-inclusive, resulting in the exclusion of much valuable evidence and the admission of some dubious evidence. A more flexible principled approach allows courts to admit only the evidence that should be admitted, in light of the governing principles. Since hearsay evidence is generally excluded primarily because its reliability cannot be tested, the courts have reasoned that it should be admitted where concerns about its reliability are minimized. The disadvantage of this principled approach is an increase in legal uncertainty. The application of the principled approach depends to a greater degree on judicial discretion than did the application of the well-defined categories of admissibility that formerly characterized hearsay law. Therefore, it is now more difficult to predict whether a given piece of hearsay evidence will be admitted. Having weighed these competing considerations, our courts have decided that the advantages of the principled approach outweigh its disadvantages.

(b) The Governing Framework of Admissibility

For some time after the Supreme Court adopted a principled approach to hearsay, it remained unclear how the necessity and reliability analysis would affect the traditional exceptions to the hearsay rule. It is now clear that the traditional exceptions continue to play a role within the context of

---

19 *R. v. Smith* (1992), 15 C.R. (4th) 133 (S.C.C.).
20 See especially *Smith, ibid.*; *R. v. B. (K.G.)* (1993), 19 C.R. (4th) 1 (S.C.C.); *R. v. Starr* (2000), 36 C.R. (5th) 1 (S.C.C.); *R. v. Mapara* (2005), 28 C.R. (6th) 1 (S.C.C.); *Khelawon, supra*, note 2.

the principled approach. Recently, the Supreme Court explained the framework governing the admissibility of hearsay as follows:

(a) Hearsay evidence is presumptively inadmissible unless it falls under an exception to the hearsay rule. The traditional exceptions to the hearsay rule remain presumptively in place.

(b) A hearsay exception can be challenged to determine whether it is supported by indicia of necessity and reliability, required by the principled approach. The exception can be modified as necessary to bring it into compliance.

(c) In "rare cases", evidence falling within an existing exception may be excluded because the indicia of necessity and reliability are lacking in the particular circumstances of the case.

(d) If hearsay evidence does not fall under a hearsay exception, it may still be admitted if indicia of reliability and necessity are established on a *voir dire*.[21]

Thus, the traditional hearsay exceptions still exist, but they can be challenged on principled grounds, and their requirements may be modified to bring them into conformity with the principled approach. Moreover, the traditional hearsay exceptions are no longer conclusive; evidence that does not fall within an exception can be admitted if it is necessary and reliable, and evidence that does fall into an exception can be excluded (in rare cases) where necessity and reliability are not present in the particular case.[22]

The Supreme Court has held that the party seeking to adduce hearsay evidence on the basis of the principled approach bears the onus of proving on a balance of probabilities that the evidence is both necessary and reliable.[23] Because it can operate to exclude relevant defence evidence or to admit Crown evidence that cannot be tested by cross-examination, the hearsay analysis can affect the accused's Charter rights to a fair trial and to make full answer and defence.[24] In exercising discretion in this area, there is authority for the proposition that courts should be more willing to receive hearsay statements where the same will exculpate.[25]

---

21 *Mapara, ibid.* at para. 15, quoted in *Khelawon, ibid.* at para. 42.

22 The Supreme Court has emphasized that hearsay falling in an exception should rarely be excluded because fails to meet the criteria of necessity and reliability. "In all but the most exceptional cases", held the majority in *Mapara, ibid.*, "the argument is spent at the point where an exception to the hearsay rule is found to comply with the principled approach to the hearsay rule."

23 *Khelawon, supra,* note 2 at para. 47.

24 *Ibid.*

25 *R. v. Finta* (1992), 14 C.R. (4th) 1 (Ont. C.A.), affirmed [1994] 1 S.C.R. 701, application for re-hearing refused (June 23, 1994), Doc. 23023, 23097 (S.C.C.).

(c) Necessity and Reliability

The twin principles underlying the principled approach to hearsay require some elaboration. The first question will be whether reception of the hearsay statement is necessary. Necessity of this nature might arise in a number of situations: the declarant whose out-of-court statement is offered may be dead, out of the jurisdiction, insane, or otherwise unavailable. But necessity, according to our courts, is not to here be equated only with the unavailability of the declarant. Necessity for these purposes means "reasonably necessary",[26] and it should be defined flexibly to apply to various situations where relevant direct evidence is not available.[27] For example, in the case of an out-of-court statement by a child, the inadmissibility of the child's evidence might be one basis for a finding of necessity; if the child is regarded as not competent to testify, her earlier statement may be seen as necessary.[28] But even if she could testify, evidence based on psychological assessments that testifying in court might be traumatic or harmful for the child might also serve to establish necessity.[29] Indeed, even though the child has testified, the trial judge might determine that it is reasonably necessary to admit the out-of-court statement in order to obtain an accurate and frank rendition of the child's version of the relevant events.[30] The courts have also said that necessity might be found if the out-of-court statement is such that one could not expect to get evidence of the same value in any other way.[31]

The second question concerns reliability. The court needs to be satisfied that the traditional dangers associated with hearsay evidence—defects in the declarant's perception, memory, communication and sincerity—are minimized in the circumstances and that the absence of contemporaneous cross-examination should affect only the weight to be given to the evidence and not admissibility. In this context, the Courts have distinguished threshold reliability from ultimate reliability.[32] Threshold reliability is a question for the judge at the admissibility stage; it concerns whether the hearsay evidence bears indicia of reliability that make it admissible under the principled approach. Ultimate reliability, by contrast, involves the question whether the jury will rely on the hearsay evidence as true. Ultimate reliability is always and only a question for the trier of fact at the end of the case, and

---

26 *R. v. Khan*, *supra*, note 18.

27 *Smith*, *supra*, note 19.

28 See *R. v. Khan*, *supra*, note 18. See also *R. v. Parrott* (2001), 39 C.R. (5th) 255 (S.C.C.), indicating that live testimony from the complainant should not be pre-empted by hearsay without a full inquiry into the complainant's testimonial competence.

29 *Khan*, *ibid.*

30 *Khan v. College of Physicians & Surgeons (Ontario)* (1992), 9 O.R. (3d) 641 (C.A.).

31 See *Smith*, *supra*, note 19; *B. (K.G.)*, *supra*, note 20.

32 See *Khelawon*, *supra*, note 2 at para. 50.

should never be decided by the judge at the admissibility stage. At one time our courts took the view that certain factors pointing to reliability were relevant only to ultimate reliability, and could not be considered in the threshold reliability analysis; for example, independent evidence corroborating the truth of a hearsay statement could not be considered by the trial judge at the admissibility stage.[33] The Supreme Court has recently, and wisely, overturned these authorities. It is now clear that threshold reliability can be established by reference to whatever indicia of reliability exist to overcome the hearsay dangers in the circumstances.[34]

Insofar as the determination of threshold reliability amounts to a judgment call dependent on the circumstances of each case, it illustrates the potential difficulty with the principled approach. There is a risk that trial judges will differ significantly in their appreciation of the factors bearing on the reliability of hearsay statements, and the lack of uniformity could make preparation for trial difficult.[35] However, the Courts have not been left entirely without guidance. The Supreme Court explained in *Khelawon* that there are essentially two ways to establish threshold reliability. First, the circumstances surrounding the making of the statement may provide sufficient assurance of its reliability. The hearsay statement of the complainant in *Khan* is a good example of this type of reliability: since the young child disclosed the sexual abuse soon after its occurrence, naturally and without prompting, and she would not have been expected to have knowledge of the sexual act described unless her allegation were true, the child's spontaneous disclosure to her mother bore a stamp of reliability. Second, there are situations where the reliability of the hearsay statement can be adequately tested even though the declarant cannot be contemporaneously cross-examined. The authorities permitting certain recanted statements of witnesses to be considered for their truth provide the best example of this second way of satisfying the threshold reliability criterion. These authorities are discussed in the following subsection.

(d) Recanted Statements of a Witness

In *R. v. B. (K.G.)*,[36] the accused and three of his young friends were involved in a fight with two men. During the course of the fight, one of the

---

33 See especially *Starr, supra,* note 20 at paras. 215, 217.

34 See *Khelawon, supra,* note 2 at para. 93.

35 For contrasting inclusive and exclusive approaches see *R. v. Kharsekin* (1994), 30 C.R. (4th) 252 (Nfld. C.A.) and *R. v. Cassidy* (1993), 26 C.R. (4th) 252 (Ont. Gen. Div.). See also *R. v. Cansanay,* [2009] 7 W.W.R. 618 (Man. C.A.) and *R. v. S. (C.E.)*, 2009 MBCA 61 (C.A.), in which two co-accused were tried separately on murder charges and the trial judges came to different conclusions about the admissibility of certain hearsay statements.

36 *Supra,* note 20.

youths pulled a knife and stabbed one of the men in the chest and killed him. The accused's friends were interviewed by the police and they told the police that the accused had made statements to them in which he acknowledged that he thought he had caused the death of the victim by the use of a knife. The accused was charged with murder. At trial, the three youths recanted their earlier statements and said they had lied to the police. Although the trial judge had no doubt that the recantations were false, the witnesses's prior inconsistent statements could not be tendered as proof that the accused actually made the admissions. Under the traditional common law position, even though the declarants were now in the witness stand, the statements could not be used for their truth but could only be used to impeach the witnesses's credibility.

The Supreme Court decided that, under the principled approach, the earlier statements could be relied on for their truth. The Court observed that relying on hearsay is dangerous because, unlike original testimony, hearsay statements are not made under oath, they are not made in the presence of the trier of fact, and they are not subject to cross-examination at the time they are made. The Court reasoned that hearsay can be admitted where there are adequate substitutes for oath, presence and contemporaneous cross-examination, provided that the statements are also necessary and voluntary. The Court identified an ideal set of substitutes to allay the reliability concerns arising from the hearsay nature of the statements: an oath administered at the time the statement was taken, a video recording of the full statement and the ability to cross-examine the declarant at trial. In *B. (K.G.)*, the Crown witnesses had all voluntarily given sworn video recorded statements to police implicating the accused, and they were all present at trial. In the circumstances, the statements were admissible for their truth.[37] The Court further held that in other cases, other substitutes for oath, presence and contemporaneous cross-examination could suffice to ground admission. The Court later recognized that where a witness does not recall making the earlier statement, or refuses to answer questions, the trial judge should take into account that the inability in the adversary to cross-examine might impede the jury's ability to assess the ultimate reliability of the statement.[38]

---

37   The Court placed great weight on the fact that the witnesses could be cross-examined at trial. Althought not equivalent to cross-examinination at the time the statements were made, cross-examination at trial would provide an opportunity for the witnesses to explain the discrepancies in their statements. The trier of fact could then consider these explanations alongside the witnesses's prior statemtents and testmony to determine the truth of the matter.

38   See *R. v. U. (F.J.)*, [1995] 3 S.C.R. 764. But see *R. v. Campbell* (2002), 1 C.R. (6th) 343 (N.S. C.A.) that "the absence of an opportunity to cross-examine the declarant does not preclude admission of the statement." See also Delisle, "*B. (K.G.)* and Its Progeny" (1998) 14 C.R. (5th) 75 and Delisle, "*Diu*: Inconsistency in *B. (K.G.)* Rulings" (2000) 33 C.R. (5th) 259.

5. Exceptions to the Hearsay Rule

As we have seen, the traditional exceptions remain presumptively in place in the context of the principled approach to hearsay. In the pages that follow, we examine many of the most important exceptions to the hearsay rule as they exist in Canadian law.

(a) Admissions

Perhaps the most frequently used exception to the hearsay rule is the admission. It helps that it's also the easiest to identify. An admission is, very simply, a statement made by a party when tendered by the opposing party. The purpose of the hearsay rule is to protect the adversary against the admission of evidence that the adversary cannot cross-examine. An adversary can hardly complain about the introduction of his own statements. He surely cannot object that he had no opportunity to cross-examine himself! It just seems fair, given our adversarial system, that one adversary is able to use any statement made by her opponent which is relevant to a material issue. Thus, the general rule is that party statements are admissible.

Given that their admissibility rests of the logic of the adversary system, it is commonly recognized that admissions require a different kind of analysis than other hearsay exceptions.[39] Some even question whether admissions should be understood as hearsay at all. The unique status of admissions has led to some confusion over whether the hearsay exception for admissions should be subject to the governing framework of the principled approach to hearsay. The traditional and still prevailing view is that admissions should be admitted without any application of the necessity and reliability analysis.[40] However, responding to suggestions from the Supreme Court that all traditional hearsay exceptions should operate within the context of the principled framework,[41] some courts have begun to subject admissions to the necessity and reliability analysis.[42]

---

39 See most recently *Khelawon, supra,* note 2 at para. 65.

40 See, *e.g., Evans, supra,* note 9n; *R. v. Foreman* (2002), 6 C.R. (6th) 201 at para. 37 (Ont. C.A.); *R. v. Osmar* (2007), 44 C.R. (6th) 276 at para. 53 (Ont. C.A.); *R. v. Terrico* (2005), 31 C.R. (6th) 161 (B.C. C.A.).

41 See especially *Starr, supra,* note 20 at para. 192.

42 See, *e.g., R. v. Wytyshyn* (2002), [2002] A.J. No. 1389, 2002 CarswellAlta 1400 (Alta. C.A.).

(i) Some Specific Rules on Admissions

To be admissible as an admission, the out-of-court statement need not have been seen by the maker to be against his interest when he made it and we don't have to worry as to whether it's against his interest when introduced at trial as we can rest assured that his opponent thinks so. There is therefore no need to style this exception as an admission against interest; an admission will do. Also, there is no absolute requirement that the maker of the statement be himself possessed of personal knowledge of the facts he has cared to admit. Since the reason for this particular exception is fairness and the adversary system, as opposed to circumstantial guarantees of trustworthiness, it is seen to be fair to receive the statement as long as the maker earlier adopted it or indicated his belief in its truth.[43] For example, in *Stowe*,[44] the plaintiff sought damages from the railway for the loss of his horses which had been hit by the defendant's train. The plaintiff was not present at the time of the accident but he had been heard to say that his brother had left open the gate to the corral. Though the plaintiff had no personal knowledge of this fact, his statement was received against him.

Continuing the thought of fairness, if one adversary chooses to use the other's statement she must use all of it. She cannot pick and choose. It would be manifestly unfair, for example, if the prosecutor introduced the accused's statement "I killed him ..." and failed to also introduce the closing words "... but I didn't mean to."[45] Once the statement has been introduced it is evidence in the case and both sides are entitled to make of it what they will.

By definition, an admission is only receivable in evidence against the person who made it. If, therefore, two persons are sued for negligence in the operation of a motor vehicle, and one gave a statement admitting fault, and that statement implicated his co-defendant, the statement though receivable is not evidence against the silent co-defendant.[46] The judge needs to give a limiting instruction to the jury to that effect. The best practice is to give the instruction immediately after the statement is introduced.

When a statement is tendered as an admission against an accused in a criminal case there is another rule that must be faced. An admission by an accused to a police office or similar authority is a confession and there are additional conditions of admissibility. These are canvassed in the final Chapter of this book.

---

43 *R. v. Streu*, [1989] 1 S.C.R. 1521; and *R. v. Schmidt*, [1948] S.C.R. 333.

44 *Stowe v. Grand Trunk Pacific Railway*, [1918] 1 W.W.R. 546 (Alta. C.A.), affirmed (1918), 59 S.C.R. 665.

45 See *Capital Trust Corp. v. Fowler* (1921), 64 D.L.R. 289 at 292 (Ont. C.A.). See also *R. v. Ferris* (1994), 27 C.R. (4th) 141 (Alta. C.A.), affirmed [1994] 3 S.C.R. 756; and *R. v. Phillips* (1995), 45 C.R. (4th) 204 (Ont. Gen. Div.).

46 *R. v. Schmidt*, [1945] S.C.R. 438; and *Chote v. Rowan*, [1943] O.W.N. 646 (C.A.).

(ii) Statements Adopted by a Party's Conduct

If an accusation is made against a party, in circumstances where it would be reasonable to expect a denial should that party regard the accusation as untrue, the party's failure to deny or protest will be received into evidence as an implied admission.[47] It needs to be emphasized that this exception does not cover all statements made in a party's presence, although that is frequently how the exception is characterized in the courtroom. The circumstances need to be such that a protest is the reasonable thing to expect. Thus it would not be reasonable to take an accused's silence in the face of an accusation by a police officer as an acceptance as to its truth.[48] To do so would fly in the face of the accused's right to silence.[49] A good rule of practice is to not allow the evidence of the accusation until the proper foundation has been laid; the judge should ensure that there is evidence from which a jury could reasonably infer that the party by his conduct in the circumstances accepted the statement as to make it his own.[50]

(iii) Statements Authorized by a Party

A person may expressly authorize another to conduct his affairs for him. When he authorizes her to act he authorizes her to speak on his behalf. Any statement made by the agent on the principal's behalf will then be receivable against the principal as a vicarious admission should litigation later follow.

If a person in the employ of another was not explicitly authorized to speak on behalf of the principal, the law of evidence has decided that an out-of-court statement made by the employee will nevertheless be receivable against the principal provided the statement was made in the course of the employment and provided it would be reasonable for the court to imply authority to speak. Just as the law of agency, or of master-servant, has constructed vicarious liability for tort based on an assessment of the agent's duties, so too the law of evidence will find a vicarious admission applying the same tests.[51] Just as vicarious liability in tort will be found if the agent or servant was acting within the scope of his duties or employment, so too authority will be found to speak on the principal's behalf. While it may not be seen as appropriate to fix a corporation with responsibility for the statement of an office boy concerning a bond issue, it might be appropriate to

---

47 *R. v. Christie*, [1914] A.C. 545 (H.L.); and *R. v. Conlon* (1990), 1 O.R. (3d) 188 (C.A.).
48 *R. v. Eden*, [1970] 2 O.R. 161 (C.A.).
49 *R. v. Chambers* (1990), 80 C.R. (3d) 235 (S.C.C.).
50 *R. v. Harrison*, [1946] 3 D.L.R. 690 at 696 (B.C. C.A.).
51 *R. v. Strand Electric Ltd.*, [1969] 1 O.R. 190 (C.A.), *per* Laskin J.

fix an employer with responsibility for a statement by his truck driver concerning his careless driving.[52] At one time[53] it was thought that to be admissible the agent's admission needed to have been made to a third party but the better view, that it is receivable as an admission even if it was made by the agent to his own principal, has now been accepted.[54]

In a partnership each partner, when acting within the scope of the partnership, is an agent for the other partners and for the partnership. Statements made by a partner while conducting the firm's business are therefore receivable as admissions against the partnership.

It is important to recognize that before there can be vicarious responsibility for any of the above statements, the fact of the agency relationship, the preliminary condition of admissibility, must be independently established. It would, of course, be a bootstrap operation of the first order, and not acceptable if the out-of-court statements were themselves tendered as evidence of the agency relationship.[55]

(iv) Co-conspirator Statements

When a partnership is formed for the purpose of carrying out a criminal enterprise, we commonly refer to the same as a conspiracy. The acts and statements of co-conspirators are receivable against their partners in crime if the same were done or said in furtherance of the conspiracy. The latter condition is very important. Statements by co-conspirators afterwards, in the form of narrative describing their mutual exercise, are not receivable under this head. Such statements are only receivable against their maker. The reception of one co-conspirator's statements against the others is frequently justified on the basis that each partner to the conspiracy has impliedly authorized the other to do these acts and to say these things. This exception is not limited to charges of conspiracy but is also applicable to any offence committed pursuant to some common design. The exception is also not limited to criminal conspiracies.[56]

One can immediately discern a problem. The preliminary condition of admissibility, the fact of a conspiracy, is also the very thing sought to be established. Our courts have devised a solution. First, the acts and statements made and said in furtherance of the conspiracy are received into evidence.

---

52 *Rudzinski v. Warner Theatres Inc.*, 114 N.W. 2d 466 at 471 (1962).

53 See *R. v. Strand Electric, supra*, note 51, *per* Laskin J.

54 *Morrison-Knudsen Co. v. British Columbia Hydro & Power Authority* (1973), 36 D.L.R. (3d) 95 (B.C. S.C.).

55 See *Strand Electric, supra*, note 51, *per* Laskin J.

56 See, *e.g.*, *Great West Uranium Mines Ltd. v. Rock Hill Uranium Mines Ltd.*, [1955] 4 D.L.R. 307 (Sask. C.A.).

At the end of the trial, the trier of fact is advised to consider all the evidence and satisfy itself beyond a reasonable doubt that the conspiracy alleged in fact existed. If the conspiracy is found to exist, the trier is advised to consider all the evidence directly admissible against the accused and decide whether, on a balance of probabilities, the accused was a member of the conspiracy. If the trier is satisfied on a balance of probabilities that the accused was a member of the conspiracy, then the trier may make use of the evidence of the acts and statements of the co-conspirators to determine whether it is satisfied beyond a reasonable doubt as to the accused's membership. This complex analysis has become known as the *Carter* test.[57]

Observe the result. During the trial, all the evidence of statements made during the conspiracy is received. The jury is then told at the end of the day that these statements are receivable against the accused if they follow the above formula. There is good reason to doubt that the jury will be able to follow the limiting instructions.[58] Nevertheless, the *Carter* test recently survived scrutiny under the principled approach. In *Mapara*,[59] the Supreme Court held that co-conspirator statements admissible under the rule were supported by indicators of reliability and necessity and that the exception should therefore be preserved.

(b) Exceptions Where Declarant Is Unavailable

Recall that the clearest case of necessity under the principled approach arises when the declarant is unavailable for some reason, for example because she is deceased. We have seen that necessity under the principled approach extends beyond these kinds of cases. However, some of the traditional hearsay exceptions still require necessity in this strict form, and we examine those here.

(i) *Declarations Against Interest*

The common law recognized an exception to the hearsay rule for a declaration made by a person concerning a matter within her personal knowledge which declaration when made was known to the declarant to be to the declarant's prejudice. The theory was that a person would not say something falsely as to which she knew the truth if the statement was against her own interest. There are grounds of necessity since the declarant must

---

57   *R. v. Carter*, [1982] 1 S.C.R. 938; and *R. v. Barrow*, [1987] 2 S.C.R. 694.

58   See Dufraimont "*R. v. Mapara*: Preserving the Co-conspirators' Exception to the Hearsay Rule" (2006) 51 C.L.Q. 169.

59   *Supra*, note 20.

be unavailable. It is well to distinguish this from an admission. A declaration against interest is not made by a party.

In the beginning, the prejudice was restricted to adverse effects to the declarant's pecuniary or proprietary interest. More recently, the courts have expanded its use to instances where the declarant's penal interest was adversely affected. It was decided that a declarant who exposed himself to criminal liability was as unlikely to be falsifying as was one who made a declaration against his pecuniary interest.[60] Nevertheless, our courts are clearly suspicious of such declarations. In *Demeter*,[61] the accused had been convicted of the murder of his wife. On appeal, the issue concerned the admissibility of evidence that a deceased declarant, who was unconnected to the accused, had confessed to the murder. The Court decided that the alleged confession was inadmissible because there was nothing in the evidence to show that when the declarant made the statement it was contrary to his interest either penal or pecuniary. At the time of the statement, the declarant was an escaped convict under sentence of life imprisonment. In the result, he could not be sentenced to a consecutive sentence so that there could be no penal consequence for the crime admitted. The Court approved the guidelines for the operation of this exception that had been set out in the Court below:

1. The declaration would have to be made to such a person and in such circumstances that the declarant should have apprehended a vulnerability to penal consequences as a result.
2. The vulnerability to penal consequences would have to be not remote.
3. The declaration must be considered in its totality and if upon the whole tenor the weight is in favour of the declarant, it is not against his interest.
4. In a doubtful case, a court might properly consider whether or not there are other circumstances connecting the declarant with the crime and whether or not there is any connection between the declarant and the accused.
5. The declarant would have to be unavailable by reason of death, insanity, grave illness which prevents the giving of testimony even from a bed, or absence in a jurisdiction to which none of the processes of the court extends.

The Supreme Court later held that such declarations against penal interest should not be admitted where they inculpate an accused.[62]

---

60 *R. v. O'Brien* (1977), 76 D.L.R. (3d) 513 (S.C.C.); and *R. v. Demeter*, [1978] 1 S.C.R. 538.
61 *Ibid.*
62 *R. v. Lucier* (1982), 65 C.C.C. (2d) 150 (S.C.C.).

(ii) Dying Declarations

At common law, a deceased's declaration regarding the cause of his death, such declaration founded on declarant's personal knowledge, was receivable in a prosecution for his death provided there was evidence that when he made the declaration he entertained a settled and hopeless expectation of death. The theory is that a person in such an extreme state would not tell a falsehood, quieting the danger of insincerity, and that since the statement is limited to the cause of his death his statement was likely accurate. The limitation to criminal prosecutions is odd. Given the quieting of the hearsay dangers, one would have assumed the exception would be available in all cases, civil and criminal. In the beginning, the exception was not so limited and the limitation, created in the nineteenth century, was by accident. One might now argue for the reception of such a statement in other cases based on the principled approach.

As an illustration of how the old exceptions are strictly construed in comparison to the principled approach, consider *Kharsekin*.[63] The accused was charged with murder. The victim died of a stab wound. Around 1 a.m., the victim, bleeding profusely, appeared at the medical centre. The doctor asked him who had wounded him. The victim said it was the accused. Just after this statement, the victim became unconscious. About 15 to 20 minutes later he was revived. The doctor asked the victim whether his assailant was the accused and the victim nodded his head in agreement. The victim died just before 3:00 a.m. The statements were tendered as dying declarations. The trial judge decided that there was no evidence of a settled hopeless expectation of death and refused to admit. That finding was not challenged on appeal. The Court of Appeal decided that the statements were receivable under the principled approach to hearsay and that the trial judge was wrong when he concluded that the indicia of reliablity under that doctrine should be the same as those for dying declarations.

(iii) Business Records and Other Declarations in the Course of Duty

Historically at common law, declarations of a deceased person were receivable if the person was under a duty to act, the declarations described the deceased's own activities in carrying out that duty, the declarations were made contemporaneously with the activity, and the deceased was then under a duty to record the same. The fact that the declaration was about the declarant's own activities quieted perception dangers, that they were made contemporaneously with the doing of the act quieted memory dangers and

---

the duty to record and the routine nature of the declaration ensured accuracy and stilled any concerns as to sincerity.

The requirement that the declarant be deceased has been eliminated. In *Ares v. Venner*,[64] the plaintiff had been injured in a skiing accident. The fracture was set by the defendant doctor and a cast applied. The cast was evidently applied too tightly and there was consequent impairment of the plaintiff's circulatory system. In the civil suit, the plaintiff sought to prove negligence by showing that the signs of impairment were manifest and that the doctor should have done something to relieve the pressure. The plaintiff tendered the nurses's notes describing the plaintiff's toes as "blue", "bluish pink" and "cold", this despite the fact the nurses were present in the court-room and this common law exception needed evidence that the declarant was deceased. The Supreme Court decided that hospital records, including nurses's notes, which were made contemporaneously, by one with personal knowledge and under a duty to record, were receivable as proof of the facts stated therein. For the Court those parameters gave assurances of trustwor-thiness. The nurses were trained observers, they made the notes contem-poraneously with their observations and their duty to keep accurate records was subject to supervision. Thus the dangers of perception, memory and sincerity were minimized. But what of the requirement of necessity? The nurses were alive and well and sitting in the courtroom! For necessity, the Court decided it was to be found in the otherwise serious interference with the convenience of hospital management. The language chosen by the Court in *Ares v. Venner* in concluding its judgment was specific to the fact situation before it and referred to hospital records; the language in the rest of the judgment invited the profession to reform the hearsay rule with a princi-pled approach. As we saw above, it took another 20 years for this to happen.

Around the time the common law was being developed in *Ares v. Venner*, the federal and provincial legislatures acted to facilitate the admis-sion of business records. The legislative provisions recognize that there are circumstantial guarantees of accuracy resident in the business context from records which are relied on in the day-to-day carrying out of business activities and which are subject to frequent routine checking. Typically these provisions require that the records be of a kind that are made in the usual and ordinary course of business and that the proponent of the evidence give notice to the other side of the intention to introduce business records into evidence. The legislation is quite detailed and the following extracts from the Ontario *Evidence Act*,[65] with references to the counterpart provi-sions in the *Canada Evidence Act*, serve as an example:

---

64 *Supra*, note 18.
65 R.S.O. 1990, c. E.23.

35.—(1) In this section,

"business" includes every kind of business, profession, occupation, calling, operation or activity, whether carried on for profit or otherwise;

"record" includes any information that is recorded or stored by means of any device.[66]

(2) Any writing or record made of any act, transaction, occurrence or event is admissible as evidence of such act, transaction, occurrence or event if made in the usual and ordinary course of any business and if it was in the usual and ordinary course of such business to make such writing or record at the time of such act, transaction, occurrence or event or within a reasonable time thereafter.[67]

(3) Subsection (2) does not apply unless the party tendering the writing or record has given at least seven days' notice of the party's intention to all other parties in the action, and any party to the action is entitled to obtain from the person who has possession thereof production for inspection of the writing or record within five days after giving notice to produce the same.[68]

(4) The circumstances of the making of such a writing or record, including lack of personal knowledge by the maker, may be shown to affect its weight, but such circumstances do not affect its admissibility.

(5) Nothing in this section affects the admissibility of any evidence that would be admissible apart from this section or makes admissible any writing or record that is privileged.[69]

Some controversies have arisen surrounding the interpretation of business records legislation. For example, cases have examined the admissibility of opinions in business records,[70] and the significance of the fact that the maker of the record has no personal knowledge of the matters recorded.[71] Little purpose would be served by examining these intricate controversies here, in light of the fact that principled approach to hearsay has changed the legal terrain in this area.

---

66 Similar broad definitions of "business" and "record" appear in s. 30(12) of the *Canada Evidence Act*, R.S.C. 1985, c. C-5.

67 *Accord*, s. 30(1) of the *Canada Evidence Act*.

68 *Accord*, s. 30(7) of the *Canada Evidence Act*.

69 *Accord*, ss. 30(10) and (11) of the *Canada Evidence Act*. For provincial and territorial provisions dealing with business records, see: R.S.B.C. 1996, c. 124, s. 42; C.C.S.M., c. E150, s. 49; R.S.N.W.T. 1988, c. E-8, s. 47; R.S.N.S. 1989, c. 154, s. 23; R.S.P.E.I. 1988, c. E-11, s. 32; S.S. 2006, c. E-11.2, ss. 49-50; R.S.Y. 2002, c. 78, s. 39.

70 See, *e.g.*, *Adderley v. Bremner*, [1968] 1 O.R. 621 (H.C.), excluding evidence of a medical diagnosis noted in a hospital record.

71 See, *e.g.*, *R. v. Martin* (1997), 8 C.R. (5th) 246 (Sask. C.A.), admitting under s. 30 of the *Canada Evidence Act* records containing statistical information of which the maker of the record had no personal knowledge.

Early on there was authority that business records could be admitted either under the legislation or under the common law criteria in *Ares v. Venner*.[72] In some cases records that would not have been admissible under the legislation have been admitted under the common law rule. For example, while the legislation applies only to written records, the common law hearsay exception covers oral declarations in the course of duty. Now, with the ascendancy of the principled approach, there is yet another basis on which to admit business records: the necessity and reliability analysis.[73] Given the complexity of the legislation and the common law requirements, some courts proceed immediately to the necessity and reliability analysis and admit business records on that basis.[74] Taken together, the common law exception for declarations in the course of duty, business records legislation and the principled approach to hearsay ensure that this type of evidence is broadly admissible.

In addition to the provisions relating to business records discussed above, the legislatures have enacted various provisions governing the admission of banking and financial records.[75]

(iv) Former Testimony

At common law, if a witness had given testimony on oath in a judicial proceeding, and the witness had thereby been open for cross-examination by the other side in that proceeding, and if that witness was not available at a later judicial proceeding, his testimony at the earlier proceeding would be receivable at a later proceeding provided it was on the same subject and tendered against the same party who earlier had the opportunity to cross-examine.[76] Grounds of necessity reside in the witness's unavailability and there are circumstances guaranteeing reliability resident in the oath and the

---

72 *Supra*, note 18. See *R. v. Monkhouse* (1987), 61 C.R. (3d) 343 (Alta. C.A.) approving the application of *Ares v. Venner* to business records in a criminal case and receiving at common law where the Crown had failed to give the notice required by statute. See also *Setak Computer Services Corp. v. Burroughs Business Machines Ltd.* (1977), 76 D.L.R. (3d) 641 at 646 (Ont. H.C.) applying *Ares v. Venner* to business records in a civil case. *Accord, Tecoglas Inc. v. Domglas Inc.* (1985), 51 O.R. (2d) 196 (H.C.). But compare *Exhibitors Inc. v. Allen* (1989), 70 O.R. (2d) 103 (H.C.).

73 See, *e.g., R. v. Larsen* (2001), 42 C.R. (5th) 49 (B.C. S.C.), where a document that did not meet the common law requirements for admissibility of declarations in the course of duty was admitted under the principled approach.

74 See, *e.g., R. v. West* (2001), 45 C.R. (5th) 307 (Ont. S.C.J.).

75 For provisions dealing with financial records, see: R.S.C. 1985, c. C-5, s. 29; R.S.A. 2000, c. A-18, s. 41; R.S.B.C. 1996, c. 124, ss. 34 and 43; C.C.S.M., c. E150, s. 48; R.S.N.B. 1973, c. E-11, s. 46; R.S.N.W.T. 1998, c. E-8, s. 51; R.S.N.S. 1989, c. 154, s. 21; R.S.O. 1990, c. E.23, s. 33; R.S.P.E.I. 1988, c. E-11, s. 30; R.S.Y. 2002, c. 78, s. 45.

76 *Walkerton (Town) v. Erdman* (1894), 23 S.C.R. 352.

earlier availability of cross-examination. In criminal cases, there is a statutory embodiment of this common law rule in s. 715 of the *Criminal Code*:

> (1) Where, at the trial of an accused, a person whose evidence was given at a previous trial on the same charge, or whose evidence was taken in the investigation of the charge against the accused or on the preliminary inquiry into the charge, refuses to be sworn or to give evidence, or if facts are proved on oath from which it can be inferred reasonably that the person
>
> (a) is dead,
> (b) has since become and is insane,
> (c) is so ill that he is unable to travel or testify, or
> (d) is absent from Canada,
>
> and where it is proved that the evidence was taken in the presence of the accused, it may be read as evidence in the proceedings without further proof, unless the accused proves that the accused did not have full opportunity to cross-examine the witness.
>
> (2) Evidence that has been taken on the preliminary inquiry or other investigation of a charge against an accused may be read as evidence in the prosecution of the accused for any other offence on the same proof and in the same manner in all respects, as it might, according to law, be read in the prosecution of the offence with which the accused was charged when the evidence was taken.
>
> . . .[77]

In *Potvin*,[78] the Supreme Court decided that a trial judge has discretion to reject evidence, although the statutory conditions set out in s. 715 are satisfied, if in her view it would be unfair to receive the same. The Court gave, as an example of unfairness, where the prosecution knew at the time the evidence was initially taken that the witness would not be available to testify at trial and failed to inform the accused so that he could make the best use of his opportunity to cross-examine the witness at the earlier proceeding. Another example of unfairness suggested by the Court would be where the credibility of the missing witness was crucial and the jury had no opportunity to observe the witness's demeanour and so assess the witness's credibility.

---

77 R.S.C. 1985, c. C-46. For a provincial provision dealing with former testimony, see R.S.N.B. 1973, c. E-11, s. 33.

78 *R. v. Potvin* (1989), 47 C.C.C. (3d) 289 (S.C.C.).

(c) Exceptions Not Dependent on the Availability of Declarant

Several exceptions to the hearsay rule operate independently of the availability of the declarant. Clearly these exceptions lack the strict necessity requirements that characterize the exceptions reviewed in the previous section. However, when we consider that under the principled approach necessity can be satisfied in circumstances where the hearsay evidence carries a value that cannot be obtained in any other way, it becomes possible to view these exceptions too as reflecting the necessity principle.

(i) *Declarations as to Physical Sensation*

The common law permitted receipt of declarations as to physical sensations.[79] The common law did not insist on the declarant's unavailability but there was a necessity of sort in the sense that there was no other source of information as to the declarant's well-being. There were seen to be circumstantial guarantees of reliability resident in the fact that the declarant should be able to accurately perceive his own sensations and that the declarations were limited to his then present feelings. Dangers of insincerity were not quieted. The declaration needed to be limited to complaints or expressions as to physical feeling and could not be extended to include narrative as to the cause of the same.[80]

(ii) *Declarations as to Mental or Emotional State*

Since the common law decided to receive declarations as to physical state, it seemed only natural that for the same reasons it would receive declarations as to mental state.

Suppose, for example, that the material issue in the case is whether the declarant was domiciled in Ontario. Suppose domicile requires residence plus an intention to make the residence one's home. An out-of-court statement by the declarant—"I plan to make Ontario my home"—is receivable to prove his intent as the hearsay dangers related to communication, memory and perception are absent and grounds of necessity exist in the sense that you couldn't get better evidence of the person's intention. In a civil suit for alienation of affections, the plaintiff could introduce the wife-declarant's out-of-court statement "I don't love you anymore". This would be receivable

---

79 *Youlden v. London Guarantee & Accident Co.* (1912), 4 D.L.R. 721 (Ont. H.C.), affirmed (1913), 12 D.L.R. 433 (Ont. C.A.).

80 *Bacon v. Charlton* (1851), 7 Cush. 586, as quoted in 6 Wigmore, *Evidence* (Chadbourn rev. 1976), s. 1718.

to prove the wife-declarant's present state of mind and further the plaintiff's suit against the defendant.

In the examples given the state of mind was a material issue. Suppose the declarant's state of mind is not the material issue but it is relevant to a material issue. For example, in a murder prosecution, evidence of the deceased's statement "I want it all to end!" indicating her intention to commit suicide may be tendered as evidence that she later did take her own life. Evidence of a deceased's statement "I'm going over to Joe's place tonight" may be tendered as evidence that the deceased did go to Joe's place. On the hearsay danger analysis, above, these statements deserve to be received. It is true that the intention manifested by the statement may not in fact have been carried out but that's not a hearsay problem. It's a problem of relevance.[81] The statement is hearsay evidence of the declarant's then state of mind and the then state of mind is circumstantial evidence from which a trier may infer that the speaker later acted in conformity with his expressed intention. The declarant's state of mind is relevant to the issue of whether the declarant in fact went to Joe's place. It is not determinative of the issue. Few pieces of evidence are. The trier will look at all the evidence in the case, including the evidence of the declarant's state of mind, and then, based on all the relevant admissible evidence, will come to a decision.

In *R. v. Starr*,[82] the Supreme Court measured the requirements of the state of mind exception against the necessity and reliability criteria. The majority held that a hearsay statement can only be admitted under the exception to show the present intentions or state of mind of the declarant if the statement was not made in circumstances of suspicion. Thus, since circumstances of suspicion raise concerns about reliability, the Court altered the requirements of the existing hearsay exception to bring them into alignment with the principled approach. On the facts of *Starr*, the hearsay statement in question was inadmissible because while it bore on the declarant's intention, the declarant had a motive to lie.

Also in *Starr* and later in *R. v. Griffin*,[83] the Supreme Court held that a hearsay statement admitted under this exception can only be used to support an inference about the declarant's own state of mind or intentions, and not the intentions of a third party. Consequently, the jury should be warned against using the declarant's hearsay statement as evidence of a third party's intentions. Somewhat confusingly, however, *Griffin* makes it clear that the hearsay statement can be some evidence of a third party's state of mind, but only indirectly. In that case, the victim in a murder case had expressed fear

---

81 *R. v. P. (R.)* (1990), 58 C.C.C. (3d) 334 (Ont. H.C.); and *R. v. Jack* (1992), 70 C.C.C. (3d) 67 (Man. C.A.).

82 *Supra* note 20.

83 *R. v. Griffin*, (2009) 67 C.R. (6th) 1 (S.C.C.).

of the accused shortly before the killing. The Court approved the trial judge's instruction to the jury that the victim's statement was only evidence of his own state of mind, and not that of the accused. However, the majority explained that in light of the pre-existing relationship between the victim and the accused, the victim's expressed fear of the accused could help support an inference that the accused had a motive to harm him.

Suppose the declaration as to state of mind was not of an intention to do some act in the future but rather a statement of the declarant's belief as to a past act done. Should such a statement be receivable? Dr. Shepard is charged with the murder of Sally Jones. A witness is prepared to testify that shortly before Sally's death the witness heard Sally say "Dr. Shepard has poisoned me." Suppose this statement was made under such circumstances that it would not qualify as a dying declaration. The statement, however, is a statement as to the declarant's then existing state of mind, *i.e.*, Sally's belief. If we, pursuant to the instant exception, receive the statement of the declarant's belief regarding Dr. Shepard having poisoned her, the hearsay rule would be finished. The exception would have swallowed the rule. Thus, we maintain a distinction between declarations of intention which illuminate the future and declarations of belief that illuminate the past. Though the distinction may be regarded as tenuous, the very existence of the hearsay rule depends upon it.[84]

(iii) Spontaneous Statements

If a declaration is made in response to an event, in circumstances of such spontaneity or involvement that one can say that there was no opportunity for the declarant to reflect on what would have been the best thing to say, then we are assured that the hearsay danger of sincerity is eliminated. The declaration being contemporaneous with the event to which the statement is relevant, the memory danger is also stilled. The common law has traditionally received such a statement although one can imagine that the very spontaneity that quiets sincerity and memory concerns may cause misperception. Who hasn't said, after an exclamation about some stirring event, "On second thought ...".

This exception was formerly referred to by most, and is still referred to by some, as the *res gestae* exception. *Res gestae* means things done, and it reflects the idea that a spontaneous statement in response to an event forms a part of that event. However, use of the Latin phrase led to considerable confusion and describing the exception in terms of its underlying rationale,

---

84   *Shepard v. U.S.*, 290 U.S. 96 (1933), *per* Cardozo J.

spontaneous declaration, is a marked improvement.[85] The statement need not be strictly contemporaneous with the event as long as it was made while the declarant was still dominated by the event.[86] In *Clark*,[87] the accused was charged with murder. Shortly after she had been injured by the accused the victim yelled "Help, I've been murdered, I've been stabbed." The Court decided that these statements were made spontaneously in circumstances where concoction or distortion could safely be excluded and were therefore admissible. The Court specifically said that the narrow test of exact contemporaneity was no longer to be followed.

In *Khan*,[88] Supreme Court decided that, applying the traditional tests for spontaneous declarations, the trial judge had correctly rejected the mother's evidence of the child complainant's statement describing the alleged sexual assault. The statement was not contemporaneous, since it was made about one-half hour after the offence was committed, and it was not made under the pressure or emotional intensity which would give the guarantee of reliability upon which the spontaneous declaration exception had traditionally rested. The Court noted that the hearsay exception for spontaneous declarations incorporated no necessity requirement, but this conclusion is now open to question in light of the more expansive idea of necessity that has since developed. As discussed above, in the result in *Khan*, the Court received the statements under the newly-minted principled approach.

(iv) Statements of Present Sense Impression

The common law has received, often with the label *res gestae*, declarations of a present sense or belief concerning a contemporaneous event witnessed by the declarant.[89] To qualify there need not be a startling event or excitement in the declarant. There must be spontaneity, however, and the statement must describe a current event. The statement must have been made in the presence of another, who is now prepared to relate the statement, and that other must have had an opportunity to see what the declarant saw, and be now open to cross-examination as to the statement and the circumstances surrounding its making.

---

85 *Ratten v. R.* (1971), [1972] A.C. 378 (Aust. P.C.).
86 *R. v. Andrews*, [1987] A.C. 281 (H.L.).
87 *R. v. Clark* (1983), 42 O.R. (2d) 609 (C.A.).
88 *Supra*, note 18.
89 *R. v. Graham* (1972), 7 C.C.C. (2d) 93 (S.C.C.).

(d) Exceptions Where Declarant is Available

Recall that an out-of-court statement does not cease to be hearsay simply because the declarant is present in the witness stand. Although the declarant is presently under oath and subject to cross-examination, the statement when made was not so subject. It is thought that the worth of cross-examination lies in its immediacy following the making of the statement, and absent such contemporaneous cross-examination the statement is hearsay. We have seen that the prior statement of a witness can sometimes be admitted under the principled approach as discussed in *B. (K.G.)*.[90] Similarly, the following two exceptions operate to admit hearsay where the declarant is also a witness in the trial.

(i) *Previous Identification*

In *R. v. Tat*,[91] the Court explained that a prior identification by a witness can be relied on for its truth in two situations. First, if a witness has previously identified the accused out-of-court and does so again in court, that fact and circumstances of the out-of-court identification may be received in evidence at trial to confirm the witness's identification at trial. Second, if the witness is unable to identify the accused at trial but testifies that an earlier identification made by her was accurate, the out-of-court identification is again admissible. In either case the identifying witness and others who saw the identification can testify and be cross-examined on the identification procedure and other circumstances affecting the value of the identification. In *Tat*, the Court of Appeal took the view that evidence admissible under these two heads was not hearsay. In *Starr*,[92] the Supreme Court adopted the two categories of admissible prior identifications but treated them as an exception to the hearsay rule. Despite this uncertainty over whether a prior identification adopted by the witness constitutes hearsay, such an identification is clearly admissible. Conversely, there is clear agreement that a prior identification disavowed by the witness is inadmissible.

(ii) *Past Recollection Recorded*

As we saw in Chapter 3, a witness may testify to a past event having reference to his earlier notes concerning the matter, though he has no present recollection of the event. This is justified on the basis that the adversary

---

90 *Supra*, note 20.
91 (1997), 14 C.R. (5th) 116 (Ont. C.A.).
92 *Supra*, note 20.

will be able to cross-examine the witness regarding his usual habits for accuracy in perception and in recording any motives for falsifying. The contemporaneity of note-taking required for the exercise also gives added assurance of the trustworthiness of the earlier statement. Describing this process as refreshment of memory masks the reception of the earlier hearsay statement, but the fact that past recollection recorded represents an exception to the hearsay rule deserves notice.[93]

---

93 See *R. v. Meddoui* (1990), 61 C.C.C. (3d) 345 (Alta. C.A.), leave to appeal to S.C.C. quashed for want of jurisdiction (1991), 69 C.C.C. (3d) vi (note) (S.C.C.).

5

Opinion and Expert Evidence

1. The Opinion Rule and Lay Witnesses

Two hundred years ago, witnesses were admonished to speak facts and not opinion. This led, in the minds of some, to the creation of a supposed rule forbidding opinion testimony from a lay witness. Expert witnesses, by contrast, have always been allowed to state opinions related to the subject of their expertise. Even with respect to lay witnesses, however, closer examination reveals that the courts never intended to absolutely bar the expression of opinion testimony. When the rule was first announced the word "opinion" had a distinct meaning. It referred to a person's persuasion as to an event, such person being without knowledge. What was being foreclosed was testimony by witnesses who had no personal knowledge of the event and so suffered from the same lack of testimonial qualification as the witness who repeated hearsay. What was forbidden were notions, guesses and conjectures. The courts were not forbidding testimony regarding reasoned conclusions from facts observed.

While we sometimes still read statements that lay witnesses cannot give their opinions but must state facts, think about the intrinsic impossibility of such a requirement.[1] When a witness speaks, facts cannot come out of his mouth. When the witness relates what he saw or heard, he is providing not facts, but rather statements about facts. A statement about a fact is a conclusion that the witness has reached about what he believes he then saw and heard. It is an opinion.[2] The intrinsic impossibility of speaking otherwise led courts to create exceptions to the supposed rule permitting lay witnesses to express opinions on matters such as the identity of an individual, the apparent age of a person, or the speed of a vehicle.[3] This approach, a rule plus exceptions, is accommodated most instances.

Nevertheless, it might be better to see the rule for what it is. It is not an absolute rule of exclusion. It is rather a preferential rule asking the witness

---

1 See generally Willard L. King & Douglass Pillinger, *Opinion Evidence in Illinois* (1942).
2 *R. v. Miller* (1959), 29 W.W.R. 124 (B.C. C.A.).
3 *R. v. German*, [1947] O.R. 395 (C.A.).

to be as precise as possible in her opinion as to what she saw or heard. For example, it is not helpful to the trier of fact for the witness to say "In my opinion the driver was negligent" or "In my opinion the driver was driving too fast considering the circumstances at the time." Those are questions of fact for the trier to decide. On the other hand, it would be helpful if the witness gave his estimate of the driver's speed, what basis he had for estimating that speed, his best description of the weather at the time and the road conditions. These expressions of estimate and description, are, of course, on reflection, expressions of opinion but that is all that the witness can do. A better formulation of the supposed rule, preferable to a rule plus exceptions, would provide that lay opinions are prohibited, in the discretion of the trial judge, when they are not helpful to the trier of fact; the corollary, of course, is that helpful opinions from lay witnesses with personal knowledge are receivable.

In *R. v. Graat*,[4] the accused was convicted of impaired driving. On appeal, it was argued that the trial judge had erred in permitting the arresting officer and the booking sergeant to give their opinions that the accused's ability to operate a motor vehicle was impaired by the use of alcohol. The Court of Appeal dismissed the appeal on the basis that the opinion was admissible because it was really a compendious mode of giving evidence as to certain facts, in this case the condition of the accused. The Supreme Court agreed and dismissed the appeal, explaining that like any lay witness, the police witnesses could testify about the accused's state of intoxication because this opinion evidence would merely communicate a set of detailed factual observations in abbreviated form. The Court confirmed that witnesses should not be allowed to offer opinions on legal issues like whether a person acted negligently, because such opinions require the application of legal standards and do not amount to a compendious statement of facts.

The appeal in *Graat* could have been resolved on the basis of a compendious statement of facts exception to the rule against lay opinion. But the Court went further, noting that there was little virtue in the tenuous and frequently false antithesis between fact and opinion. The Court explained how the admissibility problem in *Graat* could be resolved by looking first at principles. The impugned evidence was relevant to a material issue. The officers had observed the accused. Based on their personal observations as to the manner of driving and indicia of intoxication in his appearance and behaviour, they concluded that his ability to drive was impaired. The admissibility of this opinion evidence could be decided by assessing the probative value of the opinion against the possible dangers of confusing the issues, misleading the jury, surprising the adversary and excessive consumption of time. The Court decided that the evidence did not unfairly

---

4 (1982), 31 C.R. (3d) 289 (S.C.C.), affirming (1980), 17 C.R. (3d) 55 (Ont. C.A.).

surprise the accused and that adducing the evidence did not require a great deal of time. The Court rejected as unsound historically and in principle any notion that the reception of opinion testimony would usurp the function of the jury. The Court noted that the trial judge was not in as good a position as the officers to judge the accused's impairment and the officers' expression of opinion would be of real help. The judge could accept all, part or none of their evidence. Applying these basic principles, the Court decided the evidence was properly received. Moreover, the Court held that in all cases trial judges have a large measure of discretion over whether to admit opinion evidence.

2. Expert Witnesses

We normally require witnesses to have personal knowledge concerning the event at issue. Only such persons are regarded as helpful to the trier of fact. The law has long recognized, however, an exception to this general requirement when the witness has qualifications beyond those of the trier of fact. Such a witness is able to provide, through his or her expertise, assistance to the trier. Only if the subject-matter is beyond the ken of the trier of fact will the expert be permitted to speak. The courts reasoned that sometimes the trier needed expert guidance and therefore when the evidence of experts was necessary it would be received.

Originally, when expert advice was necessary the trial judge would summon the expert. The expert would advise the judge who, in turn, would direct the jury respecting the major premise that could be used by it in determining the particular fact situation. With the change to the adversary system, and the parties calling the necessary factual witnesses, it seemed to be a natural development that by the end of the eighteenth century the experts were being called as witnesses by the parties and the trier was called on to assess the worth of the opinions expressed. The role for the trial judge today is not to assess the expert's opinion and direct the jury accordingly but rather to make sure that the expert will in fact be helpful to the jury in their determinations. Is the expert testimony necessary to the correct disposal of the litigation? Is it reliable enough to be received? The trial judge acts as a gatekeeper and must ensure that expert testimony meets strict criteria for admission.

(a) Admissibility of Expert Testimony

In exercising this gatekeeping function, the trial judge must apply the four criteria for the admissibility of expert evidence laid out by the Supreme Court in *R. v. Mohan*:[5]

    (a) relevance;
    (b) necessity in assisting the trier of fact;
    (c) the absence of any exclusionary rule;
    (d) a properly qualified expert.

The latter two criteria present few problems. The reference to the absence of any exclusionary rule means that expert evidence may be excluded by operation of another rule of evidence even if it meets the criteria for the admissibility of expert evidence. This is consistent with the normal operation of exclusionary rules.

In terms of the expert's qualifications, the judge must decide whether the witness being tendered as an expert is properly qualified.[6] An expert's qualifications may be demonstrated by formal educational certificates or by practical experience gained over a period of time. The witness will be examined before the judge and jury and may also be cross-examined as to her qualifications. Submissions may be made and the judge will decide if the witness is qualified to give expert evidence on the subject at hand. If the witness is found wanting, the trier will not be misled because the supposed expert will not be allowed to testify; if the witness is accepted as an expert, the jury will have the advantage of hearing her qualifications and will be better able to assess the weight to be given to her testimony.

At the heart of the inquiry into the admissibility of expert evidence lie the first two *Mohan* criteria: relevance and necessity. Relevance in this context includes the basic standard of logical relevance required of all evidence, but it also implies a cost-benefit analysis. Expert evidence imposes burdens on the trial process. Examining and cross-examining an expert consumes a lot of time and court resources. A jury might become confused by the expert evidence or be tempted to place undeserved weight on the testimony of an expert with impressive qualifications. The expert evidence may have an effect on the trier of fact that is out of proportion to its reliability, given our "human fallibility in assessing the proper weight to be given to evidence cloaked under the mystique of science."[7] Although this danger was not addressed in *Mohan*, it is also widely recognized that expert wit-

---

5 (1994), 29 C.R. (4th) 243 (S.C.C.).

6 See *Preeper v. R.* (1888), 15 S.C.R. 401.

7 *R. v. Béland*, [1987] 2 S.C.R. 398 at 434, *per* La Forest J. See also *R. v. Melaragni* (1992), 73 C.C.C. (3d) 348 (Ont. Gen. Div.).

nesses chosen, prepared and paid by the parties may offer testimony that is biased instead of providing the impartial expert perspective that would be most helpful to the trier of fact.[8] Expert evidence should only be admitted where these costs are outweighed by the value of the expert testimony.

Moreover, to be admissible, expert evidence must be necessary to assist the trier of fact. The Supreme Court explained in *Mohan* that it is not enough for the evidence to be helpful. Rather, the evidence must be necessary in the sense that the expert has knowledge beyond the ken of the lay person, that the expertise is of a technical nature and not commonly shared. In short, in order for expert evidence to be admissible the subject-matter of the inquiry must be such that ordinary people are unlikely to form a correct judgment about it, if unassisted by persons with special knowledge.

Recently in *R. v. Abbey*,[9] the Ontario Court of Appeal suggested a new approach to determining the admissibility of expert evidence that is consistent with the Supreme Court's jurisprudence but may further assist trial judges with this difficult analytical task. *Abbey* suggests that the analysis be undertaken in two steps. First, the proponent of the evidence should establish that it meets four pre-conditions to admissibility: the evidence must relate to a matter that can properly be the subject of expert testimony, it must come from a properly qualified expert, it must not run afoul of another exclusionary rule, and it must be logically relevant. Second, the trial judge should exercise her discretion as gatekeeper and weigh the benefits of admitting the expert evidence against the costs.

(i) Novel Science

In weighing the potential costs of the expert evidence against its value, the judge must determine the reliability or validity of the science proposed to be elicited. As gatekeeper, the judge should protect the trier from so-called "junk" science.[10] New or emerging scientific theories and techniques pose a special challenge in this regard, since often their reliability remains uncertain or contested among experts. For this reason, the Supreme Court has indicated that novel science should be subjected to "special scrutiny" by the trial judge.[11]

---

8   See, *e.g.*, David M. Paciocco, "Unplugging Jukebox Testimony in an Adversarial System: Strategies for Changing the Tune on Partial Experts" (2009) 34 Queen's L.J. 565.

9   (2009) 246 C.C.C. (3d) 301.

10 See Peter W. Huber, *Galileo's Revenge: Junk Science in the Courtroom* (Basic Books, 1991).

11 *Mohan, supra* note 5.

In *Daubert v. Merrell Dow Pharmaceuticals Inc.*,[12] the United States Supreme Court dealt with the problem of determining the reliability of novel scientific evidence. The U.S. Court rejected the notion, long accepted in that country, that expert evidence on novel science should only be admitted where the science is generally accepted. The Court also recognized that it would be wrong to demand that the subject of scientific testimony be known to a certainty. To qualify as scientific knowledge, however, an inference or assertion needed to rest on a reliable foundation grounded in the scientific method. The trial judge should be expected to assess whether the reasoning or methodology underlying the testimony is scientifically sound and whether that reasoning or methodology can properly be applied to the facts in issue. In *R. c. J. (J.-L.)*,[13] the Supreme Court of Canada adopted a similar approach to novel science, one that also emphasizes scientific method the judge's role in screening out unreliable expert evidence. Drawing explicitly on *Daubert*, the Supreme Court of Canada identified four factors for trial judges to consider when assessing the soundness of novel scientific evidence:

(1) whether the theory or technique can be and has been tested. . .

(2) whether the theory or technique has been subjected to peer review and publication. . .

(3) the known or potential rate of error or the existence of standards. . .

(4) whether the theory or technique used has been generally accepted. . ..[14]

None of these factors is decisive on its own, but taken together they will assist trial judges in determining whether expert evidence on novel science is reliable enough to be admitted.

The Supreme Court examined the four factors identified in *J. (J.-L.)* in *R. v. Trochym*.[15] A witness in the case testified that she saw the accused enter the murder victim's apartment on the day of the killing, even though she had earlier told police that she saw the accused on another day. The witness's memory had changed after she underwent hypnosis, and the version of her memory emerging from hypnosis was the basis of her testimony at trial. A majority of the Supreme Court explained that the trial judge's gatekeeper function regarding scientific evidence applied not only to an expert's opinion based on scientific techniques, but also to facts extracted through the use of a scientific technique such as hypnosis. After applying the *J. (J.-L.)* factors, the majority concluded that the witness's post-hypnotic

---

12 509 U.S. 579 (1993).

13 (2000), 37 C.R. (5th) 203 (S.C.C.).

14 *Ibid.* at para. 33.

15 (2007), 43 C.R. (6th) 217 (S.C.C.).

evidence was not sufficiently reliable to be admissible. Although researchers had done decades of work on hypnosis, this research showed that hypnotically-induced memories were unreliable. *Trochym* demonstrates that the *J. (J.-L.)* factors may come into play even where the science at issue is not strictly novel. As the Supreme Court explained, many types of scientific evidence are well-established as reliable and admissible in Canadian trials. But even if the science is not new, "a technique or science whose underlying assumptions are challenged should not be admitted in evidence without first confirming the validity of those assumptions."[16]

(ii) Expert Evidence on Human Behaviour

Since expert evidence is only admissible where ordinary people are unlikely to form a correct judgment about the subject without special help, the courts are faced with a challenge of identifying subjects on which such help is needed. If the lay person understands the issue as well as the expert, the opinion will be regarded as unnecessary. That is why we often see judicial decisions denying receipt of expert opinions on the issue of what a normal or reasonable person would do in the circumstances. It is expected that a lay juror will know that as well as any other. While ordinary people obviously need help to understand biochemistry or ballistics, it seems reasonable to conclude that all of us are capable of interpreting normal human behaviour. That line, however, can be difficult to draw.[17]

Psychiatric or psychological testimony may be received as expert evidence in those circumstances where the average person may not have sufficient knowledge or experience with human behaviour to draw an appropriate inference from the facts. In *Lavallee*,[18] the accused was charged with murder. The defence was self-defence. For that defence to succeed, the *Criminal Code* requires that the accused acted under reasonable apprehension of death or grievous bodily harm.[19] The accused had been a battered woman in a volatile common law relationship. She killed her partner late one night by shooting him in the back of the head as he left her room. The shooting occurred after an argument where the accused had been physically abused and was taunted with the threat that either she kill him or he would get her. Did she act under *reasonable* apprehension of death or grievous bodily harm? The Court decided it would be difficult for the lay person to comprehend the battered wife syndrome. The average person might think

---

16 *Ibid.* at para. 32.
17 See generally David M. Paciocco, "Coping with Expert Evidence About Human Behaviour" (1999) 25 Queen's L.J. 305.
18 *R. v. Lavallee* (1990), 55 C.C.C. (3d) 97 (S.C.C.).
19 R.S.C. 1985, c. C-46, s. 34(2).

that battered women are not really beaten as badly as they claim, otherwise they would have left the relationship, or that women enjoy being beaten. The Court recognized that each of these stereotypes might adversely affect consideration of a battered woman's claim to have acted in self-defence. The Court decided that expert evidence could assist the jury in dispelling these myths. The expert testimony would provide an explanation as to why the accused did not flee when she perceived her life to be in danger. The expert testimony might also assist the jury in assessing the reasonableness of her belief that killing her batterer was the only way to save her own life. The Court decided, therefore, that it was proper for the psychiatrist to testify that in his opinion the accused's shooting of the deceased was the final desperate act of a woman who sincerely believed that she would be killed that night. The expert testimony was properly admitted in order to assist the jury in determining whether the accused had a *reasonable* apprehension of death or grievous bodily harm and believed on *reasonable* grounds that she had no alternative but to shoot.

Expert evidence on human behaviour has been admitted in various contexts, but the courts have shown reluctance to open the door too wide to its admission. For example, the Supreme Court has explained that evidence purporting to show that an accused does not conform to the psychological profile of the perpetrator can only be admitted in very limited circumstances.[20] Such evidence is typically excluded on the basis that the psychological profiles are not sufficiently standardized to be useful and reliable.[21]

(iii) Necessity and the Availability of Jury Instructions

In some contexts, courts have refused to admit expert evidence because the matter can be explained through judicial instructions to the jury. Where instructions will suffice, expert evidence is excluded as unnecessary. For example, in *R. v. D. (D.)*,[22] the Supreme Court held that jury instructions should have been employed instead of expert evidence on the issue of delayed disclosure of sexual abuse. This notion that expert evidence becomes unnecessary where jury instructions are available is also the primary reason that Canadian courts have refused to admit psychological evidence on the frailties of eyewitness testimony.[23] Eyewitness evidence is notori-

---

20 *Mohan, supra*, note 5.

21 See *ibid.*; *R. v. B. (S.C.)* (1997), 10 C.R. (5th) 302 (Ont. C.A.). See also *R. v. Olscamp* (1994), 35 C.R. (4th) 37 (Ont. C.A.) (excluding evidence that a child complainant fit the profile of a sexually abused child).

22 (2000), 36 C.R. (5th) 261 (S.C.C.).

23 See *R. v. McIntosh* (1997), 35 O.R. (3d) 97 (Ont. C.A.); *R. v. Woodard* (2009), 245 C.C.C. (3d) 522 (Man. C.A.) at para. 41; *R. v. Fengstad* (1994), 27 C.R. (4th) 383 (B.C. C.A.). But see *R. v. Henderson* (2009), 239 Man. R. (2d) 69 (Man. Q.B.).

ously unreliable. The courts have long recognized that lay jurors may hold misapprehensions on the subject and need to be educated about the psychological factors affecting the reliability of this identification evidence. While it might seem logical that this education should be delivered by experts in the field of eyewitness psychology, under our law, jury instructions are the only approved method for sensitizing the jury to the dangers of eyewitness mistakes. Where the Crown relies on contested eyewitness identification evidence, the judge is required to deliver a cautionary instruction that touches on many of the same points an expert's testimony might cover.[24]

(b) The Ultimate Issue Rule

It is not infrequent that we hear counsel and judges refer to the supposed problem of a witness speaking to the ultimate issue. The courts have at times recognized a so-called ultimate issue rule preventing expert witnesses from offering opinions on the basic questions of guilt or liability. The rule is said to be justified on the basis that to allow such an opinion would permit the expert to usurp the jury's function. It is submitted that this is a red herring.[25] Opinion evidence, like any other evidence, can be accepted or rejected by the trier of fact and their role cannot be usurped. It is much better to recognize that in those cases where the evidence was supposedly rejected as in conflict with that rule, the real reason for rejection lay in the lack of helpfulness.[26] If a witness were to testify that in his opinion the defendant was negligent, or guilty, expressions by the witness on issues which are mixed questions of fact and law, that testimony would not be helpful to the trier of fact.[27] Rather, the trier must reach its own legal conclusions in light of the witnesses' testimony regarding the facts.

In any event there is no longer any rule of general application forbidding opinion testimony going to the ultimate issue.[28] The courts have recognized, however, that the risk that a jury might accept an expert's opinion uncritically raises particular concerns when the opinion concerns guilt or liability. In other words, the usual concerns about prejudice arising from expert testimony are heightened where the expert's opinion touches on the ultimate issue. Consequently, in such cases the criteria for admissibility of expert testimony may be applied strictly to exclude the opinion.[29]

---

24 *R. v. Mezzo*, [1986] 1 S.C.R. 802 at 845; *R. v. Hibbert*, [2002] 2 S.C.R. 445 at para. 79 (Bastarache, J., dissenting).

25 7 Wigmore, *Evidence* (Chadbourn rev. 1978), s. 1921.

26 See *R. v. Fisher* (1961), 34 C.R. 320 (Ont. C.A.).

27 See, *e.g.*, *R. v. Neil*, [1957] S.C.R. 685.

28 *Mohan, supra*, note 5; *R. v. Bryan* (2003), 175 C.C.C. (3d) 285 (Ont. C.A.).

29 *Mohan, ibid.*

In *Cooper*,[30] the accused was charged with murder. In answer to a question put by the trial judge the psychiatrist testified that he did not think the accused was suffering with a disease of the mind. Nonetheless, the trial judge dealt with this issue of insanity in her charge to the jury. The majority of the Court noted that while the term "disease of the mind" in s. 16 of the *Criminal Code* was a legal concept, and what is meant by the term was a question of law for the judge, as a matter of practice the trial judge could permit the psychiatrist to be asked directly whether or not the condition in question constituted a disease of the mind.

(c) Hypothetical Questions

When an expert expresses her opinion she bases the same on her knowledge of the applicable science and on the assumption that certain facts specific to the case have been established. All expert opinions are then, in a sense, hypothetical.

The expert after being examined as to her credentials will be asked to set out the basis of her opinion. Sometimes the expert will have personally examined the person or object of the opinion and will then set out her observations of the same. At other times the expert will have no personal knowledge and will be basing her opinion on the evidence of others. In either event the trial judge will tell the jury that they must first examine the worth of the evidence concerning the basis for the opinion. If they accept that evidence, are persuaded to the requisite degree that the facts on which the opinion is based actually did exist, they will be advised to go on and determine whether they are persuaded that the opinion ought to be accepted. If they are not persuaded that the facts upon which the opinion is based actually existed the expert's opinion is valueless.

If the jury is to adequately assess the worth of an expert opinion it is essential that the basis be clearly set out. Often this is done through the technique of hypothetical questions. By asking hypothetical questions incorporating all the factual premises on which the opinion will be based, counsel can elicit an expert's opinion based on other evidence while emphasizing the jury's responsibility to find the facts.[31]

Suppose the accused is charged with murder. A psychiatrist is called as a witness. "Doctor Smith, we have heard the accused testify as to the facts that occurred on the evening in question. That before the unfortunate occurrence he had consumed 24 pints of beer. That he had had nothing to eat for the previous 24 hours. That he had not had any sleep for the previous

---

30 *Cooper v. R.*, [1980] 1 S.C.R. 1149.
31 See *R. v. G. (P.)* (2009), 63 C.R. (6th) 301 (Ont. C.A.).

24 hours. That he was not accustomed to taking in large quantities of alcohol. Based on those facts what can you tell us as to the ability of the accused to form the requisite intent to kill?" The doctor then testifies that, in his opinion, based on those facts, and based on his studies and his personal experience with intoxicated persons, the accused lacked the necessary capacity to form the required intent. The trier then has the basis for the opinion clearly set out and will be advised that their first task is to determine whether the basis of the opinion has been established to their satisfaction. The trier will then consider whether the accused's evidence ought to be accepted. If it is not accepted then the opinion must be rejected. If the facts as described are found to exist the trier will go on to determine whether to accept or reject the expert's opinion. The expert's opinion, like any other piece of evidence, is for the trier of fact to accept or reject.

(d) Expert Opinion Based on Hearsay

It is commonly said that an expert is confined to expressions of opinion based on facts proved at the trial. The opinion is then elicited based on the acceptance of those facts as true using the device of hypothetical questions. But an expert testifying to her opinion, since only permitted so to do when she possesses particular knowledge or experience not shared by the trier of fact, frequently relies on hearsay. In developing her expertise she often relied on the statements of her instructors and those of text writers without satisfying herself by personal experiment that their instruction was accurate. It is perfectly acceptable for the expert to rely on the opinions of text writers where those texts are recognized by the profession as authoritative. In cross-examination an expert witness, having first been asked whether a certain textbook is recognized as authoritative by her profession, may have read to her passages from such book expressing another opinion for the purpose of testing the value of the witness's expressed opinion.[32]

So too there is a growing recognition that an expert may be able to give his opinion though it be based partly on hearsay evidence if there are grounds of necessity and reliability. For example, a real estate assessor who is called on to give his opinion on the value of a piece of property will naturally rely on statements of others, perhaps found in the registry office, as to what other like properties fetched on the market. This is how he regularly goes about his business.[33] There are grounds of necessity: receiving his opinion rather than calling all the persons who sold their houses over a period of time. There are circumstances of reliability resident in the absence of any motive

---

32   *R. v. Anderson* (1914), 16 D.L.R. 203 at 220 (Alta. C.A.).
33   See *Saint John (City) v. Irving Oil Co.* (1966), 58 D.L.R. (2d) 404 (S.C.C.).

to falsify and in the cumulative nature of the evidence relied on. A psychiatrist asked for an opinion as to an offender's dangerousness will base his opinion not only on his own interviews and tests but will also study the individual's previous records. This is how he normally goes about his tasks.[34] Again we have circumstances of necessity and reliability.

Suppose, however, the hearsay relied on has within it concern as to trustworthiness. What then should we do? In *Lavallee*,[35] the accused was charged with murder. We saw earlier how the psychiatric expert was determined to be valuable in helping the jury decide whether her actions were reasonable. The expert in *Lavallee* based his opinion on his expertise in the area of battered woman syndrome, gained through the literature and his own experience. He also accepted as true information he had received from the accused during four hours of interviews, the police report, an interview with the accused's mother and hospital reports documenting eight of her visits to hospital emergency departments. The accused did not testify. The Crown introduced into evidence the statement she gave to the police on the evening of the shooting. That statement, inculpatory in that it described the shooting, was also exculpatory in that it detailed how frightened she was and how her partner had yelled at and hit her. Our Court, in a most pragmatic exercise, said that insofar as the opinion is based on admissible evidence the fact that it is partly based on hearsay does not impact on admissibility but rather only on weight and the trier is to be so advised. Such advice is admittedly hard to formulate and may be even more difficult to follow. Another solution might be to have the expert testify after all the other witnesses have testified and then the trial judge could ask the expert to testify solely on the basis of the admissible evidence.[36]

(e) Number of Experts

There are statutory limits on the number of expert witnesses that can be called. The *Canada Evidence Act* limits each party to five.[37] Similar provisions appear in provincial and territorial *Evidence Acts* limiting a party to three or five experts, and in all cases the legislation provides for more with leave of the court. A few jurisdictions limit the number of experts on any given issue, while other jurisdictions including the federal have merely

---

34 See *R. v. Wilband,* [1967] 2 C.C.C. 6 (S.C.C.).
35 *R. v. Lavallee, supra,* note 17.
36 See *Mizzi v. DeBartok* (1992), 9 O.R. (3d) 383 (Gen. Div.).
37 R.S.C. 1985, c. C-5, s. 7.

legislated limits on the number of expert witnesses a party can call.[38] Where the legislation purports simply to limit the number of experts, the cases conflict on whether a party may call the number specified with respect to each issue on which expert evidence is necessary as opposed to that number in the whole trial.[39]

3. Exchange of Expert Reports

In the interests of efficiency at trial and to minimize inconvenience to some experts who are regularly called on for their opinions some provinces have enacted legislation permitting the admission of written expert reports in lieu of live expert testimony. For example, the Ontario *Evidence Act* provides:

52.—(1) In this section,

"practitioner" means,

(a) a member of a College as defined in subsection 1(1) of the *Regulated Health Professions Act, 1991,*

(b) a drugless practitioner registered under the *Drugless Practitioners Act,*

(c) a person licensed or registered to practise in another part of Canada under an Act that is similar to an Act referred to in clause (a) or (b).

(2) A report obtained by or prepared for a party to an action and signed by a practitioner and any other report of the practitioner that relates to the action are, with leave of the court and after at least ten days' notice has been given to all other parties, admissible in evidence in the action.

(3) Unless otherwise ordered by the court, a party to an action is entitled, at the time that notice is given under subsection (2), to a copy of the report together with any other report of the practitioner that relates to the action.

---

38   The jurisdictions taking the former approach and limiting expert witnesses to three on any issue are New Brunswick (R.S.N.B. 1973, c. E-11, s. 23), the Northwest Territories and Nunavut (R.S.N.W.T. 1998, c. E-8, s. 9) and the Yukon Territory (R.S.Y. 2002, c. 78, s. 9). The jurisdictions taking the latter approach, in which the legislation simply purports to limit the number of experts, are Manitoba at three experts (C.C.S.M., c. E150, s. 25), Ontario at three (R.S.O. 1990, c. E.23, s. 12) and Saskatchewan at five (S.S. 2006, c. E-11.2, s. 21).

39   See *Ure v. Fagnan*, [1958] S.C.R. 377; *R. v. Higgins* (1979), 28 N.B.R. (2d) 20 (N.B. C.A.), suggesting that the limits apply to each issue. But see *British Columbia Pea Growers Ltd. v. Portage La Prairie (City)* (1964), 49 D.L.R. (2d) 91 (Man. C.A.); *Bank of America Canada v. Mutual Trust Co.* (1998), 39 O.R. (3d) 134 (Gen. Div. [Commercial List]), concluding that the specified numbers limit the number of experts in the whole trial.

(4) Except by leave of the judge presiding at the trial, a practitioner who signs a report with respect to a party shall not give evidence at the trial unless the report is given to all other parties in accordance with subsection (2).

(5) If a practitioner is required to give evidence in person in an action and the court is of the opinion that the evidence could have been produced as effectively by way of a report, the court may order the party that required the attendance of the practitioner to pay as costs therefor such sum as the court considers appropriate.[40]

---

40 R.S.O. 1990, c. E.23, s. 52. To like effect, see C.C.S.M., c. E.150, s. 50; R.S.P.E.I. 1988, c. E-11, s. 33; S.S. 2006 c. E-11.2, s. 22. See also R.S.B.C. 1996, c. 124, ss. 10 and 11, not restricting the scheme to medical experts.

6

Excluding Evidence for Purposes Other Than Truth

1. Introduction

The rules of evidence that we examined in the earlier Chapters of this book are largely designed to promote an approximation to truth. The rules we are about to examine in this Chapter, by contrast, restrict our search for truth and must therefore be justified by other values. The public has an interest in the accurate outcome of litigation; to exclude information that would assist in that regard there must be another public interest that can be identified and that can be seen to outweigh the search for truth.

2. Privileged Communications

The law of privilege protects certain communications from compelled disclosure and makes them inadmissible in evidence. Although shielding some communications from the fact finder clearly interferes with the search for truth, this interference is seen to be justified on various public interest grounds.

(a) Solicitor-Client

From the earliest times, the courts have recognized a privilege for communications between a lawyer and his or her client. In the beginning it was seen to be the lawyer's privilege and was founded in notions of honour. It was dishonourable to disclose a communication made in confidence. Later a new basis for the privilege was recognized and the privilege was seen to be that of the client. Our courts recognized that the administration of justice required counsel to assist the litigant. Litigation required professional advice. The litigant could not pursue his remedy or defence unless the litigant could make a clean breast of things to the professional he had engaged.[1] The privilege protects the client against the disclosure of any confidential communication made by the client to his lawyer and any communications made in response which communications were made while the client was seeking legal advice.[2] The privilege attaches whether or not litigation was then contemplated. The privilege may attach even to the identity of the client if the client intended the same to be confidential.[3] The privilege attaches when the client seeks legal advice—even though the lawyer has not as yet accepted a retainer the privilege is present.[4]

For the communication to be privileged, the client must be seeking legal advice from one who is,[5] or who the client reasonably believes to be,[6] professionally qualified to practise law.[7] On the other hand, the fact that one party to a communication is professionally qualified does not automatically make the communication privileged; it must be legal advice that is being sought.[8] A lawyer engaged by a corporation to give legal advice oftentimes will be called on to work for his employer in another capacity. The character of the particular work performed must be looked at to see whether the privilege attaches.[9]

If the client is seeking advice to assist in the furtherance of a criminal purpose, our courts have said that this cannot be legal advice being sought and therefore communications of such sort are not privileged.[10] To displace the privilege in such a case there must be more than just an allegation—there must be some evidence from which the judge can infer the illegal purpose.[11]

The Supreme Court has explained that the solicitor-client privilege is not absolute.[12] In certain rare circumstances other societal values must prevail. Where a solicitor had retained the services of a psychiatrist who determined that the client posed an imminent danger to public safety after the client revealed details of his plan to murder prostitutes, the privilege could be set aside. The Court created what has become known as the public

---

1   *Greenough v. Gaskell* (1833), 39 E.R. 618 at 620-621 (Ch. Div.), approved in *Solosky v. Canada* (1979), 50 C.C.C. (2d) 495 at 506 (S.C.C.). See also *Anderson v. Bank of British Columbia* (1876), 2 Ch. Div. 644 (C.A.).

2   *Descôteaux v. Mierzwinski* (1982), 70 C.C.C. (2d) 385 (S.C.C.).

3   *Thorson v. Jones* (1973), 38 D.L.R. (3d) 312 (B.C. S.C.).

4   *Descoteaux v. Mierzwinski, supra*, note 2.

5   *United States v. Mammoth Oil Co.*, [1925] 2 D.L.R. 966 (Ont. C.A.).

6   *R. v. Choney* (1908), 17 Man. R. 467 (C.A.).

7   *United States v. Mammoth Oil Co., supra*, note 5.

8   See, *e.g.*, *Alfred Crompton Amusement Machines v. Customs & Excise Commissioners (No. 2)*, [1972] 2 All E.R. 353 at 376 (C.A.), *per* Lord Denning.

9   See, *e.g.*, *Canary v. Vested Estates Ltd.*, [1930] 3 D.L.R. 989 (B.C. S.C.).

10   *R. v. Cox* (1884), 14 Q.B.D. 153 at 167, approved in *Solosky v. Canada, supra*, note 1.

11   *Re Goodman & Carr and Minister of National Revenue*, [1968] 2 O.R. 814 (H.C.).

12   See *Smith v. Jones* (1999), 22 C.R. (5th) 203 (S.C.C.).

safety exception to solicitor-client privilege. Also the Court has created another exception: the innocence at stake exception. If an accused can establish that a client's communications to his solicitor contain information that is likely to raise a reasonable doubt about the accused's guilt on a criminal charge and there is no other way to obtain the information or raise a reasonable doubt, there will be an exception requiring disclosure.[13]

Originally, solicitor-client privilege operated only to permit the lawyer to refuse to answer questions or to produce documents at trial. There has since been a recognition, however, that the privilege may operate at an earlier time. For example, some of our courts allowed that an application to quash a search warrant for a lawyer's office might be made when the purpose of issuing the warrant was to allow the seizure of documents believed to afford evidence; if such documents attracted a privilege claim they could not very well afford evidence.[14] This led some to suggest that the privilege had become a rule of property rather than just a rule of evidence. While viewing the privilege as a property right bereft of any evidentiary connection was rejected by our Court,[15] there was later recognized to be a substantive right to confidentiality broader than the privilege as an evidentiary rule and even more protective of the solicitor-client relationship. In *Descoteaux*,[16] a citizen was suspected of lying about his financial means in order to obtain legal aid. This would be a crime. The police gained a search warrant to search the legal aid bureau and seize the form filled out by the citizen at his interview. The seizure was effected and the documents taken were sealed. Descoteaux and the legal aid bureau applied to a judge to have the seizure quashed and the form returned. The Supreme Court decided that it was not necessary to wait for the trial before raising the issue of confidentiality. The Court formulated a substantive rule of confidentiality as follows:

1.   The confidentiality of communications between solicitor and client may be raised in any circumstances where such communications are likely to be disclosed without the client's consent.
2.   Unless the law provides otherwise, when and to the extent that the legitimate exercise of a right would interfere with another person's right to have his communications with his lawyer kept confidential, the resulting conflict should be resolved in favour of protecting the confidentiality.

---

13   See *R. v. McClure* (2001), 40 C.R. (5th) 1 (S.C.C.). But see *R. v. Brown* (2002), 50 C.R. (5th) 1 (S.C.C.) emphasizing that the Innocence at Stake exception allows for breach of solicitor-client privilege only in rare circumstances. For comment see David Layton, *R. v. Brown: Protecting Legal-Professional Privilege*, (2002) 50 C.R. (5th) 37.

14   For a list of citations to these cases, see *Solosky v. Canada, supra*, note 1.

15   *Solosky v. Canada, ibid.*

16   *Descoteaux v. Mierzinski, supra*, note 2.

3. When the law gives someone the authority to do something which, in the circumstances of the case, might interfere with that confidentiality, the decision to do so and the choice of means of exercising that authority should be determined with a view to not interfering with it except to the extent absolutely necessary in order to achieve the ends sought by the enabling legislation.
4. Acts providing otherwise in situations under paragraph 2 and enabling legislation referred to in paragraph 3 must be interpreted restrictively.

The Court sent the matter back for consideration in accordance with these principles. Although the substantive rule of confidentiality was originally defined as separate from and complementary to the privilege as an evidentiary rule, the Supreme Court has more recently identified the substantive right as the latest stage in the evolution of solicitor-client privilege itself.[17]

The Court's recent jurisprudence emphasizes that solicitor-client privilege is close to absolute. Privileged communications can only be disclosed where "absolutely necessary", a test just short of a full prohibition on disclosure.[18] This strong protection for solicitor-client privilege is seen to be necessary to safeguard access to justice.[19] The Supreme Court has gone so far as to recognize solicitor-client privilege as a principle of fundamental justice under s. 7 of the Charter,[20] and to strike down legislation that compromises the privilege.[21]

Traditionally, the privilege did not operate to foreclose a third-party witness, such third party not being an agent of the client or the lawyer, disclosing what he had overheard pass between the lawyer and his client.[22] The lawyer and his client were expected to take precautions against being overheard. The Court in *Descoteaux* recognized that the privilege as a rule of evidence did not prevent a third-party witness from introducing into evidence confidential communications made by a client to his lawyer. But the Court said that before allowing such evidence to be introduced the judge

---

17 See *Lavallee, Rackel & Heintz v. Canada (Attorney General)* (2002), 3 C.R. (6th) 209 at para. 18 (S.C.C.).
18 *Goodis c. Ontario (Ministry of Correctional Services)*, [2006] 2 S.C.R. 32.
19 *Canada (Privacy Commissioner) v. Blood Tribe Department of Health*, [2008] 2 S.C.R. 574.
20 See *Lavallee, Rackel & Heintz, supra*, note 17 at para. 21, recognizing this principle under the *Canadian Charter of Rights and Freedoms*, Part I of the *Constitution Act, 1982*, being Schedule B to the *Canada Act 1982* (U.K.), 1982, c. 11.
21 See *Lavallee, Rackel & Heintz, ibid.*, in which a Criminal Code provision setting out a procedure for claiming solicitor-client privilege in documents seized under warrant from law offices was struck down on the basis that it authorized searches and seizures that were unreasonable because they interfered unnecessarily with the privilege.
22 *Lloyd v. Mostyn* (1842), 152 E.R. 558 at 560 (Exch. Ct.); and *Calcraft v. Guest*, [1898] 1 Q.B. 759 at 764 (C.A.).

must satisfy herself, through the application of the third substantive rule, that what was being sought to be proved by the communications was important to the outcome of the case and that there was no reasonable alternative form of evidence that could be used for that purpose. Moreover, there is now recognition that precautions by the parties may not always be possible. The *Criminal Code* provides that information gained through electronic surveillance that, but for the interception, would have been privileged remains privileged.[23]

While solicitor-client privilege generally attaches to communications between lawyer and client, there are circumstances where agents of the client or lawyer, for example the lawyer's clerical staff, are exposed to privileged communications. Solicitor client privilege continues to attach in these circumstances. Similarly, the Supreme Court has recognized that a "permanent and substantive" privilege can attach to communications between the accused and an expert retained by the defence lawyer to assist in the preparation of the defence.[24]

(b) Litigation Privilege

The Americans decided that materials created in anticipation of litigation needed to be protected from disclosure. They labelled these materials the "work product" of the lawyer.[25] In anticipation of litigation, interviews must be conducted, statements taken, memoranda to files written. Third parties, including experts and private investigators, must often be engaged. All these together with counsel's briefs, records of her mental impressions and personal beliefs make up the file. All are necessary to the proper conduct of the litigation. Unless these materials were protected from disclosure the adversary system would break down. In Canada, as well, we have recognized the correctness of this policy and such material is protected under the rubric of "litigation privilege".

Litigation privilege has traditionally been conceived as a branch of solicitor-client privilege, and many cases and statutes use the phrase "solicitor-client privilege" in a broad sense that comprehends litigation privilege. However, the Supreme Court of Canada has recently explained that it is preferable to keep these privileges separate: the phrase "solicitor-client privilege" is best confined to the legal advice privilege discussed above, whereas litigation privilege merits separate treatment.[26] This separate treatment is warranted because litigation privilege differs from the legal advice

---

23 R.S.C. 1985 c. C-46, s. 189(6).
24 *Smith v. Jones, supra,* note 12, at para. 14.
25 *Hickman v. Taylor,* 329 U.S. 495 (1947).
26 *Blank v. Canada (Minister of Justice),* [2006] 2 S.C.R. 319.

privilege in several important respects. Whereas legal advice privilege covers communications between solicitor and client, litigation privilege can attach to communications between the lawyer and third parties, or even between an unrepresented litigant and third parties. While solicitor-client privilege is permanent and attaches whenever the client seeks legal advice from the lawyer, litigation privilege exists only in the context of the litigation. For litigation privilege to attach, the material or communication must have been generated in contemplation of litigation, and the privilege expires when the litigation ends. Instead of protecting the solicitor-client relationship, litigation privilege aims to promote and protect the adversary process by ensuring a "zone of privacy" as the litigant prepares for litigation.

(c) Marital Privilege

When spouses of parties were made competent and compellable witnesses in civil cases in England, the legislation also provided for a privilege with respect to communications between the spouses which communications were made during the marriage. This legislation was copied in Canada. The *Canada Evidence Act*, s. 4, provides:

> 4. (3) No husband is compellable to disclose any communication made to him by his wife during their marriage, and no wife is compellable to disclose any communication made to her by her husband during their marriage.[27]

It is important to note that although the spouse may be a competent and compellable witness in certain criminal cases, this fact does not affect the privilege to refuse to answer questions regarding marital communications.[28] It is noteworthy that this privilege, unlike the solicitor-client privilege, belongs, mysteriously, not to the communicant but to the recipient of the communication.

Does communication refer only to statements made or does it also cover acts and facts discovered during the relationship? In *Gosselin*,[29] the accused was charged with murder. The wife, over objection, was forced to disclose the fact that she had discovered her husband's clothes with bloodstains shortly after the incident. The Supreme Court decided this was not a "communication" within the meaning of the legislation.

---

27 R.S.C. 1985, c. C-5. For similar provincial and territorial provisions, see: R.S.A. 2000, c. A-18, s. 8; R.S.B.C. 1996, c. 124, s. 8; C.C.S.M., c. E150, s. 8; R.S.N.B. 1973, c. E-11, s. 10; R.S.N.L. 1990, c. E-16, s. 4; R.S.N.W.T. 1988, c. E-8, s. 6; R.S.N.S. 1989, c. 154, s. 49; R.S.O. 1990, c. E.23, s. 11; R.S.P.E.I. 1988, c. E-11, s. 9; S.S. 2006, c. E-11.2, s. 7; and R.S.Y. 2002, c. 78, s. 6.

28 See *R. v. Zylstra* (1995), 41 C.R. (4th) 130 (Ont. C.A.); and *R. v. Jean* (1979), 7 C.R. (3d) 338 (Alta. C.A.). See *contra, R. v. St. Jean* (1976), 32 C.C.C. (2d) 438 (Que. C.A.).

29 *Gosselin v. R.* (1903), 33 S.C.R. 255.

The legislation speaks of no husband or wife being obliged to disclose. By definition then, a widow(er) or divorced person cannot claim this privilege.[30]

The privilege allows the spouse to refuse to disclose. That is the essence of the privilege. At common law, the privilege did not foreclose a third-party witness from disclosing what the third party had overheard. In the British case, *Rumping*,[31] the accused was charged with murder. The accused, about to set sail, had given a letter to a fellow seaman to post. The letter, to the accused's wife, amounted to a confession. Instead of posting the letter it was turned over to the police. The House of Lords decided the legislation in its terms did not prevent proof of the communication; the legislation only bestowed a privilege in the spouse not to answer questions about the communication.[32] The spouses are expected to take the necessary precautions to ensure that their privileged communications are not overheard or intercepted.

The *Criminal Code* in Canada, dealing with invasion of privacy and elecronic interception of private communications, provides:

> Any information obtained by an interception that, but for the interception, would have been privileged remains privileged and inadmissible as evidence without the consent of the person enjoying the privilege.[33]

In *Lloyd*,[34] the accused, husband and wife, were charged with conspiracy to traffic in narcotics. Pursuant to lawful authority, telephone conversations between them were intercepted and introduced into evidence. The Court of Appeal, basing itself on the time-honoured tradition described above, said that while there was a privilege in a spouse to refuse to divulge the information conveyed the information itself was not privileged. The Supreme Court decided that, in order to make some sense of the *Criminal Code* provision, notwithstanding the tradition, the communications were privileged.[35]

---

30 *Shenton v. Tyler*, [1939] 1 Ch. 620 (C.A.); and *R. v. Kanester*, [1966] 4 C.C.C. 231 at 240 (B.C. C.A.) applying *Shenton v. Tyler*.

31 *Rumping v. Director of Public Prosecutions*, [1962] 3 All E.R. 256 (H.L.).

32 *Accord, R. v. Kotapski* (1981), 66 C.C.C. (2d) 78 (Que. S.C.); *R. v. Illes* (2003), 59 W.C.B. (2d) 383 (B.C. S.C.).

33 Section 189(6).

34 *R. v. Lloyd* (1981), 64 C.C.C. (2d) 169 (S.C.C.).

35 Interestingly nothing was said as to whether communications in furtherance of a crime should be excepted.

(d) Privilege for Without Prejudice Communications

There is a public interest in the out-of-court settlement of disputes.[36] If all legal disputes went to trial, our courts could not handle the workload and so our law encourages litigants to settle their differences by privileging their communications when they were made in an attempt to settle. The communications of offers to settle at a certain amount might be viewed as conduct amounting to an admission of fault and, without the privilege, be receivable in the subsequent suit.

When parties try to settle a dispute they will often label their communications to be "without prejudice". Whether labelled as "without prejudice" or not, such communications are held to be privileged if, objectively viewed, the communications were meant to come to an agreement regarding the matter. The application of the rule is not dependent on the use of the phrase.[37]

The privilege operates, not only with respect to the parties who entered into the negotiations, but also with respect to third parties. In *Waxman*,[38] there had been an attempt to settle a dispute between two parties. Waxman had purchased a hydraulic press from United Steel. This machine was used for the purpose of crushing old motor-cars. The fluid used in the machine was a special kind of oil made by Texaco. An explosion occurred. Waxman sued United Steel and also sued Texaco. Letters had been written between Waxman and United Steel. These letters were marked as being written without prejudice and their contents related to settlement negotiations between them. Texaco sought disclosure of the letters but the the the Court decided that they were privileged, holding that a party to a correspondence within the without prejudice privilege is protected from being required to disclose it on discovery or at trial in proceedings by or against a third party. The Court reasoned that, as the privilege was intended to encourage amicable settlements and to protect parties to negotiations for that purpose, it was in the public interest that it not be given a restrictive application.

Public policy also encourages compromise in criminal cases. If the vast majority of criminal cases were not settled by a guilty plea the system of criminal justice would grind to a halt. That policy should similarly then protect from disclosure admissions of culpability made by an accused to the Crown if engaged in plea bargaining.[39] The public has as much an interest

---

36 See *Middelkamp v. Fraser Valley Real Estate Board* (1992), 71 B.C.L.R. (2d) 276 (C.A.); and *Rush and Tompkins v. Greater London Council*, [1989] A.C. 1280 (H.L.).

37 See *Travelers Indemnity Co. of Canada v. Maracle* (1991), 80 D.L.R. (4th) 652 at 658 (S.C.C.).

38 *I. Waxman & Sons Ltd. v. Texaco Canada Ltd.* (1968), 67 D.L.R. (2d) 295 (Ont. H.C.), affirmed [1968] 2 O.R. 452 (C.A.).

39 Describing the American approach to this effect, see Kenneth S. Broun, ed., *McCormick on Evidence*, 6th ed. (St. Paul: West Publishing, 2006), s. 266, vol. 2 at 237-39.

in encouraging the settlement of criminal cases as it has in civil. Thus, the cases recognize that representations made by the defence or the Crown in the course of plea negotiations are privileged.[40] While statements between counsel engaged in legitimate plea bargaining are privileged, statements made by an accused to a victim should perhaps be dealt with differently. Such statements might be seen to encompass buying off the prosecuting witness or compounding the crime and should not be privileged.[41]

(e) Crown Privilege—Public Interest Immunity

In a suit between private parties, or in a suit by a private party against the government, when production of a government document is sought, the government might resist production on the grounds that production of such a document would be injurious to the public interest. This claim of immunity from disclosure was normally called a claim of Crown Privilege. More recently this phrase has been described as inapt and the same is now referred to by some as a claim for public interest immunity.[42] Some continue using the older phrase.[43]

The claim may be made for different reasons. For example, in a civil suit for damages against a shipbuilder, where the plaintiff sought production of the plans for the ship, production was resisted on the basis that disclosure of the contents of the requested document would hurt the war effort by disclosing to the enemy military secrets.[44] This would be seen as a "contents" claim to Crown privilege. In other circumstances the claim might be on the basis that while the particular document had no information the disclosure of which would be injurious to the public interest, the document belonged to a class of documents that needed to be kept confidential in order to promote candour and completeness of communication. For example, it is necessary for the proper conduct of government affairs that documents disclosing the minutes of Cabinet meetings be kept confidential. This sort of claim would be characterized as a "class" claim to Crown privilege.[45]

Claims of Crown privilege are normally made by the filing of a ministerial certificate with the court. Claims of privilege on the basis of the contents of the document are normally allowed as it would be rare for a

---

40 See *R. v. B. (D.S.)* (2006), 204 Man. R. (2d) 154 (Q.B.); *R. v. Laroque* (1998), 124 C.C.C. (3d) 564 (Ont. Gen. Div.); *R. v. Lake* (November 24, 1997), McCombs J, [1997] O.J. No. 5447 (Ont. Gen. Div.).

41 See *R. v. Pabani* (1994), 17 O.R. (3d) 659 (C.A.).

42 *Rogers v. Home Secretary*, [1973] A.C. 388 at 400 (H.L.).

43 See Martland J. in *Canada (Solicitor General) v. Royal Commission Re Health Records* (1981), 62 C.C.C. (2d) 193 at 226 (S.C.C.).

44 *Duncan v. Cammell Laird & Co.*, [1942] A.C. 624 (H.L.).

45 See *Conway v. Rimmer*, [1968] 1 All E.R. 874 (H.L.).

court to go beyond a certificate of the responsible member of the executive that it would be contrary to the public interest to make public the contents of a particular document.[46] The courts, however, have often said that a claim on the basis of class should be vetted by the judge who can balance the injury to the public interest, resident in the disclosure of such a document, against the injury to the public interest that the administration of justice not be frustrated by the non-disclosure of documents.

Much of the area concerning federal claims is now governed by statute. Section 37 of the *Canada Evidence Act* permits the Crown to object to disclosure of information before a court on the grounds of any "specified public interest." Section 38 provides a special procedure for objections to disclosure on grounds related to international relations, national defence or national security. Although the procedures under these two sections differ in some respects, both sections provide for a judge to balance the public interests weighing for and against disclosure before determining whether, to what extent, and under what conditions the information should be disclosed. In balancing the public interests, the judge may inspect the documents, although this inspection is not always necessary.[47] To provide a heightened level of protection for information related to international relations, national defence or national security, s. 38 imposes an obligation on all litigants to give notice to the Attorney General of Canada of the possibility that such information may be disclosed in a proceeding.

While there is a balancing to be done by the judiciary with respect to most claims of Crown privilege, the claim with respect to the class of documents normally referred to as Cabinet documents is absolute. Section 39 of the *Canada Evidence Act*, which governs objections to disclosure of Cabinet confidences, does not permit a judge to inspect the documents or to weigh the public interests involved. Rather, a judge must refuse any application for disclosure of information that the government has properly certified as confidential under this section.[48]

Compare a provincial class claim.[49] In *Carey*,[50] the government of Ontario became increasingly involved with Minaki Lodge, a resort in northwestern Ontario, and eventually became the owner. The previous owner launched a civil suit against the government seeking damages for breach of agreement, deceit and damage to reputation. On examination for discovery

---

46 See *Goguen v. Gibson* (1984), 10 C.C.C. (3d) 492 (Fed. C.A.).

47 See *ibid.*

48 *Babcock v. Canada (Attorney General)*, [2002] 3 S.C.R. 3.

49 For provincial and territorial provisions dealing with Crown privilege, see: R.S.A. 2000, c. A-18, s. 34; C.C.S.M., c. E150, s. 10; R.S.N.B. 1973, c. E-11, s. 68; R.S.N.W.T. 1988, c. E-8, s. 46; R.S.O. 1990, c. E.23, s. 30; R.S.P.E.I. 1988, c. E-11, s. 29; and R.S.Y. 2002, c. 78, s. 36.

50 *Carey v. Ontario*, [1986] 2 S.C.R. 637.

the defendant's witnessses claimed absolute privilege respecting all documents that went to or emanated from Cabinet. The Ontario *Evidence* Act provides:

> 30. Where a document is in the official possession, custody or power of a member of the Executive Council, or of the head of a ministry of the public service of Ontario, if the deputy head or other officer of the ministry has the document in his or her personal possession, and is called as a witness, he or she is entitled, acting herein by the direction and on behalf of such member of the Executive Council or head of the ministry, to object to producing the document on the ground that it is privileged, and such objection may be taken by him or her in the same manner, and has the same effect, as if such member of the Executive Council or head of the ministry were personally present and made the objection.

The claim in *Carey* was not based on the contents of the documents but on the class to which they belonged. Production, it was claimed, would breach confidentiality and inhibit Cabinet discussion of matters of significant public policy. The Supreme Court decided that the documents should be produced for the trial judge's inspection so that the judge, and not the executive, might decide the proper balance to be taken between the competing interests of government confidentiality and the proper administration of justice. The judge will ensure that no disclosure is made that unnecessarily interferes with confidential government communication.[51]

(f) Identity of Informers

An aspect of Crown privilege, or public interest immunity, is the long-established rule that the identity of informers should be protected from disclosure. In principle, the information is not protected from disclosure, only its source, but the privilege is broad and extends to any information that might reveal the informer's identity.[52] The public has an interest in ensuring that the lines of communication between the police and sources of information regarding the criminal activity be kept open. The privilege, born out of concerns to the administration of criminal justice, is also available now in the conduct of civil proceedings.[53]

---

51 See also *Smerchanski v. Lewis* (1981), 58 C.C.C. (2d) 328 (Ont. C.A.).

52 *Named Person v. Vancouver Sun* (2007), (sub nom. *Application to proceed in Camera, Re*) 51 C.R. (6th) 262 (S.C.C.); *R. v. Leipert* (1997), 4 C.R. (5th) 259 (S.C.C.). See also *R. v. Hardy* (1794), 24 Howell's State Trials 199; *R. v. Hunter* (1987), 34 C.C.C. (3d) 14 (Ont. C.A.); and *R. v. Scott*, [1990] 3 S.C.R. 979.

53 *Canada (Solicitor General) v. Royal Commission Re Health Records, supra,* note 38; and *Bisaillon v. Ḳeable* (1983), 7 C.C.C. (3d) 385 (S.C.C.).

Informer privilege is considered so important that it is not subject to the balancing of public interests that applies to most claims of Crown privilege.[54] Thus a court has no discretion with respect to informer privilege; this class privilege applies in every case where a confidential informer is involved.[55] Nevertheless, informer privilege is not absolute because it admits of one exception: the "innocence at stake" exception. Where the informer's identity must be disclosed to demonstrate the accused's innocence, protection of the accused will prevail.[56] Under this exception, disclosure could be ordered if the informer was a material witness to the crime, if the informer was the agent provocateur of the crime, or if an attack was made on the constitutionality of a search and the warrant was issued on information supplied by an informer.[57]

(g) Other Privileged Communications

Aside from the specific class privileges discussed above, there is a residual discretion in a trial judge to protect other confidential communications on a case-by-case basis. In *Slavutych*,[58] the Supreme Court recognized that a judge has the power to grant a privilege with respect to a communication if four criteria, originally proposed by Wigmore, are met:

1. The communication must have originated in a confidence that it would not be disclosed.
2. The element of confidentiality must be essential to the satisfactory maintenance of the relationship between the parties.
3. The relationship must be one which the community feels ought to be fostered.
4. The injury that would inure to the relationship by disclosure must be greater than the benefit gained for the correct disposal of the litigation.

Notice the difficult balancing exercise called for in the fourth criterion.

In *R. v. Gruenke*,[59] the accused was charged with murder. There had been conversations between the accused and her pastor concerning the killing. Evidence of these had been received at trial and the accused was convicted. The Supreme Court had to decide whether these conversations

---

54 *Leipert, supra*, note 52 at para. 12.

55 *Named Person, supra*, note 52 at paras. 21-23.

56 *Leipert, supra*, note 52 at para. 21; *Marks v. Beyfus* (1890), 25 Q.B.D. 494 at 498 (C.A.).

57 *Leipert, ibid.* at paras. 22, 26. See also *R. v. Davies* (1982), 1 C.C.C. (3d) 299 (Ont. C.A.); *R. v. Hunter, supra*, note 52.

58 *Slavutych v. Baker* (1975), 55 D.L.R. (3d) 224 (S.C.C.); and *R. v. S. (R.J.)* (1985), 19 C.C.C. (3d) 115 (Ont. C.A.).

59 [1991] 3 S.C.R. 263, (sub nom. *R. v. Fosty*).

were confidential communications the disclosure of which ought not to have been compelled in accordance with the principles accepted in *Slavutych*. The Court distinguished two categories of privilege: a blanket, *prima facie*, common law, or "class" privilege on the one hand, and a "case by case" privilege on the other. With the class privilege there would be a presumption of inadmissibility once it was established that the relationship fit within the class. It would be for the opposing party to persuade that the communications should not be privileged in their particular case, why their communications fitted within an exception to the general rule. The judicial creation of a class or *prima facie* privilege for religious communications would be akin to the existing class privileges for solicitor-client and marital communications. The term "case by case" privilege would apply to a situation where non-disclosure could be claimed for communications, for which there was no presumption that they were privileged, by the claimant satisfying the Wigmore criteria approved in *Slavutych*.

The majority in *Gruenke* decided that the policy reasons for protecting the confidentiality of religious communications were not sufficiently compelling to justify the creation of a class privilege, but explained that such communications might be privileged on a case by case basis. The majority then embarked on a case by case analysis and determined that the criteria were not met, indeed that the communications in *Gruenke* did not even satisfy the first requirement, because on the facts the communications did not originate in a confidence that they would not be disclosed. Since *Gruenke*, privilege claims for religious communications must be considered on a case by case basis; the same is true of communications between doctor and patient.

3. Disclosure of Third Party Records

Recent years have seen the development of a complex body of law governing disclosure to the accused of records held in the hands of third parties. In *R. v. O'Connor*,[60] the watershed case on third party records, the accused was charged with a number of sexual offences. Defence counsel obtained a pre-trial order requiring that the Crown disclose the complainants' entire medical, counselling and school records and that the complainants authorize production of such records by the third parties holding them. The accused later applied for a judicial stay of proceedings based on non-disclosure of several items. Crown counsel submitted that uninhibited disclosure of medical and therapeutic records would revictimize the victims.

---

60 (1995), 44 C.R. (4th) 1 (S.C.C.).

When the Crown was unable to guarantee that full disclosure had been made the trial judge stayed the proceedings.

The Supreme Court held that disclosure of the third party records should be governed by a two-step procedure. At the first stage, the court should determine whether the records should be produced to the court for inspection, while at the second stage, having inspected the records, the court should determine whether they should be disclosed to the accused. The majority of the Court held that given the privacy interests involved, even at the first stage where the issue is production to the court, the onus should be on the accused to satisfy the judge that the information is likely to be relevant. In the context of disclosure, the meaning of "relevance" is whether the information may be useful to the defence. While likely relevance was the appropriate threshold for the first stage of the two-step procedure, the majority determined that it should not be interpreted as an onerous burden upon the accused. If the accused satisfies this onus, the judge should examine the records to determine whether, and to what extent, it is to be produced to the accused.

The majority said that, at this second stage, when deciding whether to order production to the accused, the judge should balance the salutary and deleterious effect of such production, and the following factors should be considered:

1. the extent to which the record was necessary for the accused to make full answer and defence;
2. the probative value of the record;
3. the nature and extent of the reasonable expectation of privacy vested in that record;
4. whether production of the record would be premised upon any discriminatory belief or bias; and
5. the potential prejudice to the complainant's dignity, privacy or security of the person.

The majority specifically rejected two other factors suggested by the minority: the extent to which production of records of this nature would frustrate society's interest in encouraging the reporting of sexual offences and the acquisition of treatment by victims as well as the effect on the integrity of the trial process of producing, or failing to produce, the record. In addition to suggesting these additional factors for the judge's consideration, the minority in *O'Connor* took the view that the first stage burden on an accused was significant and, if it could not be met, the application for production should be dismissed as nothing more than a fishing expedition. For the minority the mere fact that the complainant had received treatment or counselling could not be presumed to be relevant to the trial.

Following *O'Connor*, Parliament enacted legislation to restrict the production of records in sexual offence proceedings. The legislation[61] in large measure reflects the minority position in *O'Connor*. This legislation was held constitutional by the Supreme Court, and it continues to apply to disclosure of third party records in the special context of sexual cases.[62] Outside that context, however, *O'Connor* still governs: as the Supreme Court recently explained, the *O'Connor* regime "provides a general mechanism at common law for ordering production of *any* record beyond the possession or control of the prosecuting Crown."[63]

4. Privilege Against Self-Incrimination

In the beginning years of trial by jury the accused in the common law courts was questioned concerning the charges against him. It seemed the sensible thing to do. Gradually however, during the seventeenth century, as a reaction, or perhaps an overreaction, towards the inquisitorial methods of the Ecclesiastical Courts and the Court of Star Chamber, accused persons in the common law courts began to resist such questioning and by 1700 it was recognized that no person, in any court, whether he be an accused or merely a witness, could be compelled to answer if the answer would tend to incriminate. The common law privilege against self-incrimination was born.

(a) Non-Compellability of Accused

Until the end of the nineteenth century the accused was not able to give testimony on oath for two reasons. First, he was regarded as incompetent because of his obvious interest in the outcome of the proceedings. Second, it was regarded as a violation of his privilege against self-incrimination to place him on the horns of a dilemma: should he choose to testify falsely gaining temporal relief but everlasting damnation or testify truthfully and forfeit his liberty? Perhaps a trilemma in that should he choose not to testify, and it being known that he was able, he risked an inference of guilt being drawn from his silence. By the end of the nineteenth century statutory reforms made the accused competent for the defence. The common law position of non-compellability at the instance of the prosecution remained.

---

61 See ss. 278.1 to 278.9 of the *Criminal Code*.
62 See *R. v. Mills* (1999), 28 C.R. (5th) 207 (S.C.C.). For the proper procedure in a civil case where production is sought see *M.(A.) v. Ryan* (1997), 4 C.R. (5th) 220 (S.C.C.).
63 *R. v. McNeil* (2009), 62 C.R. (6th) 1 (S.C.C.).

Section 4 of the *Canada Evidence Act* provides:

> (1) Every person charged with an offence, and, except as otherwise provided in this section, the wife or husband, as the case may be, of the person so charged, is a competent witness for the defence, whether the person so charged is charged solely or jointly with any other person.

The Charter provides: "11 (c) [any person charged with an offence has the right] not to be compelled to be a witness in proceedings against that person in respect of the offence."

It is important to recognize that this privilege, in its origins and as later interpreted in Canada,[64] operated to protect a person from being compelled to give evidence before a court or like tribunal. It was also restricted to testimonial evidence. Taking bodily samples, fingerprints or photographs were not seen as captured by the privilege.[65] In short, the privilege in Canada was seen to be reflected simply, and solely, in the accused's non-compellability at trial. The accused, pursuant to the legislation, was a competent witness for the defence. It was up to the accused to decide whether he would go into the box.

(b) Use Immunity

In Canada, the legislation also provided that no witness, including the accused who chose to become a witness, could refuse to answer a question on the grounds that the answer might tend to criminate. Rather, the legislation provided that he was obliged to answer but the answer could not be used against him in later proceedings. For example, the *Canada Evidence Act* provides:

> 5. (1) No witness shall be excused from answering any question on the ground that the answer to the question may tend to criminate him, or may tend to establish his liability to a civil proceeding at the instance of the Crown or of any person.
>
> (2) Where with respect to any question a witness objects to answer on the ground that his answer may tend to criminate him, or may tend to establish his liability to a civil proceeding at the instance of the Crown or of any person, and if but for this Act, or the Act of any provincial legislature, the witness would therefore have been excused from answering the question, then although the witness is by reason of this Act or the provincial Act compelled to answer, the answer so given shall not be used or admissible in evidence against him in any criminal trial or other criminal proceeding against him thereafter taking

---

64   *R. v. Curr* (1972), 7 C.C.C. (2d) 181 (S.C.C.), interpreting the privilege as bestowed by the *Canadian Bill of Rights*.

65   *R. v. Marcoux* (1975), 24 C.C.C. (2d) 1 (S.C.C.).

place, other than a prosecution for perjury in the giving of that evidence or for the giving of contradictory evidence.

Similar provisions exist in provincial legislation.[66]

The Charter similarly provides:

13 A witness who testifies in any proceedings has the right not to have any incriminating evidence so given used to incriminate that witness in any other proceeding, except in a prosecution for perjury or for the giving of contradictory evidence.

These statutory and Charter provisions offer the witness a protection known as "use immunity." The witness who has been compelled to answer incriminating questions at an earlier proceeding is immune from having that testimony used against her in her own subsequent criminal trial. Notice that, unlike the protection under s. 5(2) of the *Canada Evidence Act*, use immunity under s. 13 of the Charter is automatic and does not depend on the witness's objection. The Supreme Court has recently explained that the Charter only provides use immunity for testimony given under compulsion. Section 13 does not prevent an accused who testifies voluntarily in her own defence at a first trial from being cross-examined on the basis of that testimony if she once against testifies voluntarily on a retrial.[67]

(c) Other Protections Related to Compelled Testimony

Under both the statute and the Charter, the prohibition against subsequent use is limited to foreclose use of the statement; it does not foreclose use of evidence derived from the statement, such as physical evidence discovered in a place identified in the statement. In the past, this limitation frequently allowed the state to avoid the strictures of the privilege against self-incrimination. Often, by compelling a suspect or an accused to testify at some other proceeding prior to his criminal trial, the Crown could discover evidence usable against him at his trial.[68] The Supreme Court has moved, under the Charter, to foreclose that possibility.

---

66 For similar provincial and territorial provisions, see: R.S.A. 2000, c. A-18, s. 6; R.S.B.C. 1996, c. 124, s. 4; C.C.S.M., c. E.150, s. 6; R.S.N.B. 1973, c. E-11, s. 6; R.S.N.L. 1990, c. E-16, s. 5; R.S.N.W.T. 1988, c. E-8, s. 7; R.S.N.S. 1989, c. 154, s. 59; R.S.O. 1990, c. E.23, s. 9; R.S.P.E.I. 1988, c. E-11, s. 6; S.S. 2006, c. E-11.2, s. 9; and R.S.Y. 2002, c. 78, s. 7.

67 *R. v. Henry* (2005), 33 C.R. (6th) 215 (S.C.C.).

68 See generally, Ed Ratushny, *Self-Incrimination in the Canadian Criminal Process* (Toronto: Carswell, 1979) at 347-402.

The Court has recognized that the principles of fundamental justice under s. 7 of the Charter include a principle against self-incrimination.[69] This principle is reflected in the non-compellability of the accused and in s. 13 use immunity, but it offers other protections as well. In *Branch*,[70] the Supreme Court decided that the principle against self-incrimination would in some cases require that persons who were compelled to testify be provided with subsequent derivative use immunity in addition to the use immunity guaranteed by s. 13 of the Charter. Derivative use immunity protects an accused from having evidence used against her when that evidence was discovered as a result of the accused's former compelled testimony. The former testimony itself would be protected by use immunity; the derivative evidence would be covered by derivative use immunity. According to *Branch*, to benefit from derivative use immunity, the accused would have the evidentiary burden of showing a plausible connection between the compelled testimony and the evidence later sought to be adduced. Once this was done, in order to have the evidence admitted, the Crown would have to satisfy the court on a balance of probabilities that the authorities would have discovered the impugned derivative evidence absent the compelled testimony.

The judgment in *Branch* also indicates that courts can, in certain circumstances, grant exemptions from compulsion to testify. The crucial question is whether the predominant purpose for seeking the evidence was to obtain incriminating evidence against the person compelled to testify or rather some legitimate public purpose. That test is seen to strike the appropriate balance between the interests of the state in obtaining the evidence for a valid public purpose on the one hand, and the right to silence of the person compelled to testify on the other.[71]

(d) Inferences from the Accused's Silence At Trial

When the accused was made a competent witness at the end of the nineteenth century, the change brought problems for the accused. He then faced the dilemma of choosing between not going into the stand, with the trier perhaps inferring guilt from his silence, or exposing himself to the oath and cross-examination.

In *R. v. Noble*[72] the manager of an apartment building found two young men in the parking area of his building, one of whom appeared to be

---

69 See, *e.g.*, *R. v. S. (R.J.)* (1995), 36 C.R. (4th) 1 (S.C.C.).

70 *British Columbia (Securities Commission) v. Branch* (1995), 38 C.R. (4th) 133 (S.C.C.).

71 See also *R. v. Jobin* (1995), 38 C.R. (4th) 176 (S.C.C.); and *R. v. Primeau* (1995), 38 C.R. (4th) 189 (S.C.C.).

72 (1997), 6 C.R. (5th) 1 (S.C.C.).

attempting to break into a car with a screwdriver. When the manager asked the man for identification, he handed over an expired driver's licence. The manager testified that he thought the photograph on the licence accurately depicted the man in front of him in the garage and told the man that he could retrieve the licence from the police. The accused was eventually charged with breaking and entering and having in his possession an instrument suitable for the purpose of breaking into a motor vehicle. At trial, neither the manager nor anyone else could identify the accused, but the trial judge concluded that he as the trier of fact could compare the picture in the driver's licence with the accused in the courtroom and conclude that the driver's licence accurately depicted the accused. He was also satisfied that the building manager would have carefully examined the licence at the time of the incident. The trial judge noted that the accused faced an overwhelming case to meet as a result of the licence, yet remained silent. In the trial judge's view, he could draw "almost an adverse inference" that "certainly may add to the weight of the Crown's case on the issue of identification". The accused was convicted on both counts. The Court of Appeal set aside the convictions and ordered a new trial. A 5:4 majority of the Supreme Court dismissed the Crown's appeal. For the majority the use of the accused's silence to help establish guilt beyond a reasonable doubt was impermissible and contrary to the rationale behind the right to silence. The minority pointed to a number of the Court's previous judgments that seemed to indicate that the use of the accused's silence at trial was permissible.[73]

(e) Comments on the Accused's Failure to Testify

The *Canada Evidence Act* provides:

> 4(6). The failure of the person charged, or of the wife or husband of that person, to testify shall not be made the subject of comment by the judge or by counsel for the prosecution.

The first thing to notice about the Canadian provision is that our courts have decided that the comment is only prohibited in cases of trial by jury and when the comment is made in the presence of the jury.[74] Perhaps such reasoning was born of a belief that in trials by judge alone the accused's failure to testify would not be magnified out of its proper proportion, since

---

73 For comments on *Noble* see Delisle and Don Stuart at (1997), 6 C.R. (5th) 5 and 8. See also, Delisle, "Silence at Trial: Inferences and Comments" (1997) 1 C.R. (5th) 313.

74 *R. v. Binder* (1948), 92 C.C.C. 20 (Ont. C.A.), followed in *Pratte v. Maher*, [1965] 1 C.C.C. 77 (Que. C.A.); *R. v. Bouchard*, [1970] 5 C.C.C. 95 (N.B. C.A.); *Ontario (Attorney General) v. Clark*, [1967] 1 C.C.C. 131 (Ont. H.C.), affirmed [1967] 2 C.C.C. 196n (C.A.).

a trial judge is able to place it in its proper perspective. The next thing to notice is that comment by an accused on his own or his co-accused's failure to take the stand is not foreclosed by the section.[75]

Some of the case law on s. 4(6) suggests that there are comments and then there are *comments*. Sometimes, what appears to be a comment is interpreted to be rather a statement and not prohibited. In *Avon*,[76] the trial judge said to the jury:

> The accused did not testify. Evidently, he could have done so. He is not obliged to do so. I must tell you immediately .... it is not because the accused did not testify that you should believe that he could be guilty .... Actually you have merely the Crown's evidence. The defense did not call witnesses, and the accused did not testify: he did not have to. It is up to the Crown to prove its case.[77]

The Supreme Court said this was a "statement" of an accused's right not to testify, rather than a "comment" on his failure to do so and could not be construed as prejudicial to the accused or such to suggest to the jurors that his silence was used to cloak his guilt.

In *McConnell*,[78] the accused were charged with possession of house-breaking instruments. They had offered an explanation to the police at the time but they did not testify. The trial judge told the jury:

> You are not to be influenced in your decision by either of the accused not going into the witness box and testifying, but the Court does point out that these explanations ... when made were not made under oath and it is not only for that reason alone, but for any other number of reasons that may occur to you, to decide if you will accept these explanations.[79]

The accused's appeals were dismissed as the Court noted that the language used by the trial judge was not so much a "comment" on the failure of the persons charged to testify as a "statement" of their right to refrain from doing so. The Supreme Court held that a trial judge is not precluded from explaining to juries the law with respect to the rights of accused persons in this regard.[80]

---

75 See *R. v. Creighton*, [1995] 1 S.C.R. 858.

76 *Avon v. R.* (1971), 21 D.L.R. (3d) 442 (S.C.C.).

77 *Ibid.* at 455.

78 *R. v. McConnell*, [1968] 4 C.C.C. 257 (S.C.C.).

79 *Ibid.* at 260.

80 For recent discussion of the distinction between impermissible comments and permissible statements under s. 4(6), see *R. v. Biladeau* (2008), 63 C.R. (6th) 187 (Ont. C.A.); *R. v. Sparvier* (2006), 215 C.C.C. (3d) 555 (Sask. C.A.); *R. v. Knox* (2006), 209 C.C.C. (3d) 76 (Ont. C.A.). For a longer list of cases setting out what comments are within the section and what are without, see Casey Hill, David M. Tanovich & Louis P. Strezos, eds., *McWilliams' Canadian Criminal Evidence*, 4th ed. (Aurora, Ont.: Canada Law Book, 2003), s. 30:30.40.

Although s. 4(6) was not at issue in *Noble*,[81] Lamer C.J. in dissent suggested that the provision was irreconcilable with the majority's conclusion that the trier of fact may not draw an adverse inference from the accused's silence at trial. According to Lamer C.J., the majority's conclusion suggested indirectly that s. 4(6) was unconstitutional. He reasoned that if the jury was not entitled to draw any inference from the accused's failure to testify the jury should be told just that by the judge and yet the section foreclosed that advice. The majority said the issue was not before it.

(f) The Creation of a Right to Silence in Canada

While many rights are bestowed in the Charter, from the right to counsel to the right to be secure against unreasonable search and seizure, there is nothing in the Charter that speaks to a right to silence. However, there is in the Charter a broad and mysterious section:

> 7. Everyone has the right to life, liberty and security of the person and the right not to be deprived thereof except in accordance with the principles of fundamental justice.

In *Hebert*,[82] the parties agreed that s. 7 accorded a right to silence to a detained person but disagreed over the extent of the right. The Court accepted the parties' concession and occupied itself with articulating its views on the scope of the right. In that case it was decided that a detained person's pre-trial right to silence was violated when an undercover officer elicited a confession from the accused in his jail cell. The essence of the pre-trial right to silence was that a detained person must have a free choice whether to speak with the authorities; once the detainee had opted not to speak with police, is was not open to them to trick him into speaking with them by sending in an undercover officer to actively elicit information. In excluding the confession, the Court decided that the admissibility of confessions rested not just on considerations of trustworthiness but also on fairness concerns related to the privilege against self-incrimination.[83]

The pre-trial right to silence recognized in *Hebert* was defined within strict limits. Most importantly, it does not apply where the suspect is not detained. Thus, self-incriminating statements elicited from suspects by undercover officers outside the context of detention have not been excluded on this basis.[84]

---

81 *Supra*, note 72.
82 *R. v. Hebert* (1990), 77 C.R. (3d) 145 (S.C.C.).
83 Just before the Charter came into being, the Court had concluded the opposite: see *R. v. Rothman* (1981), 59 C.C.C. (2d) 30 (S.C.C.).
84 See, *e.g.*, *R. v. Osmar* (2007), 44 C.R. (6th) 276 (Ont. C.A.).

(g) A Principle Versus a Privilege

Until quite recently there was not in Canada a broad principle against self-incrimination.[85] There existed two protections: non-compellability at trial,[86] and protection against subsequent use of evidence given at a prior proceeding.[87] The right of a suspect not to say anything to the police was not the result of some general right of no self-incrimination, but was merely the exercise by him of the general right enjoyed in this country by anyone to do whatever one pleases, saying what one pleases or choosing not to say certain things, unless obliged to do otherwise by law.[88] This situation has changed dramatically with the development of Charter jurisprudence.

In *Dubois*,[89] an early Charter case, the Court addressed the admissibility into evidence of statements made by an accused at his first trial for murder into the second trial. The accused chose not to testify at his second trial, but the Crown read in his testimony from the first trial as part of its case in chief. The Court decided that this was a violation of s.13 of the Charter. In doing so, the Court noted that otherwise the Crown would be able to do indirectly what it couldn't do directly; by virtue of s.11(c) of the Charter, the Crown could not compel the accused to testify. It also was observed that permitting receipt of his earlier testimony would permit an indirect violation of the right to be presumed innocent as guaranteed by s. 11 (d) of the Charter. The Court found underlying the Charter rights in ss. 11(c), (d) and 13, and the benefit of an initial right to silence at trial, the common concept of the Crown's obligation to bring a "case to meet".[90]

In *R. v. P. (M.B.)*,[91] the Court, deciding it was wrong to permit the prosecution to re-open its case after the accused had outlined its defence, repeated the thought of a "case to meet", and spoke of the broad protection afforded to accused persons, which the Court said was best described in terms of the overarching *principle* against self-incrimination.[92] This principle, according to the Court, was firmly rooted in the common law and was a principle of fundamental justice under s. 7 of the Charter. The Court

---

85 See, *e.g.*, Ed Ratushny, "Is There a Right Against Self-Incrimination in Canada?" (1973) 19 McGill L.J. 1, and Iacobucci J. in *S. (R.J.)*, *supra* note 69.

86 Section 4 of the *Canada Evidence Act* and s. 11(c) of the Charter.

87 Section 5(2) of the *Canada Evidence Act* and s. 13 of the Charter.

88 *Per* Lamer J. in *R. v. Rothman*, *supra*, note 83.

89 *R. v. Dubois*, [1985] 2 S.C.R. 350. The Supreme Court recently reaffirmed the correctness of the result in Dubois in *Henry*, *supra* note 67.

90 This concept was taken from the analysis of Ed Ratushny, "The Role of the Accused at the Trial Stage", in Tarnopolsky & Beaudoin (eds.), *The Canadian Charter of Rights and Freedoms* (1982) at 358-359.

91 (1994), 29 C.R. (4th) 209 (S.C.C.). See also *R. v. G. (S.G.)* (1997), 8 C.R. (5th) 198 (S.C.C.).

92 *P. (M.B.)*, *ibid.* at 226.

recognized that apart from the *privilege* against self-incrimination, which grants the specific protections outlined above, there is also a *principle* against self-incrimination which may give greater protection than formerly contemplated.

In *Jones*,[93] Chief Justice Lamer expanded on what he had earlier written about the principle. He said that any state action that coerced an individual to furnish evidence against himself in a proceeding in which the individual and the state were adversaries violated the *principle* against self-incrimination. He described the *privilege* as the narrow traditional common law rule relating only to testimonial evidence at trial.

Another application of the principle against self-incrimination came in *White*,[94] where a majority of the Supreme Court recognized that the principle could ground a form of use immunity for statutorily compelled statements. A person who makes a statement in the honest and reasonable belief that she is legally obligated to do so under provincial motor vehicle legislation has the right not to have that statement used against her in her subsequent criminal trial. In the course of his majority judgment in *White*, Iacobucci J. described the principle against self-incrimination as "an overarching principle within our criminal justice system".[95]

In summary, the Supreme Court has recognized a principle against self-incrimination, rooted in s. 7 of the Charter, that can give rise to other protections for the accused not specifically mentioned in the text of the Charter. Two of these other protections, derivative use immunity and exemptions from compulsion to testify, were discussed earlier in this Chapter,[96] and a few more have been mentioned in this section. The principle against self-incrimination may well give rise to further safeguards in the future, but its creative potential seems to be in decline. The full Supreme Court recently held that the principle has a "limited scope".[97]

5. Confessions

A special rule of evidence applies to confessions made by the accused to the authorities. Confessions are, of course, a subset of party admissions,

---

93 *R. v. Jones* (1994), 30 C.R. (4th) 1 at 41 (S.C.C.). Although speaking in dissent, the Chief Justice's remarks regarding the principle against self-incrimination seem to have been adopted by, at least, most of the Court. In *R. v. S. (R.J.)*, *supra*, note 69, Iacobucci J., for himself and three others, decided that the dissent in *Jones* was only on the narrow question of whether dangerous offender proceedings serve to incriminate further a person who has already been convicted.

94 *R. v. White* (1999), 24 C.R. (5th) 201 (S.C.C.).

95 *Ibid.* at para. 44.

96 See above, Other Protections Related to Compelled Testimony.

97 *R. v. B. (S.A.)* (2003), 14 C.R. (6th) 205 at para. 57 (S.C.C.).

and admissions are generally admissible for their truth as an exception to the hearsay rule. However, our courts have long taken the view that confessions deserve to be scrutinized more closely than other admissions. This cautious attitude toward confession evidence stems from two longstanding sets of concerns: first, that confessions may be the products of official coercion, and second, that these statements may be false. The evidentiary rule that aims to address these concerns, known as the confessions rule, may be stated as follows: any out-of-court statement by an accused person to a person in authority is inadmissible against the accused unless the Crown establishes beyond a reasonable doubt that the statement was made voluntarily.[98] The confessions rule is a common law rule, but it continues to apply in the Charter era, and it remains the accused's primary defence against coercive interrogation.[99]

Note that the confessions rule only applies when the accused makes a statement to a person in authority. The Supreme Court has stated that persons in authority are those formally involved in the accused's arrest, detention, examination or prosecution.[100] A police officer is the paradigmatic person in authority, though others, including corrections officers, also meet the definition. The question whether an individual is a person in authority should be answered reasonably from the accused's perspective at the time the statements were made.[101] Consequently, statements made to undercover police are not covered by the confessions rule,[102] and neither are statements made under coercion by private individuals like members of the victim's family.[103] The rule is primarily directed at the context of police interrogation.

The meaning of the voluntariness requirement has changed over the years. Initially a confession was considered voluntary if it was not obtained as the result of promise of favour or fear of prejudice held out by a person in authority.[104] The focus was solely on the presence or absence of threats or promises from the authorities. In later decisions, courts began taking a more expansive view of voluntariness. For example, a statement by a person shortly after a motor vehicle accident, when the person was still in a state of shock, could be excluded as involuntary if there was a reasonable doubt

---

98   See, *e.g.*, *R. v. Hodgson* (1998), 18 C.R. (5th) 135 (S.C.C.).

99   See Dufraimont, "The Common Law Confessions Rule in the Charter Era: Current Law and Future Directions" (2008) 40 Sup. Ct. L. Rev. (2d) 249.

100 *Hodgson, supra*, note 98 at para. 16.

101 *Ibid.* at paras. 33-34.

102 *R. v. Grandinetti* (2005), 25 C.R. (6th) 1 (S.C.C.).

103 See *Hodgson, supra*, note 98, at para. 30, noting that where a private individual procures an accused's confessions by violence or threats, the jury should be warned of the dangers of relying upon the statement.

104 The test was articulated in *Ibrahim v. R.*, [1914] A.C. 599 (Hong Kong P.C.) and accepted in Canada in *R. v. Prosko* (1922), 63 S.C.R. 226 and *R. v. Boudreau* (1949), 7 C.R. 427 (S.C.C.).

that the words were the product of an operating mind.[105] In *R. v. Oickle*,[106] now the leading case on confessions, the Supreme Court held that the confessions rule addresses "voluntariness, broadly understood."[107] Writing for a majority of the Court, Iacobucci J. emphasized that voluntariness must be assessed in all the circumstances of the case, and identified four sets of factors that could vitiate the voluntariness of a confession: threats or promises, oppression, operating mind, and police trickery. Iacobucci J. explained each of these factors in turn.

The threats or promises that could render a confession involuntary include threats of violence against the accused, promises of lenient treatment, and threats against family or friends. These inducements might be express or implied. Alone or in combination with other factors, threats or promises vitiate voluntariness when they are strong enough to raise a reasonable doubt that the suspect's will was overborne. Ultimately, *Oickle* suggests that the key consideration is whether the interrogators have offered the suspect a *quid pro quo* for confessing.[108] In *Spencer*,[109] the Supreme Court dealt with a clear inducement: the accused confessed after police refused to allow him to see his girlfriend until he "cleaned his slate." The Supreme Court decided that, although this was an inducement in the form of a *quid pro quo*, the inducement was not strong enough to raise a reasonable doubt regarding voluntariness.

According to *Oickle*, another factor that can raise a reasonable doubt about the voluntariness of a confession is oppression. A suspect who is interrogated under oppressive conditions may be coerced into confessing. Oppression can result, for example, from withholding food, sleep, or clothing, or from the use of prolonged hostile questioning.

Next, the Court in *Oickle* explained that a confession would be involuntary if it came from a suspect who lacked an operating mind in the sense that she did not know what she was saying or did not know that she was saying it to a police officer who could use it against her. A confession by a suspect who was hypnotized could be ruled involuntary on this basis, for example.

Finally, Iacobucci J. held that a confession could be rendered involuntary by the use of trickery and deception by police. The analysis of police tricks was held to be related to the rest of the voluntariness analysis, but to constitute a "distinct inquiry" directed at maintaining the integrity of the criminal justice system. A confession will be excluded under the confessions

---

105 *R. v. Ward* (1979), 44 C.C.C. (2d) 498 (S.C.C.). To similar effect, see *R. v. Horvath* (1979), 44 C.C.C. (2d) 385 (S.C.C.).
106 (2001), 36 C.R. (5th) 129 (S.C.C.).
107 *Ibid.* at para. 27.
108 *Ibid.* at para. 57.
109 *R. v. Spencer* (2007), 44 C.R. (6th) 199 (S.C.C.).

rule where it is elicited by police trickery "so appalling as to shock the community."[110]

The voluntariness analysis laid out in *Oickle* is multifaceted and contextual, and deference will be due to the trial judge's determination. Iacobucci J. emphasized that the confessions rule aims to exclude unreliable confessions, but it is clear that the rule is also directled at ensuring fair and decent treatment of suspect in the interrogation room.[111]

The voluntariness of a statement is determined on a *voir dire* in the absence of the jury. The trial judge has a duty to hold such a voir dire whenever the Crown offers evidence of a statement made by the accused to a person in authority.[112] It is for the trial judge to decide whether the statement was voluntary. If that preliminary condition of admissibility is satisfied the evidence is given to the jury. There may be contradictory evidence as to what, if anything, was in fact said. In such a case the normal rules apply and it is for the jury to decide what, if anything, was actually said.[113] Once the judge has determined that the statement ought to be received much of the same evidence heard on the *voir dire* will be repeated for the jury's benefit so that the jury can decide what weight to give to it. If the trial is by judge sitting alone it is common practice, to save time, for the parties to agree that the evidence taken on the *voir dire* be taken as if it was given at the trial proper.

The Supreme Court recently clarified the relationship between the confessions rule and the s. 7 pre-trial right to silence recognized in *Hebert*.[114] Although *Hebert* established that s. 7 offers some protection for detainees in the context of undercover operations, for some time it was unclear whether the Charter right to silence offered any additional protection to detainees interrogated by known police. In *Singh*,[115] a majority of the Supreme Court ruled that the s. 7 pre-trial right to silence offers no protection to an accused in the interrogation room beyond that offered by the common law confessions rule. In the words of Charron J. for the majority, when a detained person is interrogated by known police, "the confessions rule effectively subsumes the constitutional right to silence".[116] *Singh* brought an abrupt end to a line of authorities in which lower courts had relied on s. 7 to exclude

---

110   *Oickle, supra*, note 106 at para 67.
111   For a critical comment see Don Stuart, "Oickle: The Supreme Court's Recipe for Coercive Interrogation" (2001) 36 C.R. (5th) 188.
112   *Hodgson, supra* note 98 at para. 41.
113   See *R. v. Park* (1981), 59 C.C.C. (2d) 385 (S.C.C.).
114   See *R. v. Hebert, supra*, note 82 and the discussion in that section.
115   *R. v. Singh* (2007), 51 C.R. (6th) 199 (S.C.C.). For commentary, see Dale E. Ives & Christopher Sherrin, "*R. v. Singh* – A meaningless Right to Silence with Dangerous Consequences" (2007) 51 C.R. (6th) 250.
116   *Singh, ibid.* at para. 39.

confessions obtained by persistent questioning of suspects who had repeatedly asserted their right to silence.[117] The majority in *Singh* rejected the suggestion that the police must cease questioning a detainee who asserts the right to silence. However, the majority also recognized that a confession obtained by unrelenting questioning of a suspect who repeatedly asserts the right to silence might be excluded as involuntary under the confessions rule. The question is whether the suspect's will was overborne.

A final issue related to confessions bears mention. Police increasingly video-record their interrogations and the confessions that result. The recording of interrogations has a number of benefits: it can eliminate disputes about what transpired in the interrogation room, deter police from using coercive tactics, and give judges and juries the best evidence with which to assess the circumstances and judge the voluntariness and reliability of a confession. The Supreme Court commented favourably on the practice in *Oickle*, but expressly disavowed the notion that unrecorded confessions would be "inherently suspect".[118] In a line of recent cases, the Ontario Court of Appeal has gone farther, suggesting that confessions are inherently suspect where the police fail to record an interrogation despite the availability of recording facilities. This failure to record can weigh against the prosecution on the voluntariness voir dire,[119] and can also be the subject of a jury instruction indicating that deliberate non-recording of an interrogation casts doubt on the value of police testimony regarding a resulting confession.[120]

6. Exclusion of Improperly Obtained Evidence

At common law there was no power in a trial judge to exclude evidence based on how the evidence was obtained. If the evidence had probative value the court was, aside from confessions, not concerned with how the evidence was obtained.[121] If real evidence—the gun, the narcotics—was obtained by illegal methods, Canadian courts said the remedy for such illegality was not to be found in excluding the evidence in the subsequent prosecution of the accused. The aggrieved could seek a remedy in the civil courts or lay a complaint with the appropriate police governing body.

---

117 See *R. v. Otis* (2000), 151 C.C.C. (3d) 416 (Que. C.A.); *R. v. Roy* (2003), 15 C.R. (6th) 282 (Ont. C.A.).

118 *Oickle, supra*, note 106 at para 46.

119 See *R. v. Moore-McFarlane* (2001), 47 C.R. (5th) 203 (Ont. C.A.); *R. v. Sabri* (2002), 166 C.C.C. (3d) 179 (Ont. C.A.); *R. v. Ahmed* (2002), 170 C.C.C. (3d) 27 (Ont. C.A.). But see *R. v. Ducharme* (2004), 184 Man. R. (2d) 36 (C.A.).

120 *R. v. Wilson* (2006), 210 C.C.C. (3d) 23 (Ont. C.A.).

121 *R. v. Wray* (1970), 11 D.L.R. (3d) 673 (S.C.C.).

Section 24(2) of the Charter gave a discretion to the trial judge to exclude if the evidence was obtained in violation of the accused's rights. That section provides:

> 24(2) Where, in proceedings under subsection (1), a court concludes that evidence was obtained in a manner that infringed or denied any rights or freedoms guaranteed by this Charter, the evidence shall be excluded if it is established that, having regard to all the circumstances, the admission of it in the proceedings would bring the administration of justice into disrepute.

As with any discretion in the law of evidence the appropriate factors for consideration have been spelled out. For more than two decades, the courts' followed an approach to s. 24(2) that was originally defined in *R. v. Collins*[122] and refined in *R. v. Stillman*.[123] As applied in subsequent cases, the *Collin/Stillman* framework resulted in the virtually automatic exclusion of any evidence that was conscripted from the accused and not otherwise discoverable by the state. The framework thus elevated the importance of the technical distinction between conscriptive and non-conscriptive evidence, rather than requiring an inquiry into the totality of the circumstances as required by the text of s. 24(2).

Recognizing these weaknesses in the former approach, the Supreme Court very recently rejected the *Collin/Stillman* framework and adopted a fresh approach to s. 24(2) in *R. v. Grant*:[124]

> When faced with an application for exclusion under s. 24(2), a court must assess and balance the effect of admitting the evidence on society's confidence in the justice system having regard to: (1) the seriousness of the *Charter*-infringing state conduct (admission may send the message the justice system condones serious state misconduct), (2) the impact of the breach on the *Charter*-protected interests of the accused (admission may send the message that individual rights count for little), and (3) society's interest in the adjudication of the case on its merits. The court's role on a s. 24(2) application is to balance the assessments under each of these lines of inquiry to determine whether, considering all the circumstances, admission of the evidence would bring the administration of justice into disrepute.

At issue in *Grant* was the admissibility of a gun recovered from the 18-year-old male accused by police who stopped and questioned him as he was walking down a street in downtown Toronto in the middle of the day. During the encounter, the accused was arbitrarily detained contrary to s. 9 of the Charter, and his right to counsel under s. 10(b) was also breached. As a result of these violations of his Charter rights, the accused made statements

---

122   (1987), 56 C.R. (3d) 193 (S.C.C.).
123   (1997), 5 C.R. (5th) 1 (S.C.C.).
124   (2009), 66 C.R. (6th) 1 (S.C.C.).

disclosing that he had a gun, which was subsequently seized by police. The accused was charged with various firearms offences. Applying its new s. 24(2) framework, the majority concluded that the gun was properly admitted in evidence. The breach of the accused's Charter rights was not deliberate or egregious and there was no bad faith on the part of the police. On the other hand, the impact on the accused's Charter-protected interests was significant. With respect to society's interests in adjudicating the case on the merits, the gun represented reliable evidence of considerable value. This last factor weighed strongly in favour of admission, while the impact on the accused weighed strongly in favour of exclusion. It was a close case, but the balance was tipped in favour of admission by the fact that the Charter breaches arose from the police making an understandable mistake on the issue of detention in circumstances of legal uncertainty.

The Supreme Court's new framework for s. 24(2) was also applied in the companion case of *R. v. Harrison*.[125] *Harrison* involved the seizure by police of 35 kg of cocaine from the back of a rental car being driven by the accused. The cocaine was found in the course of a search that violated the accused's s. 8 rights, which followed on an arbitrary detention that violated the accused's rights under s. 9. In these circumstances, the majority of the Supreme Court determined that the evidence should have been excluded under s. 24(2). The conduct of the police officer showed a blatant disregard for Charter rights, and the impact on the accused's Charter-protected liberty and privacy interests was significant. The cocaine was reliable evidence of a serious offence, a factor that weighed in favour of admission. However, the seriousness of the offence and the reliability of the evidence could not be permitted to overwhelm the s. 24(2) analysis. A contextual balancing of all the factors weighed in favour of exclusion.[126]

---

125 (2009), 66 C.R. (6th) 105 (S.C.C.).

126 For commentary on *Grant* and *Harrison*, see Don Stuart, "Welcome Flexibility and Better Criteria for Section 24(2)" (2009), 66 C.R. (6th) 82; Tim Quigley, "Was it Worth the Wait? The Supreme Court's New Approaches to Detention and Exclusion of Evidence" (2009), 66 C.R. (6th) 88; Hamish Stewart, "The Grant Trilogy and the Right Against Self-Incrimination" (2009), 66 C.R. (6th) 97.

Index

[All references are to page numbers of the text]

witness, of, 76

CHARTER OF RIGHTS AND FREEDOMS
exclusion of evidence, 157-159
presumption of innocence, 42-45
rape shield provisions, 25-28
remedy for violation of, 157-159
right to counsel, 151, 158
right to silence, 145-146, 151-153, 156-157

CHILDREN AS WITNESSES, 58-62, 86. *See also* WITNESSES

CIRCUMSTANTIAL EVIDENCE, 8-10

CIVIL ACTIONS
court's power to call witnesses, 69
liability insurance, 15
previous criminal convictions, 15-16
settlement offers, 14-15
similar fact evidence, 23-24
subsequent repairs, 14

COLLATERAL FACTS RULE, 71-72

CONCLUSIVE PRESUMPTIONS, 39

CONDITIONAL RELEVANCE, 13

CONFESSIONS, 153-157

CONFIDENTIAL COMMUNICATIONS, 131-143

CONSCIOUSNESS OF GUILT. *See* POST-OFFENCE CONDUCT

CONSPIRACY, 103-104

CORROBORATION, 83-86

CREDIBILITY, 9

CRIMINAL LAW, *See* ACCUSED, SEXUAL ASSAULT CASES

CROSS-EXAMINATION
accused, of, 78-79
leading questions, 67
one's own witness, of, 74-75
prior inconsistent statement, 72-73
refreshing memory, 67-69
scope of, 67

CROWN PRIVILEGE, 139-142

DECLARATIONS AGAINST INTEREST, 104-105. *See also* EXCEPTIONS TO HEARSAY RULE

DECLARATIONS IN COURSE OF DUTY, 106-109. *See also* EXCEPTIONS TO HEARSAY RULE

DEMONSTRATIVE EVIDENCE, 52

DERIVATIVE USE IMMUNITY, 148

DIRECT EVIDENCE, 8-10

DIRECT EXAMINIATION, 65-66

DIRECTED VERDICT OF ACQUITTAL, 38

DISCRETION, 4, 10-12

DIVISION OF DUTIES BETWEEN JUDGE/ JURY, 37

DOCTRINE OF RECENT POSSESSION, 40